A
Sanskrit Primer

Sri Garib Dass Oriental Series No. 129

A Sanskrit Primer

E. D. Perry

Sri Satguru Publications
A Division of
Indian Books Centre
Delhi– India

Published by :

Sri Satguru Publications,
Indological & Oriental Publishers
A Division of
Indian Books Centre
40/5, Shakti Nagar
Delhi– 110 007
India

Reprint : Delhi– 1991

ISBN 81–7030–281–1

Printed at:
D. K. Fine Art Press, Delhi.

Preface to the Edition of 1936.

The Primer, originally published in 1885 by Ginn and Company, Boston, is based upon an excellent little work by Professor Georg Bühler of Vienna: Leitfaden für den Elementarcursus des Sanskrit, Wien, 1883. I became acquainted with this book while in Germany, and after using it with a class in Columbia College was convinced of its great practical value. On the other hand it seemed likely to be less useful to classes in America as keeping throughout to the native system of grammar, whereas the admirable Sanskrit Grammar of William Dwight Whitney presented the language in a much more logical and scientific form. It seemed therefore advisable to attempt a combination of Bühler's practical exercises and Whitney's presentation of the actual structure of the language. To this end the book was entirely rewritten for the use of English-speaking students, nothing being retained that did not seem likely to meet the real needs of those for whom it was designed. Occasionally, however, as the book would probably be used by persons who would not have the guidance of a competent teacher, explanations were added which normally would be given by the instructor. In many cases not only the substance but also the actual wording of Whitney's rules was incorporated into the text of the Primer — of course with his consent.

The experiment tried with many misgivings in 1885 may be said to have proved successful, since the book has been in steady, though naturally in limited, demand for fifty years. Two years ago Messrs. Ginn and Company found it no longer practicable for them to continue its publication, and the Columbia University Press agreed to take it over.

In the original preface my deep obligations to Professors Bühler, Whitney and Lanman, and to the first of my former pupils in Sanskrit, Professor A. V. Williams Jackson, likewise to the printers in Berlin, Gebrüder Unger (Theodor Grimm), were expressed. Since then Professors H. F. Burton of the University of Rochester, Louis H. Gray of Columbia University, and A. W. Ryder of the University of California, with Dr. Charles J. Ogden of Columbia University, have given me similar and most welcome assistance. My further thanks are due, and most gladly expressed, to the two publishing houses mentioned above, who negotiated the transfer of rights with the greatest courtesy and skill.

The book has been carefully revised to remove all still remaining errors.

E. D. P.

Columbia University
in the City of New York:
June 2, 1936.

Table of Contents,

in systematic grammatical arrangement.

The figures in heavy type refer to paragraphs.

Suggestions for using the Primer.

The Primer can be finished by earnest students in sixteen or seventeen weeks, reckoning three lessons per week, with here and there an hour for review. After that LANMAN's Sanskrit Reader, an introduction to which this work is partly intended to be, should be taken up. Students are strongly recommended to provide themselves with WHITNEY's Sanskrit Grammar at the outset.

It seemed advisable to leave the Introduction undivided into lessons, as different teachers may prefer to impart the alphabet, etc., to their scholars at different rates of speed. Some of the exercises for translation may be found rather too long to be completed in one lesson. In such cases it will probably be better, after requiring the translation of only so many sentences as the pupil may reasonably be expected to master in the preparation of one day's lesson, to proceed directly to the next lesson in the following hour, leaving the untranslated sentences for a review.

The vocabularies prefixed to each exercise are not exhaustive, since words which have been treated of immediately before are sometimes omitted from them. The glossaries at the end of the book will, it is hoped, be found complete for the exercises; but the meaning of compound words must in most cases be learned from their elements; and proper names have often been omitted, their Sanskrit forms being discernible from the transliteration.

The table of contents in systematic grammatical arrangement is designed to facilitate the finding of any desired article; it may also be found useful as an outline for a rapid grammatical review.

Arrangement of Vocabularies. The vocabularies are arranged

in strict alphabetic order (see below). All nouns, whether substantives or adjectives, are given in the stem-form. All verb-forms are placed under the root; prepositional compounds of verbs likewise, and not in the alphabetic place of the preposition. Of verbal adjectives and nouns, some important ones have been given in their alphabetic places, but the meaning of most of them must be learned from their respective roots. Pronouns are given generally in the form of the nominative.

Alphabetic Order. The alphabetic order is that given in § 1, but the following points are to be noticed here:

The *visarga* stands next after the vowels; but a *visarga* regarded as equivalent to a sibilant and exchangeable with it has the alphabetic place of that sibilant.

The sign *ṅ*, representing "the *anusvāra* of more independent origin", has its place before all the mutes etc.; thus *daṅç* and *daṅṣṭrā* stand before *dakṣa*.

The sign *ṁ*, representing an assimilated *m*, is placed according to its phonetic value. 1. If *ṁ*, resulting from the assimilation of *m* to a semivowel, sibilant, or *h*, represent a nasal semivowel or *anusvāra*, then its place is like that of *ṅ*. Thus *puṁs* comes before *puṇya* and *saṁçaya* before *sakṛt*. 2. But if *ṁ* be the product of *m* assimilated to a mute, representing *ṅ*, *ñ*, *ṇ*, *n*, or *m*, then its place is that of the nasal so represented.

Introduction.

Alphabet.

1. Sanskrit is commonly written in what is called the *Devanāgarī* alphabet. The characters of this, and the European characters which will be used in transliterating them, are as follows:

Vowels.

		short	long
simple		अ *a*	आ *ā*
	palatal	इ *i*	ई *ī*
	labial	उ *u*	ऊ *ū*
	lingual	ऋ *ṛ*	ॠ *ṝ*
	dental	ऌ *ḷ*	
diphthongs	palatal	ए *e*	ऐ *āi*
	labial	ओ *o*	औ *āu*

Visarga **:** *ḥ*.

Anusvāra **ं** *ṅ* or *ṁ*.

Consonants.

		surd	surd asp.	sonant	sonant asp.	nasal
Mutes	guttural	क *k*	ख *kh*	ग *g*	घ *gh*	ङ *ṅ*
	palatal	च *c*	छ *ch*	ज *j*	झ *jh*	ञ *ñ*
	lingual	ट *ṭ*	ठ *ṭh*	ड *ḍ*	ढ *ḍh*	ण *ṇ*
	dental	त *t*	थ *th*	द *d*	ध *dh*	न *n*
	labial	प *p*	फ *ph*	ब *b*	भ *bh*	म *m*

Semivowels { palatal य *y* lingual र *r*
dental ल *l* labial व *v*.

Sibilants: palatal श *ç*; lingual ष *ṣ*; dental स *s*.

Aspiration ह *h*.

2. The above order is that in which the sounds are catalogued by native grammarians; and European scholars have adopted it as the alphabetic order, for dictionaries, etc. The writing runs from left to right.

3. The theory of the *devanāgarī* mode of writing is syllabic and consonantal. That is, it regards as the written unit, not the simple sound, but the syllable; and further, it regards as the substantial part of the syllable the consonant (or the consonants) preceding the vowel — this latter being merely implied, as is the case with short अ *a*, except when initial, or, if written, being written by a subordinate sign attached to the consonant.

4. Hence follow these two principles:

A. The forms of the vowel-characters given above are used only when the vowel forms a syllable by itself, or is not combined with a preceding consonant: that is, when it is initial, or preceded by another vowel. In combination with a consonant, other modes of representation are used.

B. If more than one consonant precede a vowel, forming with it a single syllable, their characters must be combined into a single character.

5. According to the Hindu mode of dividing syllables, each syllable must end in a vowel, or *visarga*, or *anusvāra*, except at the end of the word; and as ordinary Hindu usage does not divide the words of a sentence in writing, a final consonant is combined into one syllable with the initial vowel or consonant of the following word, so that a syllable ends in a consonant only at the end of the sentence.

Thus the sentence *kṣetreṣu siktābhir meghānām adbhir dhānyaṁ prarūḍham* — 'by the water which drops from the clouds upon the fields the grain grows tall' — would be considered as consisting of the syllables *kṣe tre ṣu si ktā bhi rme ghā nā ma dbhi rdhā nyaṁ pra rū ḍham*. Each of these syllables would be indicated by a single group of signs, without any reference whatever to the division of the words composing the sentence; and the syllables are always *written* independently, with more or less closeness of approach; either like this:
क्षे त्रे षु सि क्ता भि र्मे घा ना म द्भि र्धा न्यं प्र रू ढम् — or thus: क्षेत्रेषु-सिक्ताभिर्मेघानामद्भिर्धान्यंप्ररूढम्.

6. In Sanskrit works printed in Europe, the common practice is to separate the words so far as this can be done without any alteration of the written form. Thus, इन्द्राय नमः *indrāya namaḥ*; but तत्सवितुर्वरेण्यम् *tat savitur vareṇyam*, because the final त् *t* and र् *r* are not written with their full forms. But some few works have been printed, in which, by a free use of a sign called *virāma* (see below, § 8), the individual words are separated. In transliterated texts there is no good reason for printing otherwise than with all the words separated.

7. Under A. Vowels combined with preceding consonants are written as follows:

1. *a:* Short *a* has no written sign at all; the consonant-sign itself implies a following *a*, unless some other vowel-sign is attached to it (or else the *virāma* — see below, § 8). Thus the consonant-signs given above are really the signs for *ka*, *kha*, *ca*, *cha*, etc. (as far as ह *ha*).
2. *ā*: का *kā*. चा *cā*. धा *dhā* etc.
3. *i* and *ī:* कि *ki*. पि *pi*. धि *dhi*. — की *kī*. पी *pī*. धी *dhī*. The hook above, turning to the left or to the right, is historically the essential part of the character, having been originally

the whole of it; the hooks were only later prolonged, so as to reach all the way down beside the consonant. Observe that the *i*-hooks and the *u*-hooks, respectively above and below the line, are analogous in turning to the left for the short vowel and to the right for the long.

4. *u* and *ū*: कु *ku*. चु *cu*. बु *bu*. — कू *kū*. चू *cū*. भू *bhū*. Owing to the necessities of combination, consonant and vowel-sign are sometimes disguised; thus, दु *du*, दू *dū*; रु *ru*, रू *rū*; हु or हु *hu*, हू *hū*.

5. *ṛ* and *ṝ*: कृ *kṛ*. पृ *pṛ*. — कॄ *kṝ*. तॄ *tṝ*. With the *h*-sign, the vowel-hook is usually attached to the middle; thus, हृ *hṛ*. 6. *ḷ*: कॢ *kḷ*.

7. Diphthongs. *e*: के *ke*. पे *pe*. ये *ye*. *āi*: कै *kāi*. धै *dhāi*. *o*: को *ko*. भो *bho*. *āu*: कौ *kāu*. रौ *rāu*.

In some printed texts the signs for *o* and *āu* are separated, the े or ै being placed over the consonant-sign, and not over the perpendicular stroke; thus, को *ko*, कौ *kāu*.

8. A consonant-sign may be made to signify the sound of that consonant alone, without an added vowel, by writing beneath it a stroke called the *virāma* ('rest', 'stop'); thus, क् *k*, ह् *h*, द् *d*. Strictly, the *virāma* should be used only at the end of a sentence; but it is often used by scribes, or in print, in the middle of a word or sentence, to avoid awkward or difficult combinations; thus, लिड्भिः *liḍbhiḥ*, लिट्सु *liṭsu*.

9. **Under B.** The combinations of consonants are in general not difficult. The perpendicular and horizontal lines are common to almost all; and if two or more are to be combined, the following method is pursued. The characteristic part of a consonant-sign that is to be added to another is taken (to the exclusion of the perpendicular or of the horizontal framing-line, or of both), and they are put together according to convenience, either side by side,

or one above the other: in some combinations either arrangement is allowed. The consonant to be pronounced first is set first in the one arrangement, and above in the other arrangement. Only the consonant at the right of a horizontal group, and that at the top of a perpendicular group, are written in full.

Examples of the horizontal arrangement are:

ग्ग *gga*, ज्ज *jja*, प्य *pya*, न्म *nma*, त्थ *ttha*, भ्य *bhya*, स्क *ska*, ष्ण *ṣṇa*.

Examples of the perpendicular arrangement are: क्क *kka*, च्च *cca*, क्व *kva*, ञ्ज *ñja*, प्त *pta*, त्न *tna*.

10. In some combinations there is more or less abbreviation or disguise of the independent form of a consonant-sign.

Thus, of क् *k* in क्त *kta*; and in क्ण *kṇa*, क्य *kya* etc.;

of त् *t* in त्त *tta*;

of द् *d* in द्ग *dga*, द्द *dda*, द्ध *ddha*, द्भ *dbha* etc.;

of म् *m* and य् *y*, when following other consonants thus, क्य *kya*, क्म *kma*, ङ्म *ṅma*, द्म *dma*, द्य *dya*, ह्म *hma*, ह्य *hya*, ठ्य *ṭhya*, ढ्य *ḍhya*;

of श् *ç*, which generally becomes श्‍ when followed by a consonant; thus, श्च *çca*, श्न *çna*, श्ल *çla*, श्य *çya*. The same change is usual when a vowel-sign is added below; thus, शु *çu*, शृ *çṛ*.

11. Other combinations, of not quite obvious value, are ण्ण *ṇṇa*, ष्ट *ṣṭa*, ष्ठ *ṣṭha*; and the compounds of ह् *h*, as ह्ण *hṇa*, ह्न *hna*.

12. In a case or two, no trace of the constituent letters is recognizable; thus, क्ष *kṣa*, ज्ञ *jña*.

13. The semivowel र् *r*, in making combinations with other consonants, is treated in a wholly peculiar manner, analogous with that of the vowels. 1. As the first of a group of consonants it is written with a hook above, opening to the right (like the subjoined sign of *ṛ*); thus, र्क *rka*, र्प्त *rpta*. When a compound consonant thus containing *r* as its first member is followed by one of the vowels *i*, *ī*, *e*, *o*, *āi*, *āu*, with or without a nasal symbol, the *r*-sign must stand at the extreme right; thus, र्के *rke*, र्को *rko*, र्कौ *rkāu*, र्कि *rki*, र्की *rkī*, र्कं *rkaṁ*, र्कांसि *rkāṅsi*, र्भीं *rbhīṁ*.

2. If pronounced after another consonant or consonants, *r* is indicated by a slanting stroke below, to the left; thus, ग्र *gra*, प्र *pra*, स्र *sra*, द्र *dra*. And, with modifications of the preceding consonant-sign like those noted above, त्र *tra*, श्र *çra*. In the middle of a group, *r* has the same sign as at the end; thus, ग्र्य *grya*, स्र्व *srva*.

3. When र *r* is to be combined with a following ऋ *ṛ*, it is the vowel which is written in full, with its initial character, and the consonant in subordination to it; thus, र्ऋ *rṛ*, निर्ऋति *nirṛti*.

14. Combinations of three, four, or even five consonants (this latter excessively rare) are made according to the same rules; thus, त्त्व *ttva*, द्ध्य *ddhya*, द्व्य *dvya*, द्र्य *drya*, प्स्व *psva*, त्स्य *tsya*, श्च्य *çcya*, ष्ठ्य *ṣṭhya*; ङ्क्ष्व *ṅkṣva*, ष्ट्र्य *ṣṭrya*, त्स्म्य *tsmya*; र्त्स्न्य *rtsnya*.

15. Both MSS. and type-fonts differ considerably in their management of consonant-combinations, but a little practice will enable one who is thoroughly familiar with the simple signs and with the principles of combination to decipher, as well as to make for himself, all such groups.

16. A sign (ऽ) called the *avagraha*, or 'separator', is used in printed texts to mark the elision of initial *a* after final *e* or *o* (see below, § 119, 158): thus ते ऽब्रुवन् *te 'bruvan*. But some texts, especially those printed in India, dispense with this sign.

In our transliteration this sign will be represented by the inverted comma, as in the example just given. In the MSS. the ऽ is also used as a hyphen, and sometimes as a mark of hiatus.

17. The sign ° is used to mark an omission of something easily understood (whether from the context, or from previous knowledge),

and thus becomes a mark of abbreviation; thus, गतस् °तम् °तेन *gatas -tam -tena,* i. e. *gatam gatena* etc.

18. The only signs of punctuation are । and ॥.

19. The numeral figures are

१ 1, २ 2, ३ 3, ४ 4, ५ 5, ६ 6, ७ 7, ८ 8, ९ 9, ० 0.

In combination, to express larger numbers, they are used precisely as are European digits; thus, २४ 24, ४८५ 485, ७६२० 7620. This system of notation originated in India, and was brought to Europe by the Arabs, who call it the Indian system, as we style it the Arabic.

20. In writing Sanskrit the Hindus generally begin at the left of the letter, and make the horizontal top-stroke last; thus, र, ग, ग; ३, घ, घ; ।, क, क. But often the horizontal stroke is made first, and the perpendicular stroke added without raising the pen from the paper; thus, न, घ; न, क.

System of Sounds: Pronunciation.

21. The Sanskrit is used in India to this day very much as Latin was used in Europe in the previous century: it is a common medium of communication between the learned, be their native tongues what they may, and it is not the vernacular of any district whatever. Hence it is not strange that the pronunciation of Sanskrit words varies greatly among scholars from different parts of India; and probably no one system represents the true ancient mode of utterance with much exactness.

1. Vowels.

22. A. **The *a*, *i*, and *u*-vowels.** These three occur both short and long, and are to be pronounced in the 'Italian' manner — as in *(or-)gan* and *father, pin* and *pique, pull* and *rule,* respectively. The

a-vowel stands in no relation of kindred with any of the classes of consonantal sounds. But the *i*-vowel is distinctly palatal, and the *u*-vowel as distinctly labial.

23. B. **The *ṛ* and *ḷ*-vowels.** Both of these are plainly the result of abbreviating syllables containing a र *r* or ल *l* along with another vowel: *ṛ* is to be sounded like the *re* in the English *fibre*, *ḷ* like *le* in *able.*

24. C. **The diphthongs.** 1. The *e* and *o*, which are always long, should receive the long *e* and *o*-sounds of the English *they* and *bone,* without true diphthongal character. In their origin, both were doubtless in the main pure diphthongs ($e = a + i$, $o = a + u$); but they lost this character at a very early period.

2. The *āi* and *āu* are spoken like the *ai* in English *aisle* and *au* in German *Baum* (*ou* in English *house*); that is, as pure diphthongs with long prior element. They were originally, doubtless, distinguished from *e* and *o* only by the length of the first element.

II. Consonants.

25. A. **Mutes.** In each series of mutes there are two surd members, two sonants, and one nasal (also sonant); e. g., in the labial series, the surds *p* and *ph,* the sonants *b* and *bh*, and the sonant *m*.

26. The first and third members of each series are the ordinary corresponding surd and sonant mutes of European languages; thus, *k* and *g*, *t* and *d*, *p* and *b*.

27. Nor is the character of the nasal any more doubtful. What *m* is to *p* and *b*, or *n* is to *t* and *d*, that is also each other nasal to its own series of mutes: a sonant expulsion of breath into and through the nose, while the mouth-organs are in the mute-contact.

28. The second and fourth of each series are aspirates; thus, beside the surd mute *k* we have the corresponding surd aspirate *kh*, and beside the sonant *g*, the corresponding aspirate *gh*. It is usual among European scholars to pronounce both classes of aspirates as the corresponding non-aspirates with a very closely following *h*; e. g., *th* nearly as in *boathouse*, *ph* as in *haphazard*, *dh* as in *madhouse*. This is inaccurate; but the question of the original pronunciation of this entire group of sounds is one of great difficulty, and still unsettled.

29. The aspirates are not double letters.

The several mute-series will now be taken up in detail.

30. 1. **Gutturals:** *k*, *kh*, *g*, *gh*, *ṅ*. These are the ordinary English *k* and *g* ("hard")-sounds, with their corresponding aspirates and nasal; the last, like *ng* in *singing*.

31. 2. **Palatals:** *c*, *ch*, *j*, *jh*, *ñ*. This whole series is derivative, being generated by the corruption of original gutturals. (The palatal mute *c* and the sibilant *ç* often represent two successive stages of corruption of *k*; the corresponding degrees of corruption of *g* are both represented by *j*.) For this reason the euphonic treatment of the palatals is in many respects peculiar. The palatal mutes *c* and *j* are pronounced with the compound sounds of English *ch* and *j*, as in *church* and *judge*. See also § 28.

32 3. **Linguals:** *ṭ*, *ṭh*, *ḍ*, *ḍh*, *ṇ*. The lingual mutes are said to be uttered with the tip of the tongue turned up and drawn back into the dome of the palate, somewhat as the English (or rather American) smooth *r*, e. g. in *very* is pronounced. In practice European Sanskritists make no attempt to distinguish them from the dentals: *ṭ* is pronounced like *t*, *ḍ* like *d*, and so on.

33. 4. **Dentals:** *t*, *th*, *d*, *dh*, *n*. These are practically the equivalents of our so-called dentals *t*, *d*, *n*.*

---

* But the Hindus generally use linguals to represent the English **dentals**; thus, लण्डन *laṇḍana* = 'London.'

34. 5. **Labials:** *p, ph, b, bh, m.* These are exactly the equivalents of the English *p, b, m.*

35. B. **Semivowels:** *y, r, l, v.* 1. The palatal semivowel *y* stands in the closest relationship with the vowel *i* (short or long): the two exchange with one another in cases innumerable. Very probably the Sanskrit *y* had everywhere more of an *i*-character than our *y*.

36. 2. The *r* is clearly a lingual sound. It thus resembles the English smooth *r*, and like this seems to have been untrilled.

37. 3. The *l* is a sound of dental position, quite as in English.

38. 4. The labial *v* is pronounced as English or French *v* by the modern Hindus — except when preceded by a consonant (except *r*) in the same syllable, when it sounds like English *w*; and European scholars follow the same practice (with or without the same exception). But strictly the *v* stands related to an *u*-vowel precisely as *y* to an *i*-vowel: that is, it is a *w*-sound in the English sense, or perhaps more like the *ou* in French *oui.* The rules of Sanskrit euphony affecting this sound, and the name "semivowel", have no application except to such a *w*-sound: a *v*-sound (German *w*) is no semivowel, but a spirant, like the English *th*-sounds and *f*. The four semivowels are always sonant.

39. C. **Sibilants:** *ç, ṣ, s.* 1. The *s* is of plain character: a dental, and exactly like the English *s* (as in *lesson* — never as in *ease*).

40. 2. The *ṣ* is the sibilant pronounced in the lingual position. It is, therefore, a kind of *sh*-sound, and by Europeans is pronounced as ordinary English *sh*, no attempt being made to give it its proper lingual quality.

41. 3. The *ç* is by all native authorities described as palatal. It is the usual *sh*-sound of English, though the Hindus are said to speak it somewhat differently nowadays. By Europeans it is variously pronounced — perhaps oftener as *s* than as *sh*.

42. All three sibilants are always surd.

43. D. **Aspiration:** *h*. This is usually pronounced like the ordinary European *surd* aspiration *h*. But its true value in the euphony of the language is that of a sonant. It is not an original sound of the language, but comes in most cases from an older *gh*, in some few cases from *dh* or *bh*. It appears to include in itself two stages of corruption of *gh*: one corresponding with that of *k* to *c*, the other with that of *k* to *ç*.

44. E. **Visarga:** *ḥ*. The *ḥ* appears to be merely a surd breathing, a final *h*-sound (in the European sense of *h*), uttered in the articulating position of the preceding vowel. The *visarga* is not original, but always a mere substitute for final *s* or *r*.

45. F. **Anusvāra.** The *anusvāra*, *ṅ* or *ṁ*, is a nasal sound lacking that closure of the organs which is required to make a nasal mute; in its utterance there is nasal resonance along with some degree of openness of the mouth. European scholars give the *anusvāra* the value of the nasal in the French *-an*, *-on*, *-en*, *-in*, etc., which is a mere nasal coloring of the preceding vowel.

46. Two different signs, ं and ँ, are used in the MSS. to indicate the *anusvāra*. Most commonly ं is employed; ँ will not often be met with in printed texts, except to mark the change of a nasal mute to *anusvāra* before a following semivowel, particularly *l*; thus, तांल्ँ लब्धान् *tāṅl labdhān*. Cf. § 139.

47. It is convenient in transliteration to distinguish the assimilated *m* (in all cases) by a special sign *ṁ*, from the *anusvāra* of more independent origin, represented by *ṅ*.

Light and Heavy Syllables.

48. For metrical purposes syllables (not vowels) are distinguished as 'heavy' and 'light'. A syllable is heavy if its vowel is long, or short and followed by more than one consonant ("long by position"). *Visarga* and *anusvāra* are here counted as full consonants. The aspirated mutes, of course, do not count as double letters.

Changes of Sounds. Guṇa and Vṛddhi.

49. The changes to which both the vowels and the consonants of Sanskrit are subject are very numerous. Among the vowel-changes, the most regular and frequent are the so-called *guṇa* and *vṛddhi*, which are of frequent occurrence in derivation and inflection.

50. The following table exhibits these changes:

Simple vowels	अ *a* आ *ā*	इ *i* ई *ī*	उ *u* ऊ *ū*	ऋ *ṛ*
Guṇa	अ *a* आ *ā*	ए *e*	ओ *o*	अर् *ar*
Vṛddhi	आ *ā*	ऐ *āi*	औ *āu*	आर् *ār*

51. Theoretically the changes of *ṝ* would coincide with those of *ṛ*, and the *vṛddhi* of *ḷ* would be *āl*; but actual cases of these are quite unknown. The *guṇa* of *ḷ* is *al* (just as that of *ṛ* is *ar*), but it occurs only in one root, *kḷp*. As will be seen in the sequel, the *guṇa*-sound coincides with the result of the combination of an अ *a* with the simple vowel corresponding to that *guṇa*; thus, अ *a* combines with a following इ *i* or ई *ī* into ए *e*, which is also the *guṇa* of इ *i* and ई *ī*. The *vṛddhi*, in like manner, is identical with the result of combining an अ *a* with the corresponding *guṇa*; thus, अ *a* combines with a following ए *e* into ऐ *āi*, the *vṛddhi* of इ *i* and ई *ī*. For the present the table is to be learned outright.

52. In all gunating processes अ *a* remains unchanged — or, as it is sometimes expressed, **अ** *a* is its own *guṇa;* **आ** *ā* remains unchanged for both *guṇa* and *vṛddhi.*

53. The *guṇa*-increment does not, except in exceedingly rare instances, take place in a heavy syllable (see § 48) ending in a consonant: e. g., **चित्** *cit* may become **चेत्** *cet*, and **नी** *nī* may become **ने** *ne*; but **चिन्त्** *cint* or **निन्द्** *nind* or **जीव्** *jīv* may not become **चेन्त्** *cent* or **नेन्द्** *nend* or **जेव्** *jev.*

54. Other changes of vowels and consonants occur very frequently, in the making-up of single words from roots, by means of suffixes and endings, and in the formation of compound words by the union of two or more stems — a process of the very greatest frequency in Sanskrit. Furthermore, in the form in which the language is handed down to us by the literature, the words composing a sentence or paragraph are adapted to and combined with each other by nearly the same rules as those which govern the making of compounds, so that it is impossible to take apart and understand the simplest sentence in Sanskrit without understanding those rules. The most important of the rules for such combination will be given piecemeal in the lessons.

Roots and Stems.

55. A knowledge on the student's part of the meaning and application of the terms *root, stem, personal ending,* etc., is presupposed. The formative processes by which both inflectional forms and derivative stems are made, by the addition of endings to bases and roots, are more regular and transparent in Sanskrit than in any other Indo-European language.*

In the present work, which aims preeminently to give the student considerable practical acquaintance with the language within a brief compass of lessons, not every given form will be explained by analysis. But wherever any explanation of forms is given, it will of course be according to this method.

Accent.

56. The phenomena of accent are, by the Hindu grammarians of all ages alike, described and treated as depending on a variation of tone or pitch; of any difference of stress involved, they make no account. These accents are marked only in certain Vedic texts, and employed only in their recitation, whereas the accents used nowadays by Hindus in the pronunciation of Sanskrit (and left undenoted in writing) are mainly ictus-accents, i. e. variations of stress. The principles of the latter system will be given in an appendix. The older system of accents has great etymological importance; the latter none whatever; and only the older system will be referred to in the following. Here it will be enough to state that the primary tones or accent-pitches of the older system are two: a higher, or acute; and a lower, or grave. A third, called *svarita*, is always of secondary origin, being ordinarily the result of actual combination of an acute vowel and a grave vowel into one syllable. It is uniformly defined as compound in pitch, a union of higher and lower tone within the limits of a single syllable. It is thus identical in physical character with the Greek and Latin circumflex, and fully entitled to be called by the same name. Whenever, in the sequel, accent is mentioned, without further definition, the acute accent is to be understood; and it will be designated by the ordinary acute sign.

Conjugation of Verbs.

57. The Sanskrit verb exhibits the closest analogy with that of Greek, being developed in tense-systems, as outgrowths of certain tense-stems. In the older stage of the language, i. e. in the so-called Vedic period, the modal ramifications of each tense-stem are as numerous as in Greek; but in the later stage, the Sanskrit proper (also called the classical language), these outgrowths have been lopped off to so very great an extent, that with one insignificant exception, the precative or aorist optative, only the present-system still retains any modal variety whatever.

58. There is a simple or ordinary conjugation of verbal roots, which we call **primary**; and there are certain more or less fully developed **secondary** or **derivative** conjugations (§ 69).

59. Voices. There are two voices, active and middle, which extend throughout the whole system of conjugation. For the present-system alone there is a special passive inflection; the middle forms outside that system, and sometimes even within it, are liable to be used likewise in a passive sense. An active form is called by the Hindu grammarians *parasmāi padam* 'word for another'; a middle form, *ātmane padam* 'word for one's self.' Some verbs are conjugated in both voices, others in one only; sometimes some of the tenses are inflected only in one voice, others only in the other voice, or in both; of a verb usually inflected in one voice sporadic forms of the other occur; and sometimes the voice differs as the verb is compounded with certain prepositions.

60. Persons and Numbers. There are three persons: first, second, and third; and, as with substantives, adjectives, and pronouns, three numbers: singular, dual, and plural. All these persons and numbers are made from every tense and mode—except that the first persons of the imperative are really subjunctive forms.

61. The native grammarians denote as the first person what we call the third; and as we are wont to speak of the verb λέγω, the verb ἔρχομαι, the verb *amo*, etc., so the Hindus use for instance **भवति** *bhávati* (3rd sing. pres. indic. of √*bhū*) to signify the whole system of verbal forms from that root, since **भवति** heads the list of forms in the native grammar, as λέγω, or ἔρχομαι, or *amo*, does in Greek or Latin. The Hindus even make substantives out of such catchword forms, and inflect them according to the needs of expression.

62. In the following, the conjugation-class of verbs will be indicated by the 3rd sing. pres. ind., placed in parenthesis after the root; thus, भू *bhū* (भवति *bhávati*).

63. Tenses and modes. The scheme of tenses and modes put forth by the Hindus holds good only for the later language, and even there utterly confounds the ideas of mode and tense.

64. The only logical arrangement of the modes and tenses in Sanskrit is shown in the following table (which includes only the classical speech):

I. **Present-System:** **a.** Indicative. **b.** Imperfect. **c.** Imperative. **d.** Optative. **e.** Participle.

II. **Perfect-System.** **a.** Indicative. **b.** Participle.

III. **Aorist Systems** (of triple formation). **a.** Indicative. **b.** Optative (sometimes = "Precative").

IV. **Future Systems.**

A. Sibilant Future. **a.** Indicative. **b.** Preterit (= "Conditional"). **c.** Participle.

B. Periphrastic Future. **a.** Indicative.

65. The tenses here distinguished as imperfect, perfect, and aorist receive those names from their correspondence in mode of formation with tenses so called in other languages of the family, especially in Greek, and not at all from any differences of time designated by them. In no period of the Sanskrit language is there any expression of imperfect or pluperfect time — nor of perfect time, except in the older language, where the "aorist" has this value; in the later speech, imperfect, perfect, and aorist (of rare use) are so many undiscriminated past tenses or preterits.

Verbal Adjectives and Substantives.

66. Participles. The participles belonging to the tense-systems have been already indicated in the table at § 64. There is, besides, a participle formed directly from the root of the verb, which is prevailingly of **past** and **passive** (sometimes neuter) meaning. Moreover, **future passive** participles, or **gerundives**, of several different formations, are made, but without connection with the future-stems.

67. Infinitive. The classical Sanskrit has a single infinitive. It is really an accusative case of a verbal noun, having nothing whatever to do with the tense-systems.

68. Gerund. A so-called gerund, or absolutive, is especially frequent, and is, like the infinitive, a stereotyped case-form (instrumental) of a derivative verbal noun. Its value is that of an indeclinable active participle, with indeterminate, but oftenest past, temporal force.

Secondary Conjugations.

69. The secondary conjugations are as follows: 1. **Passive**; 2. **Intensive**; 3. **Desiderative**; 4. **Causative.** In these, not the simple root, but a conjugation-stem, underlies the whole system of inflections. Yet in them all is plainly visible the character of a present-system, expanded into a more or less complete conjugation; the passive is palpably a present-system. Compare § 58—59.

70. Under the same general head belong: 5. **Denominative** conjugation, which results from the conversion of noun-stems, both substantive and adjective, into conjugation-stems; 6. **Compound** conjugation, resulting from the prefixion of prepositions to roots, or from the addition of auxiliary verbs to noun-stems; and 7. **Periphrastic** conjugation, from the looser combination of auxiliaries with verbal nouns and adjectives.

71. The characteristic of a proper (i. e. finite or personal) verb-form is its personal ending. By this alone is determined its character as regards person and number, and in part also as regards mode and tense. But the distinctions of mode and tense are mainly made by the formation of mode and tense-stems, to which, instead of to the bare root, the personal endings are appended.

Conjugation-Classes.

72. Of the whole conjugation, the present-system is the important and prominent part. Its forms are very much more frequent than those of all the other systems together. As there is also great variety in the manner in which different roots form their present-stems, this, as being their most conspicuous difference, is made the basis of their principal classification; and a verb is said to be of this or that conjugation, or class, according to the way in which its present-stem is made.

73. Of these conjugation-classes there are nine, including the passive, which is really a present-system only. The first five exhibit coincidences enough to justify their inclusion into one conjugation, and the remaining four will compose likewise a second conjugation. The chief distinctions between the two groups are as follows:

74. In the **first**, the classes have in common, as their fundamental characteristic, a shift of accent: the tone is now upon the personal ending, now upon the root or the class-sign. Along with this goes a variation in the stem itself, which has a stronger, or fuller, form when the accent rests upon it, and a weaker, or briefer, form when the accent is on the ending. We distinguish these forms as the strong and the weak stem-forms respectively.

75. In the **second conjugation,** on the contrary, the accent has a fixed place, remaining always upon the same syllable of the stem, and never being shifted to the endings; and the distinction of strong and weak forms is unknown. Moreover, the present-stem of every verb in the four classes of this conjugation ends in **अ** *a*. There are also other points of difference.

76. The classification current among the Hindu, and hitherto among the European, grammarians comprises ten conjugation-classes, arranged according to no intelligible principle whatever. The native "tenth class" is really no present-class at all, but a causative, i. e. a derivative conjugation, which extends beyond the limits of the present-system. Probably the fact that by no means all conjugation-stems formed by the causative sign had really a causative value induced the natives to adopt such a present-class. The Hindu scheme also quite omits the passive.

77. The Hindu first, sixth, fourth, and tenth classes form the so-called first conjugation of their scheme, which corresponds, except as regards the tenth class, with our second conjugation. The remainder of the classes form the natives' second conjugation, which agrees in the main with our first.

78. The classes are then as follows:

First Conjugation.

I. The **root-class** (second or *ad*-class, of the Hindus); its present-stem is coincident with the root itself; thus, **अद्** *ad*, 'eat'; **इ** *i*, 'go'; **द्विष्** *dviṣ*, 'hate'.

II. The **reduplicating class** (third or *hu*-class); the root is reduplicated to form the present-stem; thus, **जुहु** *juhu* from √**हु** *hu*, 'sacrifice'; **ददा** *dadā* from √*dā*, 'give'.

III. The **nasal class** (seventh or *rudh*-class); a nasal, extended to the syllable *na* [*ṇa*] in strong forms, is inserted before the final consonant of the root; thus, **रुन्ध्** *rundh* (or **रुणध्** *ruṇadh*) from **रुध्** *rudh*, 'hinder'.

IV. **a.** The *nu*-class (fifth or *su*-class); the syllable नु *nu* is added to the root; thus, सुनु *sunu* from √सु *su*, 'press.'

b. A very small number of roots (only half-a-dozen) ending already in न् *n*, and also one very common and irregularly inflected root not so ending (कृ *kṛ*, 'make'), add उ *u* alone to form the present-stem. This is the eighth or *tan*-class of the Hindu grammarians; it is best ranked as a sub-class, the *u*-class; thus, तनु *tanu* from √तन् *tan*, 'stretch.'

V. The *nā*-class (ninth or *krī*-class); the syllable ना *nā* (or, in weak forms, नी *nī*) is added to the root; thus, क्रीणा *krīṇā* (or क्रीणी *krīṇī*) from √क्री *krī*, 'buy'. See note**, p. 32.

Second Conjugation.

VI. The *a*-class, or unaccented *a*-class (first or *bhū*-class); the added class-sign is *a* simply; and the root, which bears the accent, is strengthened by *guṇa* throughout, if it be capable of taking *guṇa* (see §§ 52—53); thus, भव *bháva* (through the intermediate stage *bhó-a*) from √भू *bhū*, 'be.'

VII. The *á*-class, or accented *a*-class (sixth or *tud*-class); the added class-sign is *a*, as in the preceding class; but it has the accent, and the unaccented root is not strengthened by *guṇa*; thus, तुद *tudá* from √तुद् *tud*, 'thrust.'

VIII. The *ya*-class (fourth or *div*-class); *ya* is added to the root, which has the accent; thus, दीव्य *dī́vya* from √दीव् *dīv* (by the Hindus given as दिव् *div*), 'play.'

IX. The passive conjugation is also properly a present-system only, having a class-sign which is not extended into the other systems; though it differs markedly from the remaining classes in having a specific meaning, and in being formable from all transitive verbs, but with endings of the middle voice only. It forms its stem by adding an accented *yá* to the root; thus, from √अद् *ad*, अद्य *adyá*; from √रुध् *rudh*, रुध्य *rudhyá*.

---

79. Roots are not wholly limited, even in the later language, to one mode of formation of their present stem, but are sometimes reckoned as belonging to two or more different conjugation-classes.

80. The verbs of our second conjugation show much greater simplicity of formation and inflection and are far more frequent and numerous than those of our first; their paradigms will therefore be given before those of our first.

Prepositions and Prepositional Prefixes.

81. Prepositions, or, more strictly speaking, adverbial prefixes, are used with verbs quite as frequently in Sanskrit as in Greek; and more than one may be prefixed. Thus when √बुध् *budh*+अनु *anu* is given in the vocabulary, this signifies that the preposition अनु is prefixed to the proper verbal form; and the 3rd sing. pres. ind. act. of the verb would then be अनुबोधति *anubodhati*; so *dhā* + सम्-आ (or समा) *sam-ā*, 3rd sing. समादधाति *samādadhāti*. The rules prevailing in Greek for the prefixion of prepositions, etc., to verbal forms will be found to hold good in Sanskrit.

82. There is in Sanskrit no proper class of prepositions (in the modern sense of the term); no body of words having as their exclusive office the "government" of nouns. But many adverbial words are used with nouns in a way which approximates them to the more fully developed prepositions of other languages. Words are used prepositionally along with all the noun-cases, except the dative (and of course the nominative and vocative). But in general their office is directive only, determining more definitely, or strengthening, the proper case-use of the noun.

Declension.

83. The declension of substantives and that of adjectives correspond so closely that the two classes of words must be treated together. The pronouns and numerals, on the other hand, exhibit here as in the kindred languages many striking peculiarities.

84. **Numbers and Genders.** There are three numbers, singular, dual, and plural; and the usual three genders, masculine, feminine, and neuter. The dual is used much more extensively than in Greek, where it appears in a moribund state.

85. **Cases.** The cases are eight in number, given generally in the following order: nominative, accusative, instrumental, dative, ablative, genitive, locative, and vocative. The object sought in the arrangement is simply to set next to one another those cases which are to a greater or less extent, in one number or another, identical in form; and, putting the nominative first, as leading case, there is no other order by which that object could be attained.

For the uses of the cases in detail see Wh. §§ 267—305.

86. The stems of substantives and adjectives may for convenience be classified as follows: I. Stems in अ *a*. II. Stems in इ *i* and उ *u*. III. Stems in आ *ā*, ई *ī*, and ऊ *ū*: namely, A. radical-stems, and a few others inflected like them; B. derivative stems. IV. Stems in ऋ *ṛ* (or अर् *ar*). V. Stems in consonants.

87. **Strong and weak cases.** In stems ending in consonants, and those in ऋ *ṛ* (or अर् *ar*), there is seen a distinction of stem-form in different cases. Sometimes the stem-forms are two, when they are called strong and weak respectively; sometimes three: strong, middle, and weakest. As is the case with verbs, this variation of stem-form often goes hand-in-hand with a shift of accent.

88. In the masculine and feminine, the strong cases are the nom. and acc., both sing. and dual, and the nom. pl. The rest

are weak; or, if there be the distinction of three stem-forms, then the instr., dat., abl., gen., and loc. sing., the gen. and loc. du., and the gen. pl. (all of which take endings beginning with a vowel), are weakest; and the instr., dat., and abl. du., the instr., dat., abl., and loc. pl. (whose endings begin with consonants), are middle.

89. In the neuter, the only strong cases are the nom. and acc. pl.; if there be the triple distinction, then the nom. and acc. sing. are middle, and the same cases in the dual are weakest. Otherwise the cases are classified as in the masculine.

90. Case-endings. The normal scheme of case-endings, as recognized by the native grammarians (and conveniently to be assumed as the basis of special descriptions), is this:

	Singular		Dual		Plural	
	m. f.	n.	m. f.	n.	m. f.	n.
N.	*s*	*m*	*āu*	*ī*	*as*	*i*
A.	*am*	*m*	*āu*	*ī*	*as*	*i*
I.	*ā*		*bhyām*		*bhis*	
D.	*e*		*bhyām*		*bhyas*	
Ab.	*as*		*bhyām*		*bhyas*	
G.	*as*		*os*		*ām*	
L.	*i*		*os*		*su*	

It applies entire to consonant-stems, and to the radical division of *ī* and *ū*-stems; and to other vowel-stems, with considerable variations and modifications. The endings which have almost or quite unbroken range, through stems of all classes, are *bhyām* and *os* of the dual, and *bhis*, *bhyas*, *ām*, and *su* of the plural.

91. Pada-endings. The case-endings *bhyām*, *bhis*, *bhyas*, and *su* — i. e. those of the middle cases — are called *pada* ("word")-endings. The treatment of stem-finals before them is generally the same as in the combinations of *words* with one another.

Lesson I.

92. Verbs. Present Indicativeactive. Unaccented *a*-class. A number of roots conjugated in this class have medial short अ *a*. Inasmuch as "अ *a* is its own *guṇa*", these roots merely add an अ *a* to form the present-stem; e. g., वद् *vad*, present-stem वद *váda*. The final अ *a* of the stem is lengthened in the three first persons.

	Sing.	Dual.	Plural.
1.	वदामि *vádāmi*	वदावस् *vádāvas*	वदामस् *vádāmas*
2.	वदसि *vádasi*	वदथस् *vádathas*	वदथ *vádatha*
3.	वदति *vádati*	वदतस् *vádatas*	वदन्ति *vádanti*

93. The ending of the 3rd plur. is properly अन्ति *anti*; it suffers abbreviation, however, by the loss of its अ *a*, in verbs whose stem ends in अ *a*.

94. As a heavy syllable ending in a consonant cannot be gunated, a root like जीव् *jīv* makes its 3rd sing. जीवति *jīvati;* निन्द् *nind* makes निन्दति *nindati*, etc. See § 53.

95. Euphonic rule. At the end of a word standing in the final position of a sentence, or alone, स् *s* and र् *r* always become *visarga* : *ḥ*; and generally also before क् *k*, ख् *kh*, प् *p*, फ् *ph*, and before sibilants [श् *ç*, ष् *ṣ*, स् *s*], whether these stand in the same word, or as initial in the following word; e. g. वदतस् पुनर् *vadatas punar* becomes always वदतः पुनः *vadataḥ punaḥ*.

96. Force of the present. The present indicative signifies 1. Present time. 2. Immediate futurity. 3. Past time, in lively narration ("historical present").

Vocabulary I.

Verbs to be conjugated like वद् *vad*:

- चर् *car* (intr.) go, wander, graze (of cattle); (tr.) perform, commit.
- जीव् *jīv* live.
- त्यज् *tyaj* leave, abandon.
- दह् *dah* burn.
- धाव् *dhāv* run.
- नम् *nam* (intr.) bow, bend one's self; (tr.) honor, reverence.
- पच् *pac* cook.
- पत् *pat* fall; fly.
- यज् *yaj* sacrifice *(c. acc. pers. et instr. rei).*
- रक्ष् *rakṣ* protect.
- वद् *vad* speak, say.
- वस् *vas* dwell.
- वह् *vah* (tr.) carry, bear; (intr.) flow, blow, proceed.
- शंस् *çaṅs* praise.

Adverbs and Conjunctions.

अतस् *atas*, इतस् *itas* — hence	ततस् *tatas* — thence, therefore, thereupon	यतस् *yatas* — whence, wherefo
अत्र *atra*, इह *iha* — here, hither	तत्र *tatra* — there, thither	यत्र *yatra* — where, whither
इत्थम् *ittham* — in this way, so	तथा *tathā* — in that way, so	यथा *yathā* — in which wa, as
कुतस् *kutas* — whence? why?	कुत्र *kutra*, क्व *kva* — where? whither?	कथम् *katham* how? कदा *kadā* when?
अधुना *adhunā* now	तदा *tadā* then	यदा *yadā* when, if
अद्य *adya* to-day	सर्वत्र *sarvatra* everywhere	सदा *sadā* always
एवम् *evam* so, thus	इति *iti* so, thus	तु *tu* but, however
एव *eva* just, exactly	च *ca* (postpos.) *-que*	पुनर् *punar* again, but

104. Force of cases. 1. The nominative is *casus subjectivus.* 2. The accusative is *casus objectivus*, denoting chiefly the nearer or direct, sometimes however the more remote, object; sometimes also the *terminus ad quem*, and extent of time and space.

105. Euphonic combination of vowels.

1. अ *a* or आ *ā* + अ or आ = आ. e. g. गता अपि *gatā api* = गतापि *gatā 'pi.*
2. अ or आ + इ *i* or ई *ī* = ए *e.* e. g. गता + इति *iti* = गतेति *gate 'ti.*
3. अ or आ + उ *u* or ऊ *ū* = ओ *o.* e. g. गता + उत *uta* = गतोत *gato 'ta.*
4. अ or आ + ऋ *ṛ* = अर् *ar.* e. g. महा *mahā* + ऋषिः *ṛṣiḥ* = महर्षिः *maharṣiḥ.*
5. अ or आ + ए *e* or ऐ *āi* = ऐ *āi.* e. g. गता + एव *eva* = गतैव *gatāi 'va.*
6. अ or आ + ओ *o* or औ *āu* = औ *āu.* e. g. गता + ओषधिः *oṣadhiḥ* = गतौषधिः *gatāu 'ṣadhiḥ.*

106. It will be the practice everywhere in this work to separate independent words in transliteration, but not in the *devanāgarī* text; and if an initial vowel of a following word has coalesced with a final of the preceding, this will be indicated by an apostrophe — single if the initial vowel be the shorter, double if it be the longer, of the two different initials which in every case of combination yield the same result. To aid the beginner, a point • will sometimes be placed, in the *devanāgarī*, under a long vowel formed by two coalescing vowels; thus, अग्निनारीणाम् *agninā 'rīṇām.*

Vocabulary II.

Verbs, *a*- class:	जि *ji* (tr. and intr.) conquer, win.
गम् *gam* (*gácchati*) go.	द्रु *dru* run.
घ्रा *ghrā* (*jighrati*) smell.	नी *nī* lead, guide.

पा *pā* (*pibati*) drink.

भू *bhū* become, be, exist.

यम् *yam* (*yácchati*) furnish, give.

वृष् *vṛṣ* rain, give rain; (fig.) shower down; overwhelm.

स्मृ *smṛ* remember, think on.

स्था *sthā* (*tiṣṭhati*) stand (intr.).

Subst. Masc.:

गज *gaja* elephant.

गन्ध *gandha* odor, perfume.

ग्राम *grāma* village.

नर *nara* man (*vir* and *homo*).

नृप *nṛpa* king.

पुत्र *putra* son.

Neut.:

क्षीर *kṣīra* milk.

गृह *gṛha* house.

जल *jala* water.

दान *dāna* gift, present.

नगर *nagara* city.

Interj.:

हे *he* O, ho.

Exercise II.

कदा देवान् स्मरसि । १ । गृहं* गच्छावः । २ । जलं पिबति पुत्रः । ३ । नृपौ भवतः । ४ । कदा फलानि यच्छथः । ५ । कुत्राधुना गजं नयामि । ६ । वर्षन्ति देवाः । ७ । जयथ हे देवाः । ८ । नरः फले यच्छति । ९ । अधुना जिघ्रामि गन्धम् । १० । देवं नमावः । ११ । पुत्र ग्रामं गच्छन्ति । १२ । नृप गृहे भवतः । १३ । सर्वत्र दानानि वर्षन्ति नृपाः ॥ १४ ॥

15. The man[1] drinks[3] milk[2]. 16. The king[3] leads[2] the elephant[1]. 17. *Two* houses[1] fall[2]. 18. The god[3] gives[2] water[1]. 19. Ye *both* think[2] on (स्मृ) the *two* gods[1] (*accus.*). 20. The king[3] wins[2] the village[1]. 21. The *two* elephants[1] smell[3] the perfume[2]. 22. They cook[2] fruits[1]. 23. The man[3] reverences[2] the gods[1]. 24. The *two* elephants[1] live[2]. 25. The gods[2] give[1] rain (वृष्).

---

* Final म् *m* is commonly written as *anusvāra* if the following word begins with a consonant; but the Hindus pronounce it as म् *m* in such cases. At the end of a sentence *anusvāra* should not be written for म् *m*, though this is a habit common in the MSS.

Final radical म् *m*, in internal combination, is assimilated to a following mute or spirant. In the former case it becomes the nasal of the same class with the mute; in the latter it becomes *anusvāra*.— Final radical न् *n*, in internal combination, becomes *anusvāra* before a sibilant.

Lesson III.

107. Verbs. Accented á-class. Roots of this class form their present-stem by adding an accented अ *á* to the root, which is not gunated. The inflection of these stems is precisely like that of stems belonging to the preceding class, except as to the position of the accent; thus, क्षिप् *kṣip*, present-stem क्षिप *kṣipá*, pres. ind. क्षिपामि *kṣipámi*, क्षिपसि *kṣipási*, क्षिपति *kṣipáti*, etc.

108. Several roots in ऋ *ṛ* of this class (by the Hindus written with ॠ *ṝ*) form stems in इर् *ira*; e. g., कॄ *kṝ*, 'strew', किरति *kiráti*. The roots in इ *i* and उ *u* and ऊ *ū* change those vowels into इय् *iy* and उव् *uv*, respectively. before the class-sign; thus, क्षि *kṣi*, क्षियति *kṣiyáti*; सु *su*, सुवति *suváti*; धू *dhū*, धुवति *dhuváti*.

109. For the root इष् *iṣ*, 'desire', इछ् *ich* is regarded as a substitute in the present-stem; thus, इच्छति *iccháti* (§ 100, note). Likewise, ऋ *ṛ* makes its present ऋच्छति *ṛccháti*; and प्रछ् *prach*, sometimes given as पृछ् *pṛch*, makes पृच्छति *pṛccháti*.

110. A number of roots following this class are strengthened in the present by a penultimate nasal; thus, सिच् *sic*, present ind. सिञ्चति *siñcáti*. The nasal is always assimilated in class to the following consonant; thus ञ् *ñ* is used before palatals, न् *n* before dentals, म् *m* before labials; and ं *ṅ* before sibilants and ह् *h*.

111. Masculines and Neuters in अ *a*, **cont'd.**

a. Masculines:

	Singular.	Dual.	Plural.
I.	देवेन *devena*	देवाभ्याम् *devābhyām*	देवैस् *devāis*
D.	देवाय *devāya*	„ „	देवेभ्यस् *devebhyas*
Ab.	देवात् *devāt*	„ „	„ „
G.	देवस्य *devasya*	देवयोस् *devayos*	देवानाम् *devānām*
L.	देवे *deve*	„ „	देवेषु *deveṣu*

b. Neuters follow exactly the declension of masculines in the above cases; thus, फलेन *phalena*, फलाय *phalāya*, etc.

112. **Force of cases.** 1. The instrumental answers the questions wherewith? and whereby? and expresses accompaniment, agent, or means. 2. The dative denotes the remoter object, and direction. It is also used as *dativus commodi;* very frequently also to denote end or purpose. Sometimes (and oftenest with copula omitted) it is predicative, in the sense of 'makes for, tends toward'. 3. The ablative answers the question whence? and very frequently denotes cause. 4. The genitive is *casus adjectivus,* denoting all kinds of belonging (e. g. *gen. subjectivus, objectivus, partitivus).* 5. The locative denotes the place where, or the time when, an action occurs. It is often used absolutely, in agreement with a participle expressed or understood, as the ablative is used in Latin and the genitive in Greek. It is also used as *terminus ad quem.*

Vocabulary III.

Verbs, *á*-class:

इष् *iṣ (icchāti)* wish, desire.

कृष् *kṛṣ (kṛṣáti)* plough.

क्षिप् *kṣip (kṣipáti)* hurl, cast, throw.

दिश् *diç (diçáti)* show, point out.

प्रछ् *prach (pṛcchāti)* ask, ask about.

विश् *viç (viçáti)* enter.

सिच् *sic (siñcáti)* drip, drop; moisten.

सृज् *sṛj (sṛjáti)* let go; create.

स्पृश् *(spṛçáti)* touch; (in certain connections) wash.

a-class:

गुह् *guh (gūhati,* § 101) hide, conceal.

सद् *sad (sīdati,* § 101) sit.

Subst. Masc.:

कट *kaṭa* mat.

कुन्त *kunta* spear.

बाल *bāla* child, boy.

मार्ग *mārga* road, way, street.

मेघ *megha* cloud.

शर *çara* arrow.

हस्त *hasta* hand.

Neut.:

क्षेत्र *kṣetra* field.

धन *dhana* money, riches.

लाङ्गल *lāṅgala* plough.

विष *viṣa* poison.

सुख *sukha* fortune, luck, happiness.

Exercise III.

धनानि गृहेषु गूहन्ति ।१। कुन्तान् हस्ताभ्यां क्षिपामः ।२। नृपाय नरौ मार्गं दिशतः ।३। मार्गेण** ग्रामं गच्छावः ।४। सुखेनेह गृहे तिष्ठति पुत्रः ।५। जलं सिञ्चति मेघः ।६। धनेन सुखमिच्छन्ति नराः ।७। हस्तयोः फले तिष्ठतः ।८। जलं हस्तेन स्पृशसि ।९। नरौ कटे सीदतः ।१०। क्षेत्राणि लाङ्गलैः कृषन्ति ।११। नगरं नृपौ विशतः ।१२। नरः पुत्रेण मार्गे गच्छति ।१३। नरान्सृजति देवः ॥१४॥

15. The boy[4] asks[3] the men[1] *about* the road[2] *(acc.)*. 16. The clouds[1] drop[4] water[3] *on* the fields[2] *(loc.)*. 17. The *two* men[1] go[4] *by two* roads[2] *(instr.) into* the city[3]. 18. The king[4] gives[3] the *two* men[1] money[2]. 19. The man's[1] sons[2] sit[4] *on* mats[3]. 20. The gods[4] give[3] the water[2] of the clouds[1]. 21. We wash[3] *(use* स्पृश्) *both* hands[2] *with* water[1]. 22. *Both* men[1] lead[4] *their* sons[2] *(dual)* home[3] (गृह). 23. The *two* boys[3] point out[4] the road[2] *to the* city[1] *(gen.)*.

Lesson IV.

113. **Masculines in** इ *i*. अग्नि *agni*, 'fire'.

	Singular.	Dual.	Plural.
N.	अग्निस् *agnis*	अग्नी *agnī*	अग्नयस् *agnayas*
A.	अग्निम् *agnim*	„ „	अग्नीन् *agnīn*
I.	अग्निना *agninā*	अग्निभ्याम् *agnibhyām*	अग्निभिस् *agnibhis*
D.	अग्नये *agnaye*	„ „	अग्निभ्यस् *agnibhyas*
A.	अग्नेस् *agnes*	„ „	„ „
G.	„ „	अग्न्योस् *agnyos*	अग्नीनाम् *agnīnām*
L.	अग्नौ *agnāu*	„ „	अग्निषु *agniṣu**
V.	अग्ने *agne*		

* See note to § 102.

** The dental nasal न् *n*, when immediately followed by a vowel, or by न् *n* or म् *m* or य् *y* or व् *v*, is turned into the lingual ण् *ṇ* if preceded in the same word by the lingual sibilant or semivowel or vowels — i. e. by ष् *ṣ*, र् *r*, ऋ *ṛ*, or ॠ *ṝ*: and this, not

114. Neuters in इ *i*. वारि *vāri*, 'water'.

	Singular.	Dual.	Plural.
N.	वारि *vāri*	वारिणी *vāriṇī*	वारीणि *vārīṇi*
A.	„ „	„ „	„ „
I.	वारिणा *vāriṇā**	वारिभ्याम् *vāribhyām*	वारिभिस् *vāribhis*
D.	वारिणे *vāriṇe*	„ „	वारिभ्यस् *vāribhyas*
Ab.	वारिणस् *vāriṇas*	„ „	„ „
G.	„ „	वारिणोस् *vāriṇos*	वारीणाम् *vārīṇām*
L.	वारिणि *vāriṇi*	„ „	वारिषु *vāriṣu*
V.	वारे *vāre* or वारि *vāri*		

115. Masculine and neuter adjectives in इ *i* are declined like the substantives above. But neuter adjectives (never substantives) may, in the dat., abl., gen., and loc. sing., and the gen. and loc. dual, substitute the corresponding forms of masculines.

116. Euphonic changes of स् *s* and र् *r*. These two sounds stand to each other in the practical relation, *in external combination*, of corresponding surd and sonant: in countless cases स् *s* becomes र् *r* in situations requiring or favoring the occurrence of a sonant; and, less often, र् *r* becomes स् *s* where a surd is required. In internal combination the two are far less interchangeable. The *s* is extremely common as an etymological final, the *r* not common.

117. A. Final स् *s*. 1. Before a sonant, either vowel or consonant (except र् *r* — see below), स् *s* is changed to the sonant र् *r* — unless, indeed, it be preceded by अ *a* or आ *ā*; thus, अग्निस्

---

only if the altering letter stands immediately before the nasal, but at whatever distance before the latter it may be found: unless, indeed, there intervene a palatal (except य *y*), a lingual, or a dental. Thus, नगरेण *nagareṇa*, मार्गेण *mārgeṇa*, पुष्पाणि *puṣpāṇi*.

* See preceding note.

अत्र *agnis atra* becomes अग्निरत्र *agnir atra;* अग्निस् दहति *agnis dahati* becomes अग्निर्दहति *agnir dahati.* See also § 95.

118. 2. Final अस् *as*, before any sonant consonant or before initial short अ *a*, is changed to ओ *o* — and the initial अ *a* is dropped; thus, नृपस् जयति *nṛpas jayati* becomes नृपो जयति *nṛpo jayati;* नृपस् अत्र *nṛpas atra* = नृपो ऽत्र *nṛpo 'tra.*

119. It is the practice in our system of transliteration to render the sign ऽ, which denotes this dropping of an initial अ *a*, by an inverted comma.

120. 3. Before any initial vowel other than short अ *a*, final अस् *as* loses its स् *s*, becoming simple अ *a;* and the hiatus thus occasioned remains; thus, नृपस् इच्छति *nṛpas icchati* becomes नृप इच्छति *nṛpa icchati;* ततस् उदकम् *tatas udakam* = तत उदकम् *tata udakam.*

121. 4. Final आस् *ās* before any sonant, whether vowel or consonant, loses its स् *s*, becoming simply आ *ā;* and the hiatus thus occasioned remains; thus, नृपास् इच्छन्ति *nṛpās icchanti* = नृपा इच्छन्ति *nṛpā icchanti;* नृपास् जयन्ति *nṛpās jayanti* = नृपा जयन्ति *nṛpā jayanti.*

122. B. Final र् *r*. 1. Final र् *r* in general shows the same form which स् *s* would exhibit under the same conditions: thus पुनर् *punar* standing at the end of a sentence becomes पुनः *punaḥ;* गीर् *gīr*, गीः *gīḥ*. But *original* final र् *r*, after अ *a* or आ *ā*, maintains itself before vowels and sonant consonants; thus, पुनरत्र *punar atra*, पुनर्जयति *punar jayati.*

123. 2. A double र् *r* is nowhere admitted: if such would occur, either by retention of an original र् *r* or by conversion of स् *s* to र् *r*, the first र् *r* is omitted, and the preceding vowel, if short, is made long by compensation; thus, पुनर् रामः *punar rāmaḥ* = पुना रामः *punā rāmaḥ;* अग्निस् रोचते *agnis rocate* = अग्नी रोचते *agnī rocate;* धेनुस् रोचते *dhenus rocate* = धेनू रोचते *dhenū rocate.*

Vocabulary IV.

Verbs:

कृत् *kṛt (kṛntáti)* cut, cut off.

मुच् *muc (muñcáti)* free, deliver, release.

रुह् *ruh (róhati)* grow.

लिप् *lip (limpáti)* smear.

लुप् *lup (lumpáti)* break to pieces, devastate, plunder.

Subst.:

अग्नि *agni*, m., fire; (as proper name) Agni, the god of fire.

अरि *ari*, m., enemy.

असि *asi*, m., sword.

ऋषि *ṛṣi*, m., seer.

कवि *kavi*, m., poet.

गिरि *giri*, m., mountain.

जन *jana*, m., man; (pl.) people.

दुःख *duḥkha*, n., misery, misfortune.

पाणि *pāṇi*, m., hand.

पाप *pāpa*, n., sin.

राम *rāma*, m., *nom. pr.*, name of a hero.

वृक्ष *vṛkṣa*, m., tree.

शिव *çiva*, m., *nom. pr.* name of a god.

सत्य *satya*, n., truth, righteousness.

हरि *hari*, m., *nom. pr.*, name of a god.

Exercise IV.

कदा देवा जनान्मुञ्चन्ति पापात् ।१। नृपस्य पुत्रौ क्व वसतः ।२। अग्निर्दुःखात्पुत्रं रक्षति ।३। नृपो ऽसिनारेः* पाणी कृन्तति ।४। कवयो हरिं स्तुवन्ति ।५। अरयो जनानां धनं लुम्पन्ति ।६। जनो गिरेः (abl.) पतति ।७। शरान्विषेण लिम्पथ ।८। वृक्षा गिरौ रोहन्ति ।९। ऋष्योः पुत्रौ तत्र मार्गे तिष्ठतः ।१०। हरिः कविभ्यां दानानि यच्छति ।११। ऋषिभी (§ 123) रामो वसति ।१२। असिनाऽरीणां गृहाणि नृपा दहन्ति ।१३। हरिं वीरेण यजतः ॥१४॥

15. Çiva[1] dwells[3] in the mountains[2]. 16. *Both* enemies[1] hurl[4] spears[2] *at* the king[3] (*dat.*) 17. Rāma[1] touches[4] *his two* sons[3] *with his* hands[2]. 18. Fire[1] burns[3] the trees[2]. 19. Seers[1] speak[2] the truth[3]. 20. *Through* righteousness[1] happiness[3] arises[4] (भू) for man-

* Modifiers generally precede the word which is modified.

kind[2] (जन, *gen. pl.*). 21. The seer's[1] *two* hands[2] touch water[3]. 22. Fruits[1] are[3] (*use* स्था) *on* the trees[2]. 23. People[1] remember[3] Hari[2]. 24. Rāma[1] hurls[4] the sword[3] from *his* hand[2] (*abl.*).

Lesson V.

124. Verbs. Unaccented *ya*-class. Roots of this class form their present-stem by adding य *ya* to the root, which bears the accent. Thus from नह् *nah* is made the present-stem नह्य *náhya*; from लुभ् *lubh*, लुभ्य *lúbhya*.

125. The inflection of stems of this class follows the model of वद् *vad*.

126. Certain आ *ā*-roots, because of their peculiar exchanges with इ *i* and ई *ī*-forms, especially in the formation of the present-stem, are given by the Hindu grammarians as ending in ए *e* or ऐ *ai* or ओ *o* (cf. § 132), and by them assigned to the भू *bhū*, or *a*-class. Thus धा *dhā*, 'suck' (Hindu धे *dhe*), forms धयति *dháyati*; the root हू *hū* or ह्वा *hvā* (Hindu ह्वे *hve*) forms ह्वयति *hváyati*; गा *gā* (Hindu गै *gāi*) makes गायति *gáyati*.

127. For the root दृश् *dṛç*, 'see', is substituted in the present-system another root पश् *paç*, which makes पश्यति *páçyati*.

128. Masculines in उ *u*. भानु *bhānu*, 'sun'.

	Singular.	Dual.	Plural.
N.	भानुस् *bhānus*	भानू *bhānū*	भानवस् *bhānavas*
A.	भानुम् *bhānum*	" "	भानून् *bhānūn*
I.	भानुना *bhānunā*	भानुभ्याम् *bhānubhyām*	भानुभिस् *bhānubhis*
D.	भानवे *bhānave*	" "	भानुभ्यस् *bhānubhyas*
Ab.	भानोस् *bhānos*	" "	" "
G.	" "	भान्वोस् *bhānvos*	भानूनाम् *bhānūnām*
L.	भानौ *bhānāu*	" "	भानुषु *bhānuṣu*
V.	भानो *bhāno*		

Masculine adjectives in उ *u* are similarly declined.

129. **Euphonic Changes of** स् *s*, **cont'd.** 1. Final स् *s*, the dental sibilant, whether original or representing final र् *r*, before the palatal surd mutes [च् *c*, छ् *ch*], is assimilated, becoming palatal श् *ç*. Thus नरस् चरति *naras carati* becomes नरश्चरति *naraç carati;* नरस् छलेन *naras chalena* becomes नरश्छलेन *naraç chalena.* 2. Before a lingual surd mute [ट् *ṭ*, ठ् *ṭh*], in like manner, it would become lingual ष् *ṣ*, but the case almost never occurs. 3. Before the dental surd mutes [त् *t*, थ् *th*], since it is already of the same class with them, it of course remains unchanged; thus, रामस् तिष्ठति *rāmas tiṣṭhati.*

---

130. The preposition आ *ā* is sometimes used with the ablative (much less often with the accusative), in the sense of 'hither from', 'all the way from'; but far more usually to signify 'all the way to', 'until'. As a prefix to verbs, आ *ā* means 'to', 'unto', 'at'.

Vocabulary V.

Verbs:

अस् *as (ásyati)* throw, hurl.

कुप् *kup* (*kúpyati* — w. gen. or dat.) be angry.

क्रुध् *krudh* (*krúdhyati* — w. gen. or dat.) be angry.

गम् *gam* + आ *ā (āgácchati)* come.

तॄ *tṝ* (*tárati*) cross over.

नश् *naç (náçyati)* perish.

पश् *paç (páçyati)* see.

रुह् *ruh (róhati)* rise, spring up, grow.

+ आ *ā (āróhati)* climb, mount, ascend.

लिख् *likh (likháti)* scratch; write.

लुभ् *lubh* (*lúbhyati* — w. dat. or loc.) desire, covet.

शुष् *çuṣ (çúṣyati)* dry up.

स्निह् *snih* (*sníhyati* — w. gen. or loc.) feel inclined to, love.

हू *hū* or ह्वा *hvā (hváyati)* call.

Subst.:

अन्न *anna*, n., food, fodder.

अश्व *açva*, m., horse.

उदधि *udadhi*, m., ocean.

गुरु *guru*, m., teacher.

पत्त्र *pattra*, n., leaf, letter.

परशु *paraçu*, m., axe.

पाद *pāda*, m., foot; quarter; ray, beam.

बाहु *bāhu*, m., arm.

बिन्दु *bindu*, m., drop.

भानु *bhānu*, m., sun.

मणि *maṇi*, m., jewel.

रत्न *ratna*, n., jewel.

राशि *rāçi*, m., heap.

वायु *vāyu*, m., wind.

विष्णु *viṣṇu*, m., *nom. pr.* name of a god.

शत्रु *çatru*, m., enemy.

शिखर *çikhara*, m., summit.

शिष्य *çiṣya*, m., pupil, scholar.

सूक्त *sūkta*, n., Vedic hymn.

Exercise V.

कवयो धने लुभ्यन्ति । १ । ऋषिः सूक्तानि पश्यति* । २ । गुरू शिष्ययोः क्रुध्यतः । ३ । नृपा अरिभ्यः कुप्यन्ति । ४ । अग्निरुदधौ तिष्ठति । ५ । परशुना वृक्षान्कृन्तथ । ६ । जलस्य बिन्दवो गिरेः पतन्ति । ७ । विष्णुभूतिर्यजति नृपाय । ८ । नृपोऽश्वमारोहति । ९ । क्षेत्रेषु जलं शुष्यति । १० । गुरवः शिष्याणां स्निह्यन्ति । ११ । नृपाणां शत्रवोऽसिना नश्यन्ति । १२ । बालो गुरवे पत्त्रं लिखति । १३ । जना मणीनां राशीनिच्छन्ति । १४ । आ गिरेर्वृक्षा रोहन्ति । १५ । बाहुभ्यां जलं नरास्तरन्ति । १६ । बाली गृहे द्रुह्यति नरः । १७ । कवेः पुत्रौ ग्रामस्य मार्गे गजं पश्यतः ॥ १८ ॥

19. Now[4] the sun's[1] rays[2] climb[5] the mountains[3]. 20. A drop[2] of water[1] falls[4] *down from* the cloud[3]. 21. O[1] men[2], we see[4] the city[3]. 22. *Both* kings[1] love[3] poets[2] *(gen. or loc.)*. 23. The wind[1] blows[4] (वह्) *from* the summits[3] of the mountains[2]. 24. The king[1] hurls[4] spears[3] *at his* enemies[2] *(dat. or loc.)*. 25. The scholar[1] bows[3] *before his* teacher[2] *(acc.)*. 26. *Two* men[1] come[3] *with their* sons[2] *(instr.)*. 27. The *two* kings[1] desire[4] the poet's[2] jewels[3] *(dat. or loc.)*. 28. O[1] seer,[2] we sacrifice[4] *to* Viṣṇu[3] (*acc.*). 29. The *two*

* Orthodox Hindus maintain that the Vediç hymns, etc., were revealed to their reputed authors, who thus 'saw' them.

cook[3] food[1] *with* fire[2]. 30. The seers[1] praise[4] Viṣṇu[2] *with* hymns[3]. 31. *In* the city[1] the king[2] calls[4] *his* enemies[3].

Lesson VI.

131. Verbs. *ya*-**class, cont'd.** The roots of this class which end in अम् *am* lengthen their अ *a* in forming their present-stem; thus, तम् *tam*, ताम्यति *tāmyati*; भ्रम् *bhram*, भ्राम्यति *bhrāmyati* — but this last makes also forms according to the unaccented *a*-class; thus भ्रमति *bhrámati*, etc. The root मद् *mad* has the same lengthening: माद्यति *mádyati*.

132. Certain *ā*-roots (five — by the Hindus written with final *o*) make present-stems with an accented *yá*; thus, दा *dā*, द्यति *dyáti*.

133. The root व्यध् *vyadh* is abbreviated to विध् *vidh* in the present-system: विध्यति *vidhyati*.

134. The root क्रम् *kram*, said by the natives to form its present-stem according to this class, really forms it only according to the *a*-class, and the root-vowel is lengthened in the active voice, but not in the middle; thus, क्रामति *krāmati*, but middle क्रमते *krámate*.

135. The root चम् *cam*, used only with the preposition आ *ā*, forms आचामति *ācāmati*.

136. Neuters in उ *u*. मधु *madhu*, 'honey'.

	Singular.	Dual.	Plural.
N.	मधु *madhu*	मधुनी *madhunī*	मधूनि *madhūni*
A.	„ „	„ „	„ „
I.	मधुना *madhunā*	मधुभ्याम् *madhubhyām*	मधुभिस् *madhubhis*
D.	मधुने *madhune*	„ „	मधुभ्यस् *madhubhyas*
Ab.	मधुनस् *madhunas*	„ „	„ „
G.	„ „	मधुनोस् *madhunos*	मधूनाम् *madhūnām*
L.	मधुनि *madhuni*	„ „	मधुषु *madhuṣu*
V.	मधु or मधो		

137. Neuter adjectives (but not substantives) in उ *u* may take the forms proper to the masculine in the dat., abl.-gen., loc. sing., and gen.-loc. dual.

138. Changes of final न् *n*. Before initial ज् *j* and श् *ç*, न् *n* becomes ञ *ñ*; thus, तान् जनान् *tān janān* becomes ताञ्जनान् *tāñ janān*; तान् शत्रून् *tān çatrūn* = ताञ्शत्रून् *tāñ çatrūn*. In the last case, however, छ *ch* is almost always substituted for the initial श् *ç*, thus, ताञ्छत्रून् *tāñ chatrūn*.

139. Final न् *n*, before an initial ल् *l*, is assimilated and becomes nasalized *l*, which is written ल्ँ *ṅl*, or (what is the same thing) ं *ṅ*; thus तान् लोकान् *tān lokān* becomes ताल्ँ लोकान् *tāṅl lokān* or तां लोकान् *tāṅ lokān*.

140. Before the surd palatal, lingual, and dental mutes there is inserted after final न् *n* a sibilant of each of those classes respectively, before which न् *n* becomes *anusvāra*; thus for तान् च *tān ca* we find तांश्च *tāṅç ca*; for तान् तथा *tān tathā*, तांस्तथा *tāṅs tathā*.*

Vocabulary VI.

Verbs:

ऋ *r* (*ṛcchati* — § 109) go to; fall to one's lot, fall upon.

क्रम् *kram* + आ *ā* (*ākrāmati*) stride up to, attack.

चम् *cam* + आ *ā* (*ācāmati*) sip, drink, rinse the mouth.

तम् *tam* (*tāmyati*) be sad.

तुष् *tuṣ* (*tuṣyati*) rejoice, take pleasure in (w. instr.).

दीव् *dīv* (*dīvyati*) play.

---

* This rule really involves an historic survival, the large majority of cases of final न् *n* in the language being for original *ns*. Practically, the rule applies only to न् *n* before च् *c* and त् *t*, since cases involving the other initials are excessively rare.

भ्रम् *bhram* (*bhrấmyati* — § 131) wander about.

मद् *mad* (*mấdyati*) get drunk.

व्यध् *vyadh* (*vídhyati*) hit, pierce.

शम् *çam* (*çấmyati*) become quiet, be extinguished, go out.

श्रम् *çram* (*çrấmyati*) become weary.

हृ *hṛ* (*hárati*) take away, steal, plunder.

Subst.:

अक्ष *akṣa*, m., die, dice.

अधर्म *adharma*, m., injustice, wrong.

अलि *ali*, m., bee.

अश्रु *açru*, n., tear.

ऋक्ष *ṛkṣa*, m., bear.

कोप *kopa*, m., anger.

क्षत्रिय *kṣatriya*, m., warrior, man of the second caste.

नृपति *nṛpati*, m., king.

नेत्र *netra*, n., eye.

मधु *madhu*, n., honey.

मुख *mukha*, n., mouth, face.

मृत्यु *mṛtyu*, m., death.

वसु *vasu*, n., wealth, money.

Exercise VI.

ऋक्षा मधुने लुभ्यन्ति ।१। ऋषिरधुना पाणिना अम्भ आचामति ।२। नृपा अक्षैश्च दीव्यन्ति ।३। अलिर्मधुना माद्यति ।४। नरा विषेणासीं लिम्पन्ति ।५। रामः क्षत्रियान्परशुनाक्रामति ।६। गुरूञ्छिष्यांश्च शंसामः ।७। अरयो जनानां वसूनि हरन्ति ।८। नरौ मृत्युमृच्छतः ।९। बालस्य नेत्राभ्यामश्रूणि पतन्ति ।१०। जलेनाग्निः शाम्यति ।११। ऋषेरश्वौ श्राम्यतः ।१२। गुरुः शिष्यस्य पापात्ताम्यति ।१३। गजा नगरे भ्राम्यन्ति ।१४। मधुना क्षीरेण च तुष्यन्ति बालाः ॥१५॥

16. The warriors[1] play[3] *for* money[2] (*instr.*). 17. The king's[2] horses[3] become weary[5] *on* the road[4] to-day[1]. 18. The warrior[1] pierces[4] *his* enemy[3] *with* the spear[2]. 19. Bees[1] are fond of[3] (तुष्) honey[2]. 20. *The* water[2] *of his* tears[1] moistens[4] (सिच्) *his* feet[3]. 21. There[2] bees[1] are flitting about[3] (भ्रम्). 22. *Two* men[1] are cooking[5] honey[2] and[4] fruits[3]. 23. When[1] the teacher's[2] anger[3] ceases[4], then[5] the scholars[7] rejoice[6]. 24. Tears[1] stand[4] *in* the warriors'[2]

eyes[3]. 25. The enemies[1] overwhelm[4] (वृष्) the king[2] *with* arrows[3]. 26. A quarter[2] of the injustice[1] falls upon[4] (ऋ) the king[3] (*acc.*).

Lesson VII.

141. Causative Verbs (native "*cur*-class"). The Hindu grammarians describe a certain present-system which they assign to a so-called "*cur*-class". This is, however, in fact no present-class at all, but a causative or secondary conjugation, which is not confined to the present-system. But many formations of this sort have no causative value; and it is chiefly these that are grouped by the Hindus in their *cur*-class, which also includes some *denominative*-stems in *áya*, with causative accent. For practical purposes it is well enough to consider these verbs here.

142. The causative-stem is formed by adding अय *áya* to the root, which is usually strengthened; and the strengthening process is in the main as follows:

143. 1. Medial or initial इ *i*, उ *u*, and ऋ *ṛ* have the *guṇa*-strengthening, if capable of it; thus, चुर् *cur*, चोरयति *coráyati;* विद् *vid*, वेदयति *vedáyati;* but पीड् *pīḍ*, पीडयति *pīḍáyati.*

144. 2. A final vowel has the *vṛddhi*-strengthening; thus, धृ *dhṛ*, धारयति *dhāráyati.* Before अय *aya*, ऐ *āi* and औ *āu* become आय् *āy* and आव् *āv* respectively; thus, भी *bhī*, भाययति *bhāyáyati;* भू *bhū*, भावयति *bhāváyati.*

145. 3. Medial or initial अ *a* in a metrically light syllable is sometimes lengthened, and sometimes remains unchanged; thus, क्षल् *kṣal*, caus. क्षालयति *kṣāláyati;* but जन् *jan*, caus. जनयति *janáyati.*

146. The inflection is the usual one of *a*-stems.

147. Rules of euphonic combination. In external combination, an initial sonant of whatever class (even a vowel or semivowel or nasal) requires the conversion of a preceding final surd to a sonant.

148. Final त् t. 1. Final त् t becomes द् d, before any initial sonant, except the palatals, the nasals, and ल् l: thus, मेघात् अत्र *meghāt atra* becomes मेघादत्र *meghād atra;* पापात् रक्षति *pāpāt rakṣati* or भ्राम्यति *bhrāmyati* or गोपायति *gopāyati* becomes पापाद्रक्षति *pāpād rakṣati* or पापाद्भ्राम्यति *pāpād bhrāmyati* or पापाद्गोपायति *pāpād gopāyati.*

149. 2. Final त् t is assimilated to an initial palatal, lingual, or ल् l in the next word; thus it becomes च् c before च् c and छ् ch, ज् j before ज् j, and ल् l before ल् l: e. g., मेघात् च *meghāt ca* becomes मेघाच्च *meghāc ca*; मेघात् जलम् *meghāt jalam* becomes मेघाज्जलम् *meghāj jalam;* पापात् लोकात् *pāpāt lokāt* becomes पापाल्लोकात् *pāpāl lokāt.*

150. 3. Before initial श् ç, final त् t becomes च् c, and the श् ç then becomes छ् ch; thus, नृपात् शत्रुः *nṛpāt çatruḥ* becomes नृपाच्छत्रुः *nṛpāc chatruḥ.*

151. 4. Before initial nasals त् t becomes न् n: thus, गृहात् नयति *gṛhāt nayati* becomes गृहान्नयति *gṛhān nayati.* But the change into द् d is also permitted, though hardly used; thus, गृहाद्नयति *gṛhād nayati.*

Vocabulary VII.

Verbs:

कथय *kathaya* (denom. stem — *katháyati*) relate, tell.

क्षल् *kṣal* (*kṣāláyati*) wash.

गणय *gaṇaya* (denom. — *gaṇáyati*) number, count.

चुर् *cur* (*coráyati*) steal.

तड् *taḍ* (*tāḍáyati*) strike, beat.

तुल् *tul* (*toláyati*) weigh.

दण्डय *daṇḍaya* (denom. — *daṇḍáyati*) punish.

नी + आ *nī* + *ā* (*ānáyati*) bring.

पीड् *pīḍ* (*pīḍáyati*) torment, vex.

पूज् *pūj* (*pūjáyati*) honor.

पृ *pṛ* (*pāráyati*) overcome evils; prevail.

Subst.:

जनक *janaka*, m., father.

दण्ड *daṇḍa*, m., stick; punishment.

पुण्य *puṇya*, n., merit.

फल *phala*, n., fruit; reward.

रामायण *rāmāyaṇa*, n., a noted poem.

रूपक *rūpaka*, n., gold-piece.

लोक *loka*, m., world, people (sing. and pl.).

साधु *sādhu*, m., holy man, saint.

सुवर्ण *suvarṇa*, n., gold.

सूत *sūta*, m., driver, charioteer.

स्तेन *stena*, m., thief.

Adverb: इव *iva* as, like (postpos.).

Exercise VII.

स्तेनः सुवर्णं नृपस्य गृहाच्चोरयति।१। गुरुर्दण्डेन शिष्यांस्ताडयति।२। सूतो ऽश्वान्पीडयति।३। ऋषिर्जलेन पाणी क्षालयति।४। ग्रामाज्जनान्नगरं नयन्ति।५। नरौ रूपकाणि गणयतः।६। नृपाच्छत्रूणां दण्डो भवति।७। रामस्य पुत्रौ जनेभ्यो रामायणं कथयतः।८। सुवर्णं पाणिभ्यां तोलयामः।९। जनकः पुत्रान्कोपाद्दण्डयति।१०। गृहाल्लोका आगच्छन्ति।११। पुण्येन साधुर्दुःखानि पारयति।१२। देवानिव नृपतीं लोकः पूजयति॥१३॥

14. Thieves[1] steal[4] the people's[2] money[3]. 15. The two boys[1] wash[3] their mouths[2]. 16. The father[1] tells[5] his sons[2] (*dat.*) the reward[4] of sin[3]. 17. The scholars[1] honor[3] and[5] reverence[4] their teacher[2]. 18. Ye both bring[3] fruits[1] in your hands[2] and[5] count[4] *them*. 19. Merit[1] protects[3] from misfortune[2] (*abl.*). 20. The charioteers[1] strike[4] the horses[2] with sticks[3]. 21. In anger[1] (*abl.*) the king[2] pierces[5] the thief[3] with a spear[4].

Lesson VIII.

152. Verbs, *a*-conjugation. Present Indicative Middle. The present indicative middle of verbs whose stems end in *a* is inflected as follows:

	Singular.	Dual.	Plural.
1.	वदे *váde*	वदावहे *vádāvahe*	वदामहे *vádāmahe*
2.	वदसे *vádase*	वदेथे *vádethe*	वदध्वे *vádadhve*
3.	वदते *vádate*	वदेते *vádete*	वदन्ते *vádante*

153. The ending of the 3rd pl. is properly **अन्ते** *ante* (cf. **न्ति** *nti* for **अन्ति** *anti* in the act.); before the **ए** *e* of the 1st sing. the stem-final is dropped. **एथे** *ethe* and **एते** *ete* are hard to explain.

154. With verbs inflected in both voices, the chief force of the middle is this, that the action is performed for the benefit of the actor himself; thus, **यजति** *yájati* 'he sacrifices' (for some one else); **यजते** *yájate* 'he sacrifices for himself'. But many verbs are conjugated only in the middle, like the Latin and Greek deponents.

155. The verb **मृ** *mṛ*, 'die', makes **म्रियते** *mriyáte* in the present; and **जन्** *jan*, 'give birth', substitutes as present mid. **जायते** *jáyate*, 'be born'.

156. Combination of final and initial vowels. Two simple vowels, either or both of them short or long, coalesce and form the corresponding long vowel. For the *a*-vowels, see above, § **105**. Thus: 1. **इ** *i* or **ई** *ī* + **इ** *i* or **ई** *ī* = **ई** *ī*; e. g. **गच्छति इति** *gacchati iti* becomes **गच्छतीति** *gacchatī 'ti*. 2. **उ** *u* or **ऊ** *ū* + **उ** *u* or **ऊ** *ū* = **ऊ** *ū*; e. g. **साधु उक्तम्** *sādhu uktam* becomes **साधूक्तम्** *sādhū 'ktam**.

157. The *i*-vowels, the *u*-vowels, and **ऋ** *ṛ*, before a dissimilar vowel or diphthong, are regularly converted each into its own corresponding semivowel, **य्** *y* or **व्** *v* or **र्** *r*. Thus, **तिष्ठति अत्र** *tiṣṭhati atra* becomes **तिष्ठत्यत्र** *tiṣṭhaty atra* (four syllables); **नदी अत्र** *nadī atra* becomes **नद्यत्र** *nady atra*; **मधु अत्र** *madhu atra* becomes **मध्वत्र** *madhv atra*; **कर्तृ इह** *kartṛ iha* becomes **कर्त्रिह** *kartr iha*.

---

* And theoretically 3. **ऋ** *ṛ* + **ऋ** *ṛ* = **ॠ** *ṝ*, but probably this has no occurrence.

158. Final ए *e* and ओ *o* remain unchanged before an initial *short* अ *a*, but the अ *a* disappears. Thus, वने अत्र *vane atra* becomes वने ऽत्र *vane 'tra;* भानो अत्र *bhāno atra* becomes भानो ऽत्र *bhāno 'tra.* By far the commonest case of final ओ *o* is where it represents final अस् *as* (see § 118).

159. The final इ *i* or उ *u*-element of a diphthong is changed to its corresponding semivowel य् *y* or व् *v*, before any vowel or diphthong, except when the rule of § 158 would apply. Thus, ए *e* becomes अय् *ay*, and ऐ *āi*, आय् *āy*; ओ *o* becomes अव् *av*, and औ *āu*, आव् *āv*. Thus, in internal combination, ने-अ *ne-a* becomes नय *naya*; भो-अ *bho-a* becomes भव *bhava;* so नै-अय *nāi-aya* yields नायय *nāy-aya*, and भौ-अय *bhāu-aya* yields भावय *bhāv-aya.*

160. In *external* combination, the resulting semivowel is in general dropped; and the resulting hiatus remains. Thus, वने इति *vane iti* becomes वन इति *vana iti* (through the intermediate stage वनयिति *vanay iti*); भानो इति *bhāno iti* becomes भान इति *bhāna iti* (through भानविति *bhānav iti*). The case of final ए *e* is by far the more frequent. See also § 164.

161. Certain final vowels maintain themselves unchanged before any following vowel. Such are 1. ई *ī*, ऊ *ū*, and ए *e* as dual endings, both of declension and of conjugation; thus, गिरी इह *girī iha*, साधू अत्र *sādhū atra*; फले अत्र *phale atra.* 2. The final, or only, vowel of an interjection; thus, हे इन्द्र *he indra*, हे अग्ने *he agne.*

Vocabulary VIII.

Verbs (deponents):

अर्थय *arthaya* (denom. — *arthá-yate*) ask for (w. two accus.).

ईक्ष् *īkṣ* (*íkṣate*) see, behold.

कम्प् *kamp* (*kámpate*) tremble.

जन् *jan* (*jāyate*) be born, arise, spring up (mother *in loc.*).

भाष् *bhāṣ* (*bhā́ṣate*) speak.

मृ *mṛ* (*mriyáte*) die.

यत् *yat* (*yátate*) strive for (w. dat.).

युध् *yudh* (*yúdhyate*) fight (w. instr. of accompaniment).

रभ् *rabh* + आ *ā* (*ārábhate*) take hold on, begin.

रुच् *ruc* (*rócate*) please (dat., gen.).

लभ् *labh* (*lábhate*) receive, take.

वन्द् *vand* (*vándate*) greet, honor.

शिक्ष् *çikṣ* (*çíkṣate*) learn.

सह् *sah* (*sáhate*) endure.

सेव् *sev* (*sévate*) serve, honor.

Subst.:

अनर्थ *anartha*, m., misfortune.

उद्योग *udyoga*, m., diligence.

कल्याण *kalyāṇa*, n., advantage; salvation.

तरु *taru*, m., tree.

द्विज *dvija*, m., Aryan.

द्विजाति *dvijāti*, m., Aryan.

धर्म *dharma*, m., right; law; virtue.

धैर्य *dhāirya*, n., steadfastness.

पशु *paçu*, m., beast.

बल *bala*, n., strength, might.

मनुष्य *manuṣya*, m., man (*homo*).

यज्ञ *yajña*, m., sacrifice.

वन *vana*, n., woods, forest.

विनय *vinaya*, m., obedience.

वीचि *vīci*, m., wave.

शास्त्र *çāstra*, n., science; text-book.

शूद्र *çūdra*, m., man of the fourth caste.

हित *hita*, n., advantage.

Adverb: न *na*, not.

Exercise VIII.

वायोर्बलेन तरवः कम्पन्ते । १ । असिनाद्यारयो म्रियन्त इत्यत्र* नृपो भाषते । २ । वसूनां राशीन्नृपतीन्कवयो ऽर्थयन्ते । ३ । शास्त्रे (§ 161) अधुना शिक्षामह इति पत्त्रे हरिर्लिखति । ४ । पापाद्दुःखं जायते । ५ । शिष्याणां विनय उद्योगश्च गुरुभ्यो रोचेते । ६ । अधर्माय न धर्माय यतेथे । ७ । विष्णोः (abl.) सूक्ते ऋषी लभेते । ८ । अत्रर्षिर्भानुं वन्दते । ९ । अग्नी ईक्षते बालः । १० । धनेन पशूं लभध्वे यज्ञाय । ११ । सदा गुरोः पादौ बालाः सेवन्ते । १२ । फले अत्र मनुष्यस्य पाण्योस्तिष्ठतः । १३ । सहेते अनर्थं साधू । १४ । वनेष्विहर्द्वा वसन्ति । १५ । क्षत्रिया ऋषी सेवन्ते ॥ १६ ॥

17. The two houses[4] yonder[5] tremble[6] by the power[3] (*instr.*)

---

* इति, 'thus', is very commonly used as a particle of quotation, following the words quoted.

of the ocean's[1] waves[2]. 18. The father[3] beholds[4] his son's[1] face.[2] 19. "We strive[3] after the advantage[2] of the scholars[1];" thus[4] (इति) speak[6] the teachers[5]. 20. The children[2] ask[4] their father[1] for food[3] (*accus.*). 21. In the forest[1] yonder[2] elephants[3] are fighting[5] with bears[4]. 22. The two Çūdras[3] serve[4] the two Aryans[1] here[2]. 23. Fruits[1] please[3] the children[2]. 24. Whence[1] do ye receive[3] money[2]? 25. Now[1] the two seers[2] begin[4] the sacrifice[3].

Lesson IX.

162. Feminines in आ *ā*, declined like सेना *senā*, 'army.'

	Singular.	Dual.	Plural.
N.	सेना *senā*	सेने *sene* (*ā* + *ī*)	सेनास् *senās*
A.	सेनाम् *senām*	" "	" "
I.	सेनया *senayā*	सेनाभ्याम् *senābhyām*	सेनाभिस् *senābhis*
D.	सेनायै *senāyāi*	" "	सेनाभ्यस् *senābhyas*
Ab.	सेनायास् *senāyās*	" "	" "
G.	" "	सेनयोस् *senayos*	सेनानाम् *senānām*
L.	सेनायाम् *senāyām*	" "	सेनासु *senāsu*
V.	सेने *sene*		

163. Adjectives in अ *a* are declined in the masc. like देव, in the fem. like सेना, in the neuter like फल. But often the fem. stem ends in ई *ī*, and is declined like नदी (in Less. XI).

164. Final ऐ *āi* and औ *āu*, according § 159, become आय् *āy* and आव् *āv* respectively before any following vowel or diphthong. The य् or व् may then be dropped, leaving a hiatus. The य् is in fact always dropped, but the व् not often. Thus, सेनायै अत्र becomes, through the medium of सेनायाय् अत्र, सेनाया अत्र; देवौ अत्र becomes देवावत्र.

165. Initial छ्, after short vowels, the preposition आ, and the

prohibitive particle मा, becomes च्छ्: thus, अव छाया becomes अव च्छाया; आ + छादयति = आच्छादयति.

166. An initial न् of a root generally becomes ण् after a verbal prefix containing र्, either original or representing स्; such as अन्तर् 'between', निस्, परा, etc. Thus, प्रणयति, निर्णयति.

167. The following prefixes are often used before verbs: अनु 'after, along, toward'; अव 'down, off'; उद् 'up, up forth or out'; उप 'to, toward'; नि 'down; in, into'; निस् 'out, forth'; परा 'to a distance, away'; परि 'round about, around'; प्र 'forward, forth'; सम् 'along with, completely.'

Vocabulary IX.

Active Verbs:

गम् + अव (*avagácchati*) understand.

तृ + अव (*avatárati*) descend.

नी + उप (*upanáyati*) introduce, consecrate.

+ परि (*pariṇáyati*) lead about; marry.

पत् + उद् (*utpátati*) fly up.

रुह् + अव (*avaróhati*) descend.

Deponents:

गम् + सम् (*saṁgácchate*) come together, meet (*w. instr.*).

जि + परा (*parājáyate*) be conquered (*rarely w. act. sense:* conquer).

पद् + प्र (*prapádyate*) flee for refuge (*acc.*) to (*acc. of person*).

भिक्ष् (*bhikṣate*) beg, get by begging.

मृगय (denom. — *mṛgáyate*) hunt for, seek.

वृत् (*vártate*) exist, subsist, be, become.

शुभ् (*çóbhate*) be brilliant, shine; be eminent.

Subst.:

इषु m., arrow.

कन्या f., daughter, maiden.

गङ्गा *gañgā* f., *n. pr.*, the Ganges.

गृहस्थ m., householder, head of family.

छाया f., shade.

प्रयाग m., *nom. pr.*, Prayāga (a city, Allahābād).

भय n., fear.

भार्या f., wife, woman.

भाषा f., speech, language.

भिक्षा f., alms.

यमुना f., *n. pr.*, Yamunā (a river, the Jumna).

रण m., n., battle.

रथ्या f., street.

विद्या f., knowledge, learning.

विहग m., bird.

व्याध m., hunter.

शरण n., protection.

संध्या f., twilight.

स्वर्ग m., heaven.

हृदय n., heart.

Adj.:

कृष्ण, f. **°ष्णा**, black.

पाप, f. **°पा**, bad, wicked.

प्रभूत, f. **°ता**, much, abundant; pl. many.

Adv.:

सह together with (*postpos.*, *w. instr.*).

सहसा suddenly, quickly.

Exercise IX.

रत्नं रत्नेन संगच्छते*।१। यदा विहगा व्याधं पश्यन्ति तदा सहसो-
त्पतन्ति।२। सत्यं हृदयेषु मृगयन्त ऋषयः।३। हरेः कन्यां रामः परि-
णयति।४। विष्णोर्हरेश्च भार्ये कन्याभिः सहागच्छतः।५। रामो वि-
ष्णुश्च देवाञ्शरणं प्रपद्येते।६। भिक्षया रामस्य शिष्यौ वर्तेते।७।
यदा जना गङ्गायां म्रियन्ते तदा स्वर्गं लभन्ते।८। कन्याया (§164) अन्नं
यच्छत्यृषेर्भार्या।९। वन ऋक्षेष्विषून्मुञ्चन्ति व्याधाः कृष्णौ च म्रियेते।१०।
द्विजातीनां भाषां शूद्रा नावगच्छन्ति।११। हे शिष्या नगरस्य रथ्यासु
साधूनां भार्याभ्यो ऽद्य भिक्षां लभध्वे।१२। अत्र छायायां प्रभूता विह-
गास्तिष्ठन्ति।१३। क्षत्रियस्य बालावृषिरुपनयति॥१४॥

15. The two scholars[1] beg[6] much[2] alms[3] from the wives[5] of the householders[4]. 16. At Prayāga[1] the Ganges[2] unites[4] with the Yamunā[3]. 17. Bad[1] men[2] do not[4] reach[5] (लभ्) heaven[3]. 18. O Viṣṇu[1], to-day[3] Çiva[2] marries[7] Gaṅgā[6], Hari's[4] daughter[5]. 19. In the battle[1] the kings[3] fight[4] with arrows[2] and[6] conquer[7] *their* enemies[5].

* "Birds of a feather flock together".

20. Here[2] in the street[3] the two kings[1] dismount[6] from *their* black[4] horses[5]. 21. The seer's[2] two sons[3] are eminent[4] in learning[1] (*instr.*). 22. From fear[3] of the wicked[1] hunters[2] (*abl.*) two birds[4] fly up[5]. 23. At twilight[1] (*loc. du.*) the seers[2] (§ 13, 3) reverence[4] the gods[3]. 24. In the street[2] of the village[1] the teacher[3] and[5] the scholar[4] meet[6]. 25. We two sacrifice[2] to the gods[1] *for ourselves*; we do not[4] sacrifice[5] for Hari[3].

Lesson X.

168. Verbs. Passive Inflection. A certain form of present-stem, inflected with middle endings, is used only with a passive meaning, and is formed from all roots for which there is occasion to make a passive conjugation. Its sign is an accented **य** *yá* added to the root, without any reference to the class s according to which the active and middle forms are made. The inflection is precisely like that of other *a*-stems Thus, **तन्ये** *tanyé*, **तन्यसे** *tanyáse*, **तन्यते** *tanyáte*, etc.

169. Outside the present-system middle forms may be used in a passive sense; but there is a special form for the aor. pass. in the 3rd sing.

170. The form of root to which the passive-sign is appended is usually a weak one. Thus a penultimate nasal is dropped; and certain abbreviations which are made in the weak forms of the perfect, or in the past passive participle, are found also in the passive present-system. E. g. from **अञ्ज्**, pass. **अज्यते**; from **बन्ध्**, **बध्यते**.

171. In the roots **वच्**, **वद्**, **वप्**, **वस्**, **वह्**, and **स्वप्**, the **व** *va* becomes **उ** *u* in the pres.; thus, **उच्यते**, **उप्यते**, **उष्यते** (see note to § 102), **सुप्यते**. Similarly, **यज्** makes **इज्यते**, and **ग्रह्** and **प्रछ्** make **गृह्यते** and **पृच्छ्यते**; **शास्** makes **शिष्यते**.

172. Final इ and उ of roots are generally lengthened; thus, जि, जीयते; स्तु, स्तूयते.

173. Final ऋ is in general changed to रि; thus, कृ, क्रियते; but if preceded by two consonants it takes *guṇa;* thus, स्मृ, स्मर्यते. The roots in "variable ṛ", which the natives write with ॠ ṝ, change ॠ to ईर्, or, if a labial letter precede, to ऊर्; thus, तॄ, तीर्यते; कॄ, 'strew', कीर्यते; but पॄ, पूर्यते.

174. Final आ of roots is usually changed to ई; thus, दा, दीयते; गा, गीयते; धा, धीयते. But ध्या makes ध्यायते; and so some other roots in आ.

175. The roots तन् and खन् usually form their passives from parallel roots in आ; thus, तायते. But तन्यते and खन्यते occur.

176. Verbs of causative inflection, and denominatives in अय, form their passive by adding य to the causative or denominative stem after अय has been dropped; thus, चोर्यते 'is stolen'; गण्यते 'is counted'.

177. The personal passive construction, with the logical subject in the instrumental, is particularly common with transitive verbs; and not less so the impersonal passive construction, both with transitive and intransitive verbs. Thus, नरेण स्वर्गो लभ्यते 'Heaven is reached by the man'; आगम्यते 'one comes hither'; सुप्यते 'one sleeps'; श्रूयते 'it is heard', i. e. 'they say'. The predicate to the instrumental subject of such a construction is of course also instrumental; thus, रामेणर्षिणा जीव्यते 'Rāma lives as a seer'.

Vocabulary X.

Verbs, with passives:

कृ (p. *kriyáte*) make, do, perform.

खन् (*khánati;* p. *khāyate, khanyáte*) dig.

गा (*gāyati;* p. *gīyáte*) sing.

ग्रह् (p. *gṛhyáte*) take, receive, seize.

दंश् (*dáçati;* p. *daçyáte*) bite.

2दा (*dyáti;* p. *dīyáte*) cut.

दीव् (*dīvyati;* p. *dīvyáte*) play.

1धा (p. *dhīyáte*) put, place.

2धा (*dháyati; p. dhīyáte*) suck.

ध्या (*dhyā́yati; p. dhyāyáte*) think, ponder.

1पा (p. *pīyáte*) drink.

1पृ (Hindu पॄ; p. *pūryáte*) fill.

बन्ध् (p. *badhyáte*) bind; entangle; catch.

1मा (p. *mīyáte*) measure.

वच् (p. *ucyáte*) speak.

वप् (*vápati;* p. *upyáte*) sow, scatter.

शास् (p. *çiṣyáte*) rule; punish.

श्रु (p. *çrūyáte*) hear.

स्तु (p. *stūyáte*) praise.

स्वप् (p. *supyáte*) sleep.

1हा (p. *hīyáte*) abandon, give up; neglect.

ह्वे or ह्वा (*hváyati*; p. *hūyáte*) call.
+ आ call, summon.

Subst.:

आज्ञा f., command.

आशा f., hope.

काष्ठ n., fagot; wood.

गीत n., song.

घट m., pot, vessel.

घृत n., melted butter; *ghee.*

धान्य n., grain.

पाश m., noose, cord, snare.

भार m., burden.

भिक्षु m., beggar, ascetic.

भृत्य m., servant.

माला f., garland.

राज्य n., kingdom.

शिशु m., child.

सर्प m., snake.

Adj.:

विधेय, f. °आ, obedient.

Exercise X.

रामेण पुत्रावद्योपनीयेते इति श्रूयते । १ । ऋषिर्नृपेण धर्मं पृच्छ्यते । २ । घटौ घृतेन पूर्येते । ३ । विहगाः पाशैर्बध्यन्ते । ४ । जनैर्नगरं गम्यते । ५ । हे शिष्या गुरुणाहूयध्वे । ६ । नरैः कटाः क्रियन्ते । ७ । कविभिर्नृपाः सदा स्तूयन्ते । ८ । प्रभूता भिक्षा गृहस्थस्य भार्यया भिक्षुभ्यो दीयते । ९ । कन्याभ्यां गीतं गीयते । १० । स्तेनैर्लोकानां वसु चोर्यते । ११ । इषुभी रणेऽरयो नृपतिना जीयन्ते । १२ । हे देवौ साधुभिः सदा स्मर्येथे । १३ । दण्डेन बालाः शिष्यन्ते । १४ । प्रभूतः काष्ठानां भारो नरेणोह्यते । १५ । अश्वेन जलं पीयते । १६ । धर्मेण राज्यं शिष्यते नृपेण । १७ । सर्पेण दश्येते नरौ । १८ । सूतेनाश्वस्ताड्यते ॥ १९ ॥

(*Use passive constructions throughout.*)

20. Grain[2] is scattered[3] for the birds[1]. 21. Garlands[1] are twined[3] (*use* बन्ध्) by the maidens[2]. 22. Again[2] Hari[1] is praised[4] by Rāma[3]. 23. Viṣṇu[1] drinks[4] water[3] from *his* hand[2]. 24. 'Pleasantly[1] (सुखेन) one sleeps[3] in the shade[2]'; so[4] say[5] the people[6]. 25. Both seers[1] sacrifice[2]. 26. The father[1] sets[4] hopes[2] on his child[3] (*loc.*). 27. The scholar[3] neglects[4] the teacher's[1] command[2]. 28. The two scholars[1] think[3] about *their* text-book[2] (*nom.*). 29. Grain[2] is sown[3] in the fields[1]. 30. They play[2] with dice[1] (*impers. pass.*). 31. The king's[1] commands[2] are received[5] by the obedient[3] servants[4]. 32. The man[1] digs[3] in the field[2].

Lesson XI.

178. Verbs. Imperfect Active, *a*-conjugation. The imperfect is formed from the present-stem by prefixing the augment अ, and adding a set of secondary endings.

179. If the present-stem begin with a vowel, the augment unites with it to form always the *vṛddhi*-vowel, not the *guṇa:* thus अ + इ or ई or ए = ऐ; अ + उ or ऊ = औ; अ + ऋ = आर्.

180. If a preposition be prefixed, the augment comes between preposition and verb, as in Greek; thus, from उप-नी, impf.-stem उपानय, i. e. उप + अ + नय; वि-नी, impf.-stem व्यनय.

181. The inflection in the active is as follows:

	Sing.	Dual.	Plural.
1.	अवदम् *ávadam*	अवदाव *ávadāva*	अवदाम *ávadāma*
2.	अवदस् *ávadas*	अवदतम् *ávadatam*	अवदत *ávadata*
3.	अवदत् *ávadat*	अवदताम् *ávadatām*	अवदन् *ávadan*

182. The imperfect is the tense of narration; it expresses past time simply, without any further implication.

183. Polysyllabic Feminines in ई *ī*, declined like नदी, 'river.'

	Sing.	Dual.	Plural.
N.	नदी *nadī*	नद्यौ *nadyāu*	नद्यस् *nadyas*
A.	नदीम् *nadīm*	„ „	नदीस् *nadīs*
I.	नद्या *nadyā*	नदीभ्याम् *nadībhyām*	नदीभिस् *nadībhis*
D.	नद्यै *nadyāi*	„ „	नदीभ्यस् *nadībhyas*
Ab.	नद्यास् *nadyās*	„ „	„ „
G.	„ „	नद्योस् *nadyos*	नदीनाम् *nadīnām*
L.	नद्याम् *nadyām*	„ „	नदीषु *nadīṣu*
V.	नदि *nadi*		

184. Final nasals. The nasals ङ्, ण्, and न्, occurring as finals *after a short vowel,* are doubled before any initial vowel: thus, अतिष्ठन् अत्र becomes अतिष्ठन्नत्र.

Vocabulary XI.

Verbs:

कृत् + अव (*avakṛntáti*) cut off or down.

पठ् (*páṭhati*) recite, read.

विश् + प्र (*praviçáti*) enter.

+ उप seat oneself.

हृ + आ (*āhárati, -te*) fetch, bring.

Subst.:

अर्थ m., purpose; meaning; wealth.

इन्द्र m., *nom. pr.*, the god Indra.

इन्द्राणी f., *nom. pr.*, the goddess Indrāṇī.

काव्य n., poem.

ग्रन्थ m., literary work, book.

जननी f., mother.

दासी f., female slave, servant.

देवी f., goddess, queen.

नगरी f., city.

नारी f., woman, wife.

पत्नी f., wife, consort.

पुत्री f., daughter.

पुस्तक n., book (manuscript).

पूर m., flood, high water.

पृथिवी f., earth; ground.

ब्राह्मण m., priest, Brāhman.

मत्स्य m., fish.

वापी f., cistern.

सभा f., council, meeting.

सेना f., army.

स्तोत्र n., song of praise.

Exercise XI.

नृपतिर्नगरीं सेनयाऽजयत् ।१। कवयः सभायां काव्यान्यपठन् ।२। दास्यो ऽन्नमानयन् ।३। देवीर्देवांश्च हरिरपूजयत् ।४। साधोः पत्न्या भिक्षवे रूपकाणि दीयन्ते ।५। नदीषु मत्स्यानपश्याम ।६। पुस्तकं पुत्र्या अयच्छद्विष्णुः ।७। नगर्या रथ्यासु गजावभ्राम्यताम् ।८। पृथिव्याः प्रभूता विहगा उदपतन् ।९। गृहं नद्याः पूरेणोऽह्यते ।१०। पत्नीभिर्नरा नगर आगच्छन् ।११। यदा शिवो विष्णुश्च ग्रन्थमपठतां तदाऽर्थं नाऽवागच्छाव ।१२। शिष्या गुरोर्गृहं प्राविशन्नुपाविशंश्च कटयोः पृथिव्याम् ॥१३॥

14. When[1] ye besought[4] (**प्रपद्**) the king[2] for protection[3] (*acc.*), then[5] ye were[7] (**स्था**) in misfortune[6]. 15. In the two rivers[1] Gaṅgā[2] and[4] Yamunā[3] it is[6] (**वर्तते**) high-water[5]. 16. The two women[1] sang[4] a song of praise[3] about Rāma[2] (*gen.*). 17. O[1] seers[2], why[3] do ye both sacrifice[6] to the goddesses[4] with melted butter[5]? 18. The queen's[1] women-servants[2] brought[6] jewels[3] and[5] precious stones[4]. 19. In anger[1] (*abl.*) the teacher[2] struck[4] the scholar[5] with his hand[3]. 20. The two servants[1] brought[5] water[4] from the cistern[3] in pots[2]. 21. Ye cut off[4] (*impf.*) wood[3] from the trees[2] with the axe[1]. 22. The seer[1] praised[6] Indrāṇī[4], Indra's[2] consort[3], with hymns[5].

Lesson XII.

185. Feminine Substantives in इ *i* and उ *u* are declined as in the paradigms on the next page. The two series of forms exhibit complete parallelism: where the one shows *i*, *y*, *e*, or *ay*, the other shows respectively *u*, *v*, *o*, or *av*; cf. §§ **50, 51**. In the D., Ab.-G., and L. sing., these stems sometimes follow **नदी**; thus *matyāi*, *-yās*, *-yām*; *dhenvāi*, *-vās*, *-vām*.

186. Feminines in इ *i* and उ *u*: मति 'opinion'; **धेनु** 'cow'.

	Sing.	Dual.	Plural.
N.	मतिस् *matis*	मती *matī*	मतयस् *matayas*
A.	मतिम् *matim*	" "	मतीस् *matīs*
I.	मत्या *matyā*	मतिभ्याम् *matibhyām*	मतिभिस् *matibhis*
D.	मतये *mataye*	" "	मतिभ्यस् *matibhyas*
Ab.	मतेस् *mates*	" "	" "
G.	" "	मत्योस् *matyos*	मतीनाम् *matīnām*
L.	मतौ *matāu*	" "	मतिषु *matiṣu*
V.	मते *mate*		

	Sing.	Dual.	Plural.
N.	धेनुस् *dhenus*	धेनू *dhenū*	धेनवस् *dhenavas*
A.	धेनुम् *dhenum*	" "	धेनूस् *dhenūs*
I.	धेन्वा *dhenvā*	धेनुभ्याम् *dhenubhyām*	धेनुभिस् *dhenubhis*
D.	धेनवे *dhenave*	" "	धेनुभ्यस् *dhenubhyas*
Ab.	धेनोस् *dhenos*	" "	" "
G.	" "	धेन्वोस् *dhenvos*	धेनूनाम् *dhenūnām*
L.	धेनौ *dhenāu*	" "	धेनुषु *dhenuṣu*
V.	धेनो *dheno*		

187. Adjectives in इ *i* and उ *u* are often inflected in the feminine like मति and धेनु. But adjectives in उ *u* preceded by one consonant often form a derivative feminine stem by adding ई *ī*. Thus, बहु 'much', N. masc. बहुस्, f. बह्वी, n. बहु; गुरु 'heavy', m. गुरुस्, f. गुर्वी, n. गुरु. This fem. is then declined like नदी.

Vocabulary XII.

Verbs:

क्लृप् (*kálpate*) be in order; tend or conduce to (*w. dat.*).

दिश् + उप (*upadiçáti*) teach, instruct.

2विद् (*vindáti*, *vindáte*) acquire.

Subst.:

कलह m., quarrel.

काव्य n., poem.

कीर्ति f., glory.

गोप m., cowherd; shepherd; guardian.

जाति f., birth; caste; kind.

धृति f., decision of character; courage.

पार्थिव m., prince.

बुद्धि f., prudence, intelligence.

भक्ति f., devotion, honor.

भाग m., part, piece.

भूति f., prosperity, blessing.

भूमि f., earth, ground, land.

मक्षिका f., fly, gnat.

मुक्ति f., salvation, deliverance.

यष्टि f., stick, staff.

रश्मि m., ray; rein.

रात्रि f., night.

व्रण m., wound.

शान्ति f., repose.

श्रुति f., hearing; holy writ.

स्मृति f., tradition; law-book.

स्वप्न m., sleep; dream.

हनु f., jaw.

Adj.:

नीच, f. °आ, low.

मुख्य, f. °आ, principal, first.

लघु m., f., n., or f. °घ्वी, light.

Exercise XII.

मक्षिका व्रणमिच्छन्ति धनमिच्छन्ति पार्थिवाः।
नीचाः कलहमिच्छन्ति शान्तिमिच्छन्ति साधवः ॥ १ ॥

शान्त्यर्षय इह शोभन्ते। १। श्रुतौ बह्वीषु स्मृतिषु च धर्म उपदिश्यते। २। रात्र्यां स्वप्नं न लभामहे। ३। बह्वीं कीर्तिं धृत्याविन्दन्नृपतिः। ४। पुण्येन मुक्तिं लभध्वे। ५। बह्वनिषून्रणेऽरिष्वक्षिपन्नृपतिः। ६। हन्वामश्वां लघ्वा यष्ट्याताडयम्। ७। नृपतेर्बुद्ध्या क्षत्रियाणां कलहोऽशाम्यत्। ८। शूद्राणां जातयो नीचा गण्यन्ते। ९। द्विजातीनां जातिषु ब्राह्मणा मुख्याः। १०। धर्मो भूत्यै कल्पते। ११। जात्या क्षत्रियौ वर्तेथे। १२। भूमेर्भागं ब्राह्मणायायच्छत्पार्थिवः। १३। अश्वा अश्राम्यन्भूमावपतंश्च ॥ १४ ॥

15. Viṣṇu[3] rejoices[4] at the devotion[2] (*instr.*) of the pious[1] (*pl.*), and[6] gives[7] deliverance[5]. 16. Men[3] of many[1] castes[2] dwelt[5] in the city[4]. 17. The birds[1] see[3] the hunter[2], and[5] fly up[6] from the ground[4]. 18. By the power[2] of intelligence[1] we overcame[4] advers-

ity[3]. 19. The cowherd[1] guards[4] the cows[3] in the wood[2]. 20. By intelligence[1] and[3] diligence[2] ye acquire[6] much[4] glory[5]. 21. The poem[1] tends[4] to the poet's[2] glory[3] (*two datives*). 22. For prosperity[1] we bow before[3] Çiva[2] (*acc.*). 23. The reins[1] are being fastened[4] (बन्ध्) to the horse's[2] jaws[3] (*loc.*). 24. In the night[1] we both read[5] (*impf.*) holy writ[2].

Lesson XIII.

188. Verbs, *a*-conjugation. Imperfect Middle. The imperfect middle of verbs in *a* is as follows:

	Sing.	Dual.	Plural.
1.	अलभे *álabhe* (*a* + *i*)	°भावहि *álabhāvahi*	°भामहि *álabhāmahi*
2.	अलभथास् *álabhathās*	°भेथाम् *álabhethām*	°भध्वम् *álabhadhvam*
3.	अलभत *álabhata*	°भेताम् *álabhetām*	°भन्त *álabhanta*

With एथाम् and एताम् of the dual, cf. एथे and एते of the pres. ind. mid. The impf. pass. is similarly inflected.

189. Root-words in ई *ī* are declined as follows:

	Sing.	Dual.	Plural.
N. V.	धीस् *dhīs*	धियौ *dhiyāu*	धियस् *dhiyas*
A.	धियम् *dhiyam*	" "	" "
I.	धिया *dhiyā*	धीभ्याम् *dhībhyām*	धीभिस् *dhībhis*
D.	धिये *dhiye*	" "	धीभ्यस् *dhībhyas*
Abl.	धियस् *dhiyas*	" "	" "
G.	" "	धियोस् *dhiyos*	धियाम् *dhiyām*
L.	धियि *dhiyi*	" "	धीषु *dhīṣu*

In the D., Ab.-Gen., and L. sing., and G. pl., these stems sometimes follow नदी; thus, *dhiyāi*, *dhiyās*, *dhiyām*, *dhīnām*. Cf. § 185 Observe that where the case-ending begins with a vowel the stem-final *ī* is split into *iy*.

190. The following additional prefixes are used with verbs: **अधि** 'over, above, on'; **अपि** 'unto, close upon'*; **अभि** 'to, unto', 'against' (often with implied violence); **नि** 'down, into, in'; **प्रति** 'back to, against, in return'; **वि** 'apart, away, out'.

191. Both in verbal forms and in derivatives, the final **इ** or **उ** of a prefix ordinarily lingualizes the initial **स्** of a root to which it is prefixed; and, in a few cases, the **ष्** remains even after an interposed **अ** of augment or reduplication; thus, from **सद् + नि**, **निषीदति**; **स्था + अधि**, pres. pass. **अधिष्ठीयते**, impf. pass. **अध्यष्ठीयत**.

192. The final **स्** of prefixes in **इस्** and **उस्** becomes **ष्** before initial **क्**, **ख्**, **प्**, **फ्**; thus, from **पद् + निस्**, **निष्पद्यते**.

Vocabulary XIII.

Verbs:

क्रम् + अति (*atikrámati, -krámate*) pass beyond or by, transgress.

जन् + उद् (*ujjáyate*) be born, arise from (*abl.*).

+ **प्र** arise, come into existence.

धा + अपि cover, keep shut.

नश् + वि (*vináçyati*) disappear, perish.

नह् + सम् (*saṁnáhyati*) gird; equip.

पद् + निस् (*niṣpádyate*) grow; arise from (*abl.*).

भाष् + प्रति (*pratibháṣate*) answer (*w. acc. of pers.*).

भू + प्र arise; rule.

रच् (*racáyati*) arrange, compose (a literary work).

सिध् + प्रति (*pratiṣédhati*) hold back; forbid.

सेव् + नि (*niṣévate*) dwell; devote oneself to; attend.

स्था + अधि mount, stand above or over; rule, govern.

हन् + प्रति hinder; injure; offend.

---

* Sometimes, with the verbs **नह्** and **धा**, abbreviated to **पि**; but in classical Skt. most commonly used as a conjunction: 'also', 'too'.

Subst.:

अनुज्ञा f., permission.
ईश्वर m., god; lord.
कपोत m., dove.
कर्ण m., ear.
काम m., love, desire.
कारण n., reason, cause.
क्रोध m., anger.
जाल n., net.
धी f., understanding, insight.
नाश m., destruction.
पद्म m., n., lotus.
पुरुष m., man (*homo*).
महाराज m., great king.
मुनि m., sage; ascetic.
मेखला f., girdle.
मोह m., infatuation.
रथ m., wagon.
लोभ m., desire, avarice.
वसति f., dwelling.
श्री f., luck, fortune, riches; *as nom. pr.*, goddess of fortune.
समुद्र m., ocean.
सृष्टि f., creation.
ह्री f., modesty, bashfulness.

Adj.:

कृत्स्न, f. °आ, whole.
चारु, f. °रु, beautiful.
धीर, f. °आ, steadfast, brave.
श्वेत, f. °आ, white.

Exercise XIII.

लोभात्क्रोधः प्रभवति लोभात्कामः प्रजायते ।
लोभान्मोहश्च नाशश्च लोभः पापस्य कारणम् ॥ २ ॥

नृपतिर्ऋषिणा पापात्प्रत्यषिध्यत । १ । हरेर्भार्यायां चारवः पुत्रा अजायन्त । २ । धीरं पुरुषं श्रियः सदा निषेवन्ते । ३ । पार्थिवस्याश्वां शत्रू अत्यक्रमेताम् । ४ । पद्मं श्रिया (*gen.*) वसतिः । ५ । धियो बलेन पुरुषा दुःखानि पारयन्ति । ६ । रथो ऽध्यष्ठीयत रामेण । ७ । कवेर्गृहं श्रियाशोभत । ८ । शिशू आह्वयेथां जनन्या । ९ । भानुमैक्षतर्षिः । १० । गुरोरनुज्ञया कटे शिष्यावुपाविशताम् । ११ । मुनिरीश्वरस्य सृष्टिं ध्यायति । १२ । क्षेत्रेषु धान्यं निष्पद्यते । १३ । गुरवो ग्रन्थान्रचयन्ति शिष्याश्च पुस्तकानि लिखन्ति ॥ १४ ॥

15. *The goddess of fortune was born from the ocean. 16. Why did ye hold *your* ears shut? (*pass. constr.*) 17. "The Çūdras spoke

---

* As the principal euphonic rules have now been stated and

the language of the Aryans": thus answered (*impers. pass.*) the Brāhmans. 18. By its cleverness the dove was freed from the net. 19. The teacher girded both boys with the girdle. 20. When the scholar's modesty disappeared, then the law was offended *against*. 21. Whence did ye get (लभ्) the white cows? 22. The whole earth was ruled by the great king. 23. For prosperity (*dat.*) we took refuge with the king (प्र-पद्). 24. Two law-books were composed by Viṣṇu. 25. The milk of the black cow is drunk by both children.

Lesson XIV.

193. Verbs, *a*-conjugation. Present Imperative Active. The inflection of this mode is as follows:

	Sing.	Dual.	Plural.
1.	वदानि *vádāni*	वदाव *vádāva*	वदाम *vádāma*
2.	वद *váda*	वदतम् *vádatam*	वदत *vádata*
3.	वदतु *vádatu*	वदताम् *vádatām*	वदन्तु *vádantu*

194. The three first persons are properly subjunctive forms, and accordingly often express a wish or future action.

195. The second and third persons of the imperative express oftenest a command; sometimes a wish or future action. The negative used with the imv. is मा.

196. A rare imv. form, either 2nd or 3rd pers. sing. (or plur.), is made with the ending तात्; thus, भवतात्. Its value is that of a posterior or future imv. (like the Latin forms in *to* and *tote*).

197. Root-words in ऊ *ū*, inflected like भू f., 'earth'.

---

exemplified in the exercises, no further indication need be made, except in special instances, of the position of the words in the Sanskrit.

	Sing.	Dual.	Plural.
NV.	भूस् *bhūs*	भुवौ *bhuvāu*	भुवस् *bhuvas*
A.	भुवम् *bhuvam*	" "	" "
I.	भुवा *bhuvā*	भूभ्याम् *bhūbhyām*	भूभिस् *bhūbhis*
D.	भुवे *bhuve*	" "	भूभ्यस् *bhūbhyas*
Ab.	भुवस् *bhuvas*	" "	" "
G.	" "	भुवोस् *bhuvos*	भुवाम् *bhuvām*
L.	भुवि *bhuvi*	" "	भूषु *bhūṣu*

In the D., Ab.-G., and L. sing., and G. pl., these stems sometimes follow नदी; thus, *bhuvāi*, *bhuvās*, *bhuvām*, *bhūnām*. Cf. §§ 185, 189.

198. Polysyllabic Feminines in ऊ *ū*, inflected like वधू f., 'woman'.

	Sing.	Dual.	Plural.
N.	वधूस् *vadhūs*	वध्वौ *vadhvāu*	वध्वस् *vadhvas*
A.	वधूम् *vadhūm*	" "	वधूस् *vadhūs*
I.	वध्वा *vadhvā*	वधूभ्याम् *vadhūbhyām*	वधूभिस् *vadhūbhis*
D.	वध्वै *vadhvāi*	" "	वधूभ्यस् *vadhūbhyas*
Ab.	वध्वास् *vadhvās*	" "	" "
G.	" "	वध्वोस् *vadhvos*	वधूनाम् *vadhūnām*
L.	वध्वाम् *vadhvām*	" "	वधूषु *vadhūṣu*
V.	वधु *vadhu*		

Vocabulary XIV.

Verbs:

अस् + अभि (*abhyásyati*) repeat, study, learn.

+ प्र (*prásyati*) throw forward or into.

दिश् + आ (*ādiçáti*) command.

दृश् *in pass.* (*dṛçyáte*) seem, look.

वस् + नि (*nivásati*) inhabit; dwell.

वृत् + प्र (*pravártate*) get a-going, break out. arise.

शुच् (*çócati*) sorrow, grieve.

सद् + नि (*niṣīdati*) seat oneself.

Subst.:

अतिथि m., guest.

अनृत n., untruth.

अभ्यास m., study; recitation.

आदेश m., command, prescription.

आसन n., seat, chair.

जुहू f., spoon, esp. sacrificial spoon.

पाठ m., lecture, lesson.

प्रजा f., creature; subject.

भू f., earth, ground.

भूषण n., ornament.

भ्रू f., eyebrow.

वधू f., woman, wife.

वेदि f., altar.

श्वश्रू f., mother-in-law.

स्तुति f., song of praise; praise.

स्नुषा f., daughter-in-law.

Adj.:

अपर, f. °**आ**, lower; other.

पर, f. °**आ**, highest; other.

वक्र, f. °**आ**, crooked, bent.

सुन्दर, f. **ई**, beautiful.

Adv.:

अधस्तात् under, underneath (*gen.*).

चिरम् long (of time).

दीर्घम् far, afar.

मा prohibitive particle, like Greek μή, Latin *ne*.

वा (*postpos.*) or.

ह्रस्वम् near by.

Exercise XIV.

धर्मं चरत माऽधर्मं सत्यं वदत माऽनृतम् ।
दीर्घं पश्यत मा ह्रस्वं परं पश्यत माऽपरम् ॥ ३ ॥

जयतु महाराजश्चिरं च कृत्स्नां भुवमधितिष्ठतु । १ । प्रयागं गच्छतं सु-
खेन च तत्र निवसतम् । २ । सुन्दर्या (*gen.*) भ्रुवौ वक्रे दृश्येते । ३ ।
गुरव आसने निषीदन्तु भुवि शिष्याः । ४ । स्नुषाभिः सह श्वश्रूणां कलहः
प्रावर्तत । ५ । हे क्षत्रियाः कुन्तान्क्षिपतेषूनमुञ्चत पापाञ्शत्रून्दण्डयतेति
क्रोधान्नृपतिरभाषत । ६ । अतिथिं पृच्छतु रात्रौ कुत्र न्यवस इति । ७ ।
श्वश्र्वाः कोपाच्छोचतः स्नुषे । ८ । वध्वाः स्निह्यत्यृषिः । ९ । पाठस्याऽभ्या-
साय शिष्यावागच्छतामिति गुरोराज्ञा । १० । जुह्वाऽग्नौ घृतं प्रास्या-
नि । ११ । हे वधु वाप्या जलमानय । १२ । जुह्वां घृतं तिष्ठति । १३ ।
भ्रुवोरधस्तान्नेत्रे वर्तेते ॥ १४ ॥

15. The women sing the praises (*singular*) of Indrāṇī (*pass. constr.*). 16. "Study ye holy writ and the sciences, speak the

truth, honor your teachers": thus[1] *is* the prescription[3] of the text-books[2] for scholars[4] (*gen.*). 17. Let kings protect *their* subjects and punish the wicked: thus is the law not offended (हा *pass.*). 18. O women, reverence *your* mothers-in-law. 19. Let not the coachman strike or torment the horses. 20. "Bring the jewels": thus the two maid-servants were commanded by the queen. 21. Let us with two spoons drop water on the altar. 22. "Let us play with dice for money" (*instr.*): thus spoke the two warriors (*pass.*). 23. "To-day let me initiate (*imv.*) my two sons": thus says the Brāhman. 24. Let the men dig a cistern.

Lesson XV.

199. Verbs, *a*-conjugation. Present Imperative Middle. The present imperative middle is inflected thus:

	Sing.	Dual.	Plural.
1.	लभै *lábhāi*	लभावहै *lábhāvahāi*	लभामहै *lábhāmahāi*
2.	लभस्व *lábhasva*	लभेथाम् *lábhethām*	लभध्वम् *lábhadhvam*
3.	लभताम् *lábhatām*	लभेताम् *lábhetām*	लभन्ताम् *lábhantām*

200. The first persons are really subjunctive forms. The inflection of the passive imv. is precisely similar; thus, क्रियै, क्रियस्व, क्रियताम्, etc.

201. Nouns in ऋ *r*. These stems, like many belonging to the consonant-declension, exhibit in their inflection a difference of stem-form: strong, middle, and weak. (For the cases called strong, etc., see Introd., § 87). In the weak cases (except loc. sing.) the stem-final is ऋ *r*, which in the weakest cases is changed naturally to र् *r*. But as regards the strong cases, the stems of this declension fall into two classes: in the one — which is much the larger, comprising all the *nomina agentis*, and a few others — the ऋ is vriddhied, becoming आर् *ār*; while in the other class, containing most nouns of relationship, the ऋ is gunated, becoming अर् *ar*. In both classes, the loc. sing. has अर् *ar* as stem-final. The abl.-gen. sing. is of peculiar formation; and the final र् *r* is dropped in the nominative singular.

202. Nomina agentis in ऋ *ṛ*, like कर्तृ m., 'doer'.

	Sing.	Dual.	Plural.
N.	कर्ता *kartā*	कर्तारौ *kartārāu*	कर्तारस् *kartāras*
A.	कर्तारम् *kartāram*	„ „	कर्तॄन् *kartṝn*
I.	कर्त्रा *kartrā*	कर्तृभ्याम् *-tṛbhyām*	कर्तृभिस् *kartṛbhis*
D.	कर्त्रे *kartre*	„ „	कर्तृभ्यस् *kartṛbhyas*
Ab.	कर्तुर् *kartur* (or *-us*)	„ „	„ „
G.	„ „	कर्त्रोस् *kartros*	कर्तॄणाम् *kartṝṇām*
L.	कर्तरि *kartari*	„ „	कर्तृषु *kartṛṣu*
V.	कर्तर् *kartar*		

203. Two nouns of relationship, स्वसृ f., "sister", and नप्तृ m., 'grandson', follow this declension; but स्वसृ makes the acc. pl. स्वसॄस् *svasṝ-s*.

204. The nouns of agency are sometimes used participially, or with adjective value. The corresponding feminine-stem is made in ई *ī*, and declined like नदी; thus, कर्त्री *kartrī*.

205. The grammarians prescribe a complete neuter declension also for bases in ऋ, precisely analogous with that of वारि or मधु, but such forms are rare.

Vocabulary XV.

Verbs:

गम् + अनु (*anugácchati*) follow.

चर्+सम्-आ (*samācárati*) commit, perform, do.

वद् + वि (*vivádate*) dispute, argue.

श्रि + आ (*āçráyate*) go for protection to, take refuge with (*acc.*).

Subst.:

आचार्य m., teacher.

कर्तृ m., doer, maker, author; *as adj.*, doing, making.

काल m., time.

कृपा f., graciousness, pity.

दातृ m., giver; *as adj.*, generous.

दुर्जन m., scamp, rogue.

द्रष्टृ m., seer, author (of Vedic books); *as adj.*, seeing.

धातृ m., creator.

निश्चय m., decision; certainty.

नेतृ m., leader.

पण्डित m., learned man; *pandit.*

पद n., step.

प्रायश्चित्त n., penance, expiation.

भर्तृ m., supporter, preserver; lord, husband; master.

रक्षितृ m., protector.

व्यवहार m., trial, law-suit.

शास्तृ m., punisher, governor.

स्रष्टृ m., creator.

नमस् n., honor, glory (*often as indecl., w. foll'g dat.*).

Adj.:

दरिद्र, f. °**आ**, poor.

वर, f. °**आ**, best, most excellent: better (*w. foll'g abl.*).

Exercise XV.

दुर्जनस्य च सर्पस्य वरं सर्पो न दुर्जनः ।
सर्पो दशति कालेन दुर्जनस्तु पदे पदे* ॥ ४ ॥

आचार्यं लभस्व प्रायश्चित्तं समाचरेति पापं द्विजातय आदिशन्ति।१। काव्यानि रचयाम कीर्तिं विन्दाम नृपतीनाश्रयामहै श्रियं लभामहा इति कवयो वदन्ति । २ । स्वसुर्गृहे कन्ये न्यवसताम् । ३ । नृपे रक्षितरि** सुखेन प्रजा वसन्ति ।४। धर्माय देवान्यजावहा अर्थाय कीर्तये च सभासु पण्डितैः सह विवदावहा इति ब्राह्मणस्य पुत्रयोर्निश्चयः । ५। मुक्तय (*dat.*) ईश्वरः सृष्टेः कर्ता मनुष्यैर्भक्त्या सेव्यताम् । ६। नृपतयः प्रजानां रक्षितारो दुर्जनानां च शास्तारो वर्तन्ताम्।७। शास्त्रस्य कर्त्रे पाणिनये नमः । ८ । लोकस्य स्रष्टृभ्यो वसूनां दातृभ्यो देवेभ्यो नमो नमः ॥ ९ ॥

---

* Words are often repeated, to give an intensive, a distributive, or a repetitional meaning. So here: "at every step". The position of **च** is very unusual; it would naturally follow **सर्पस्य**.

** Loc. absol. — supply "being".

10. Let the wife love *her* husband. 11. Let the warriors follow *their* leaders and fight with the enemy (*pl.*). 12. At the river the boy is to meet his two sisters (*instr.*). 13. The world was created by the creator. 14. In the houses of pious givers alms is given to ascetics. 15. King Bhoja was (अवर्तत) generous toward the author (*loc.*) of the eulogies. 16. Let servants always be useful to (सेव्) *their* masters (*acc.*). 17. For protection[4] (*acc.*) betake yourselves[5] to the gods[3], the protectors[2] of the pious[1]. 18. Men live by the graciousness of the creator. 19. O generous one, the poor bend *before thee*! 20. The man leads his sisters to the city (*pass. constr.*).

Lesson XVI.

206. Verbs, *a*-conjugation. Present Optative Active. The present optative is formed from the general present-stem by the addition of a mode-sign, after which are used secondary endings (in 3rd pl. act. उस् *us*, in 1st sing. mid. अ *a*, in 3rd pl. mid. रन् *ran*). After an *a*-stem, this mode-sign, in all voices, is ई *ī*, unaccented, which blends with the final *a* to ए *e* (accented, or not, according to the accent of the *a*): and the ए is maintained unchanged before a vowel-ending (अम्, उस्, आथाम्, आताम्) by means of an interposed euphonic य् *y*. The inflection in the active voice is as follows:

	Sing.	Dual.	Plural.
1.	वदेयम् *vádeyam*	वदेव *vádeva*	वदेम *vádema*
2.	वदेस् *vádes*	वदेतम् *vádetam*	वदेत *vádeta*
3.	वदेत् *vádet*	वदेताम् *vádetām*	वदेयुस् *vádeyus*

Similarly, विशेयम् *viçéyam*, नह्येयम् *náhyeyam*, चोरयेयम् *coráyeyam*, etc.

207. The optative expresses: 1. wish or desire; 2. request or entreaty; 3. what is desirable or proper; 4. what may or might, can or could be. It is also largely used in conditional sentences. The subject is often indefinite and unexpressed. The negative used with the opt. is न *na*. Both the prescriptive and the prohibitive optative are very common.

208. The nouns of relationship in ऋ (except स्वसृ and नप्तृ — see § 203) gunate ऋ in the strong cases; thus, पितृ m., 'father', मातृ f., 'mother', declined as follows:

	Sing.	Dual.	Plural.
N.	पिता माता	पितरौ मातरौ	पितरस् मातरस्
A.	पितरम् मातरम्	" "	पितॄन् मातॄस्
I.	पित्रा मात्रा	पितृभ्याम् मातृभ्याम्	पितृभिस् मातृभिस्
	etc.	etc.	etc.
V.	पितर् मातर्		

209. The stem गो m., f., 'bull' or 'cow', is declined thus:

	Sing.	Dual.	Plural.
NV.	गौस् *gāus*	गावौ *gāvāu*	गावस् *gāvas*
A.	गाम् *gām*	" "	गास् *gās*
I.	गवा *gavā*	गोभ्याम् *gobhyām*	गोभिस् *gobhis*
D.	गवे *gave*	" "	गोभ्यस् *gobhyas*
Ab.	गोस् *gos*	" "	" "
G.	" "	गवोस् *gavos*	गवाम् *gavām*
L.	गवि *gavi*	" "	गोषु *goṣu*

Vocabulary XVI.

Verbs:

मन् (*mányate*) think, suppose.

मुद् (*módate*) rejoice.

शंस् (*çáṅsati*) proclaim (see also in Vocab. I.).

स्मृ (*smárati*; p. *smaryáte*) remember; think of; teach, *esp. in pass.* 'it is taught', i. e. 'traditional'.

Subst.:

गो m., f., bull, steer, cow; f., speech.

गोत्व n., ox-nature; stupidity.

घास m., fodder, hay.

जामातृ m., son-in-law.

दुहितृ f., daughter.

पङ्क n., mud, bog.

पितृ m., father; du., parents; pl., *manes*.

प्रयोक्तृ m., user, arranger.

बुध m., wise man, sage.

भ्रातृ m., brother.

मातृ f., mother.

मास m., month.

युग्म n., pair.

रक्षण n., protection.

श्राद्ध n., an oblation to the *manes*, accompanied by a sacrificial meal and gifts to the Brāhmans.

Adj.:

अधिक, f. °**आ**, more, greater, greatest.

कामदुघ, f. °**आ**, granting wishes; as f., *sc.* **धेनु**, the fabulous Wonder-cow.

दुष्प्रयुक्त, f. °**आ**, badly arranged or used.

प्रयुक्त, f. °**आ**, arranged, used.

श्रेष्ठ, f. **आ**, best.

Pron.:

सा f., she, it.

Adv. and Conj.:

चेत् if.

नित्यम् always, daily.

यदि if.

सम्यक् well, properly.

Exercise XVI.

गौर्गौः कामदुघा* सम्यक् प्रयुक्ता स्मर्यते बुधैः ।
दुष्प्रयुक्ता पुनर्गोत्वं प्रयोक्तुः सैव शंसति ॥ ५ ॥

भर्तारं भर्तुश्च पितरं मातरं च पत्नी देवानिव पूजयेत् ।१। मा स्त्री-
णां रक्षणेन सुखं भवतीति द्विजातयो मन्यन्ते । २ । यदा प्रयागं ग-
च्छेव तदा पित्रे पत्त्रं लिखेव । ३ । पितृभ्यो मासे मासे श्राद्धं यच्छेयुः । ४ ।
ग्राममद्य गच्छेतमिति मातरौ पुत्रावभाषेताम् । ५ । गोः क्षीरेण शि-
शवो मोदन्ताम् । ६ । गामतिथये पचेमेत्यृषिर्भार्यामवदत् । ७ । दुहि-

* Predicate. Play upon words throughout the verse.

तरं पितरौ रक्षेतां स्वसारं भ्रातरौ मातॄः पुत्राश्च रक्षेयुः । ८ । यदि शास्त्रमभ्यस्येयं तदा गुरवस्तुष्येयुः । ९ । हे स्वसः पित्रोर्गृहे तिष्ठेः । १० । बाहुभ्यां नदीं न तरेत् । ११ । हे शिशवः पितॄन्सेवध्वं भ्रातॄणां स्निह्यत ॥ १२ ॥

13. By Ṛṣabhadatta, son-in-law of Nahapāna, many cattle and villages and much money were given to the Brāhmans. 14. Thou shalt give the mother's jewels to the sisters (*opt. or imv.*). 15. Let the coachman bring (आ-हृ) fodder for the horses; let him not torment the horses. 16. Of the father's property a greater part is to be given (*imv.*) to the eldest of the brothers. 17. "Children, bring wood and water into the house daily"; thus *was* the father's command. 18. Let the cows graze in the forest. 19. Let both live on the milk (*instr.*) of the black cow. 20. The wagon is drawn by two steers. 21. The seer rejoices over the pair (*instr.*) of white steers. 22. Hari and Çiva marry two sisters, the daughters of Rāma.

Lesson XVII.

210. Verbs, *a*-conjugation. Present Optative Middle. The optative middle (and passive) of *a*-stems, formed as shown in the preceding lesson, is inflected as follows:

	Sing.	Dual.	Plural.
1.	लभेय *lábheya*	लभेवहि *lábhevahi*	लभेमहि *lábhemahi*
2.	लभेथास् *lábhethās*	लभेयाथाम् *lábheyāthām*	लभेध्वम् *lábhedhvam*
3.	लभेत *lábheta*	लभेयाताम् *lábheyātām*	लभेरन् *lábheran*

Similarly चोरयेय *corayeya*, संगच्छेय *saṁgaccheya*, etc.

211. Declension. The stem नौ f., 'ship, boat', is entirely regular, taking throughout the normal endings, as given in § 90. Thus: नौस्, नावम्, नावा, etc.; नावौ, नौभ्याम्, etc.; नावस्, नौभिस्, etc.

212. The stems ending in long vowels (**आ, ई, ऊ**) fall into two well-marked classes: A. **root-stems** — mostly monosyllabic — **and their compounds,** with a comparatively small number of others inflected like them; B. **derivative feminine stems** in **आ** and **ई**, with a few in **ऊ**, inflected like **जाया, नदी** and **वधू**. The stems of class A take the normal endings throughout, with optional exceptions in dat., abl.-gen., and loc. sing. fem., and with **न्** inserted before **आम्** of the gen. pl. The simple words are as nouns with few exceptions fem.; as adjectives (rare), and in adjective compounds, they coincide in masc. and fem. forms. The declension of the simple words in **ई** and **ऊ** has been given (in §§ **189, 197**); those in **आ** are so rare that it is not possible to make up a whole scheme of forms in actual use.

213. When any root in **आ** or **ई** or **ऊ** is found as final member of a compound word, these root-finals are treated as follows: 1. Roots in **आ** lose that vowel before vowel-endings, except in the strong cases and in the acc. pl., which is like the nominative. Thus, **विश्व-पा** m., f., 'all-protecting':

	Sing.	Dual.	Plural.
N.V.	**विश्वपास्** *-pās*	**दिश्वपौ** *-pāu*	**विश्वपास्** *-pās*
A.	**विश्वपाम्** *-pām*	**विश्वपाभ्याम्**	,, ,,
I.	**विश्वपा** *riçvap-ā*	**विश्वपोस्** *viçvap-os*	**विश्वपाभिस्** etc.

214. 2. Roots in **ई** and **ऊ** change their final vowel, before vowel-endings, into **य्** and **व्**, if but one consonant precede the final vowel; but if two or more consonants precede, the change is into **इय्** and **उव्**. Thus, **यव-क्री** m., f., 'corn-buying': nom.-voc. **यवक्रीस्**, acc. **यवक्रियम्**; **खल-पू** m., f., 'street-sweeper': nom. sing. **खलपूस्**, acc. **खलप्वम्**.

Vocabulary XVII.

Verbs:

ईक्ष् + **प्रति** (*pratīkṣate*) expect.

नन्द् + **अभि** (*abhinándati*, poet. *-te)* rejoice in, greet with joy (*acc.*).

रम् (*rámate*) amuse oneself.

+ **वि** (*virámati*) cease from (*abl.*); cease.

स्था + **अनु** (*anutiṣṭhati*) follow out, accomplish.

Subst.:

उद्यान n., garden.

कृषि f., agriculture.

जीवित n., life.

निदेश m., command.

पाशुपाल्य n., cattle-raising.

पुरोहित m., domestic priest, chaplain.

भक्षण n., eating.

भृतक m., servant.

मरण n., death.

मित्र n., friend.

युद्ध n., battle.

वाणिज्य n., trade.

विधि m., rule; fate.

श्वशुर m., father-in-law.

Adj.:

भद्र, f. **°आ**, good, pleasant, dear; *as n. subst.*, fortune.

संदिग्ध, f. **°आ**, doubtful; unsteady.

Exercise XVII.

नाभिनन्देत मरणं नाभिनन्देत जीवितम् ।
कालमेव प्रतीक्षेत निदेशं भृतको यथा* ॥ ६ ॥

भ्रातरि स्तेनाः शरानमुञ्चन् । १ । यदि नराः श्रुतेः स्मृतेश्च विधीननुतिष्ठेयुस्तदा साधुभिः शस्येरन् । २ । वैश्याः कृष्या वाणिज्येन पाशुपाल्येन वा वर्तेरन् । ३ । संदिग्धां नावं नारोहेत् । ४ । यदि गङ्गाया वारिणि म्रियेध्वं तदा स्वर्गं लभेध्वम् । ५ । जामातरः श्वशुरान्स्नुषाः श्वश्रूर्दुहितरश्च पुत्राश्च पितरौ सेवेरन् । ६ । ब्राह्मणैर्नावोदधिर्न तीर्येत । ७ । शत्रुभिर्न पराजयेथा इति नृपतिं प्रजा वदन्ति । ८ । नृपती अरिभिर्युध्येयाताम् । ९ । नौषु युद्धमभवत् । १० । बालावुद्याने रमेयाताम् ॥ ११ ॥

---

* Rule for an ascetic, who is to put aside all earthly desires and passions.

12. Let fodder be brought (आ-हृ) *(opt., imv.)* by the brother for the horses of the all-protecting king. 13. May ye see good fortune (*pl.*); may ye acquire (लभ्) glory. 14. The king with his warriors crossed the sea in a ship. 15. Tell (*opt., imv.*) where our friends may meet with their brothers. 16. You may amuse yourselves in the garden, but cease eating (*abl. of* भक्षण) the fruits (*gen.*). 17. Mayest thou be saved (*ud-hṛ*: cf. § 267) by the all-protector from thy misfortune. 18. To-day let the king's two sons be consecrated (*opt., imv.*) by the house-priest. 19. Ye both shall greet (*opt., imv.*) your parents. 20. If we two should speak untruth, then we should be punished by the king. 21. May I conquer the enemies with my brave warriors: thus is the king's wish (*use* इष् *pass.*). 22. May we receive the reward of virtue.

Lesson XVIII.

215. Causative. The chief points to be noticed in the formation of causative-stems have been given already (in Less. VII); some additional ones follow.

216. Most roots in आ and ऋ add प् before the conjugation-sign; thus, दापयति from 1दा; धापयति; गापयति; अर्पयति from ऋ. श्रा makes श्रपयति; ग्ला and स्ना, sometimes ग्लापयति, etc., sometimes ग्लपयति, etc. 1पा, 'drink', makes पाययति (as though from पी). A few roots in इ and ई take the same प्, with various irregularities; thus, अध्यापयति from अधि-इ.

217. Medial or initial अ in a light syllable is commonly lengthened, but sometimes remains unchanged. Thus, पत्, पातयति; कम्, कामयते; चम्, चामयति. But most roots in अम्, and जन्, त्वर्, प्रथ्, व्यथ्, with other rarer ones, generally keep the अ short thus, गम्, गमयति.

218. Final vowels take *vṛddhi* before अय; thus, भू, भावयति; कृ, कारयति.

219. Some verbs of causative meaning are by formation denominatives; thus पालयति, 'protect', called causative to 2पा; प्रीणयति, to प्री; भीषयति, to भी; घातयति, to हन्.

220. For the passive of causatives, see Less. X.

221. The causatives of intransitive verbs are transitive. The causatives of transitive verbs are construed sometimes (*a*) with two accusatives, sometimes (*b*) with an acc. of the object and an instrumental of the agent. Thus, "he causes the birds to eat the cakes" may be rendered either (*a*): विहगान् पिष्टान् खादयति, or (*b*) विहगैः पि॰ खा॰.

222. Participles. The general participial endings are अन्त् (weak form अत्) for the active, and आन for the middle. But after a tense-stem in अ, the active suffix is virtually न्त्, one of the two अ's being lost; and the middle suffix is मान (except आन sometimes in causative forms). Thus, भवन्त् *bhávant*, तुदन्त् *tudánt*, दीव्यन्त् *dī́vyant*, चोरयन्त् *coráyant;* भवमान *bhávamāna*, etc. For the declension of the participles in अन्त् see below, Less. XXIII.

223. Pronoun of the First Person. The pronominal declension exhibits some striking peculiarities which are not easily explained. The pronoun of the first person is declined thus:

	Sing.	Dual.	Plural.
N.	अहम्	आवाम्	वयम्
A.	माम्, मा	आवाम्, नौ	अस्मान्, नस्
I.	मया	आवाभ्याम्	अस्माभिस्
D.	मह्यम्, मे	,, , नौ	अस्मभ्यम्, नस्
Ab.	मत्	,,	अस्मत्
G.	मम, मे	आवयोस्, नौ	अस्माकम्, नस्
L.	मयि	,,	अस्मासु

224. The forms मा, मे, नौ, नस् are enclitic, and are never used at the beginning of a sentence, or before the particles च, एव, वा.

225. In pronouns of the first and second persons the plural is often used for the singular. Pronouns (and other words as well) show in Sanskrit a curious tendency to agree in form with the predicate rather than with the subject to which they refer.

Vocabulary XVIII.

Verbs, with causatives:

अश् eat; caus. (*āçáyati*) make eat; give to eat.

इ + अधि study, read; caus. (*adhyāpáyati*) teach.

क्लृप् in caus. (*kalpáyati, -te*) make; ordain, appoint.

जन् in caus. (*janáyati*) beget.

ज्ञा + आ in caus. (*ājñāpáyati*) command.

1दा give; caus. (*dāpáyati*) make give or pay.

दृश् see; in caus. (*darçáyati*) show.

1धा + परि, in caus. (*dhāpáyati*) make put on, clothe in (*two acc.*).

नी + अप lead away (caus. *apanāyáyati*).

प्रथ् in caus. (*pratháyati*) spread, proclaim.

मृ die; caus. (*māráyati*) kill.

यज् sacrifice; caus. (*yājáyati*) make to sacrifice; offer sacrifice for (*acc.**).

वद् + अभि in caus. (*abhivādayati*) greet.

विद् know; caus. (*vedáyati*) inform (*dat.*).

+ नि in caus. inform (*dat.*).

वृध् (*várdhate*) grow; caus. (*vardhayáti, -te*) make grow; bring up.

व्यथ् in caus. (*vyatháyati*) torment.

श्रु hear; in caus. (*çrāváyati*) make hear, i. e. recite, proclaim (*acc. of pers.*).

स्था stand; in caus. (*sthāpáyati*) put, place; appoint; stop.

+ प्र (*pratiṣṭhate*) start off; in caus. (*prasthāpáyati*) send.

---

* The priest who performs sacrifice for the benefit of another person is said to "make that person sacrifice", as though the latter (who is called यजमान) were celebrating the sacrifice for himself.

Subst.:

अमृत n., nectar.

उपनयन n., initiation, investiture.

कर m., hand; trunk (of elephant); ray; toll, tax.

कालिदास m., *nom. pr.*, a noted poet.

काशी f., *nom. pr.*, the city of Benares.

गुण m., quality; excellent quality, excellence.

दशरथ m., *nom. pr.* (Rāma's father).

दास m., slave, groom.

दूत m., messenger, envoy.

पाटलिपुत्र n., *nom. pr.*, the city of Patnā.

मनोरथ m., wish.

वस्त्र n., garment.

विधि m., Brahman (the deity).

वृक m., wolf.

वेद m., science, knowledge; esp. sacred knowledge, holy writ.

Adj.:

नवीन, f. **०आ**, new.

स्व, f. **०आ**, own, one's own.

Exercise XVIII.

सूत । अधुना स्थापय रथम् । १ । यथाज्ञापयति देवः ॥ २ ॥ दशरथश्चारून्पुत्रानजनयत् । ३ । कालिदासस्य काव्यं मां श्रावयेः । ४ । वैश्यान्करान्दापयेन्नृपः । ५ । उपनयने बालान्नवीनानि वस्त्राणि परिधापयेयुः । ६ । भ्रातरो ऽस्मान्नगरं प्रास्थापयन् । ७ । स्वसार आगच्छन्तीति मह्यं न्यवेदयत । ८ । वायोर्बलेन तरवो ऽपात्यन्त । ९ । क्षत्रिया युद्धे ऽरीन्मारयन्ति । १० । कवयो ऽस्माकं गुणान्प्रथयेयुः कीर्तिं च वर्धयेयुरिति पार्थिवैरिष्यते । ११ । अहं प्रयागे निवसामि रामः काश्यां तिष्ठति । १२ । ग्रन्थो ऽस्माभी रच्यते पुस्तकं रामेण लेखयामः ॥ १३ ॥

14. I cause a mat to be made *(caus. pass.)*. 15. Show me *(dat.)* the books. 16. Let Brāhmans teach us both and offer sacrifice for us. 17. The king determined (ordained) the taxes in *his* kingdom. 18. I have my field ploughed by slaves. 19. Give me water and food. 20. They had the boy taken (led) away from me *(abl.)*. 21. The kings sent envoys to Pāṭaliputra. 22. Thieves stole our *(gen.)* cows, and wolves killed our* flocks. 23. The king made the

---

* The expression of possession, etc., on the part of pronouns

poet recite (*use* श्रावयति) a eulogy of Viṣṇu. 24. We torment our hearts with wishes. 25. Both scholars greet the teacher.

Lesson XIX.

226. Pronoun of the Second Person. This pronoun (for which the natives assume त्वद् and युष्मद् as bases) is declined thus:

	Singular.	Dual.	Plural.
N.	त्वम्	युवाम्	यूयम्
A.	त्वाम्, त्वा	युवाम्, वाम्	युष्मान्, वस्
I.	त्वया	युवाभ्याम्	युष्माभिस्
D.	तुभ्यम्, ते	„ वाम्	युष्मभ्यम्, वस्
Ab.	त्वत्	„	युष्मत्
G.	तव, ते	युवयोस्, वाम्	युष्माकम्, वस्
L.	त्वयि	„	युष्मासु

227. The forms त्वा, ते, वाम्, वस् are enclitics, subject to the same rules as मा, मे, etc. (§ 224).

228. The Pronoun of the Third Person (for which the natives assume तद् as base — the base is really त) is declined as follows (note nom. sing., m. and f.):

	Masculine:			**Feminine:**		
	Sing.	Dual.	Plural.	Sing.	Dual.	Plural.
N.	सस्	तौ	ते	सा	ते	तास्
A.	तम्	„	तान्	ताम्	„	„
I.	तेन	ताभ्याम्	तैस्	तया	ताभ्याम्	ताभिस्
D.	तस्मै	„	तेभ्यस्	तस्यै	„	ताभ्यस्
Ab.	तस्मात्	„	„	तस्यास्	„	„
G.	तस्य	तयोस्	तेषाम्	„	तयोस्	तासाम्
L.	तस्मिन्	„	तेषु	तस्याम्	„	तासु

---

is made almost entirely by the genitive case, not by a derivative possessive adjective. But often the unemphatic possessive pronoun of the English is omitted in Sanskrit.

Neuter:

	Sing.	Dual.	Plural.
N.	तद्	ते	तानि
A.	"	"	"
I.	तेन	ताभ्याम्	तैस् etc., as in the masculine.

229. The nom. sing. masc. सस्, and its compound एषस्, lose their final स् before *any* consonant; before vowels, and at the end of a sentence, they follow the usual euphonic rules. Thus, स गच्छति, स तिष्ठति; स इच्छति; सो ऽस्ति; गच्छति सः.

230. The third personal pronoun is used oftenest as a weak or indefinite demonstrative, especially as antecedent to a relative; and often like the English "definite article."

231. Like त are declined: (*a*) एत, 'this', formed by prefixing ए to the forms of त, throughout; thus, nom. sing. m. एषस्, f. एषा, n. एतद्; (*b*) the relative pronoun (and adj.) य, 'which, who'; (*c*) comparatives and superlatives from pronominal roots, such as कतर, which (of the two)?' and कतम 'which (of the many)?' So यतर and यतम; एकतम 'one of many'; अन्य 'other', with its comparative अन्यतर; and इतर 'different'. — Yet other words are so inflected, but with अम् instead of अद् in nom.-acc.-voc. sing. neut.: as, सर्व, विश्व, 'all'; एक 'one', in pl. 'some'; उभय, f. °यी (only sing. and pl.), 'both'.

232. The interrogative pronoun क (for which the Hindus give the base as किम्) follows precisely the declension of त, except nom.-acc. sing. neut. किम्; nom. sing. m. कस्, f. का.

233. A number of words follow the pronominal declension in some of their significations, or optionally; but in other senses, or without known rule, lapse into the adjective inflection. Such are comparatives and superlatives from prepositional stems, as अधर 'lower', अधम 'lowest'; पर 'chief', पूर्व 'earlier', उत्तर 'upper',

'northern', दक्षिण 'southern', etc. Occasional forms of the pronominal declension are met with from numeral adjectives, and from other words having somewhat of a numeral character, as अल्प 'few', अर्ध 'half', etc.

234. Peculiarities in the use of relative pronouns, etc. The Sanskrit often puts the relative clause before the antecedent clause, and inserts the substantive to which the relative refers into the same clause with the relative, instead of leaving it in the antecedent clause. In translating into Sanskrit, a relative clause is to be placed either before or after the whole antecedent clause; but not inserted into the antecedent clause, as is done in English. Thus, "the mountain which we saw yesterday is very high" would be in Sanskrit either: यं पर्वतं वयं ह्यो ऽपश्याम सो ऽतीव तुङ्गः, or: स पर्वतो ऽतीव तुङ्गो यं ह्यो ऽपश्याम; but not स पर्वतो यं वयं ह्यो ऽपश्याम, etc., according to the English idiom.

235. The relative word may stand anywhere in its clause; thus, शिव आदिर्येषां ते देवाः "the gods whose chief is Çiva". Sometimes relative or demonstrative adverbs are used as equivalents of certain case-forms of relative or demonstrative pronouns; thus, यत्र वने = यस्मिन्वने.

236. The repetition of the relative gives an indefinite meaning: 'whosoever, whatever'. The same result is much more commonly attained by adding to the relative the interrogative pronoun, with (or, less usually, without) one of the particles च, चन, चिद्, अपि, वा. Sometimes the interrogative alone is used with these particles in a similar sense. Thus; यद्यदेषा कथयति "whatever this woman relates"; यो यस्य भावः स्यात् "whatever any one's disposition may be"; यस्मै कस्मै चिद्यच्छति "he gives to some one or other"; यस्मात्कस्माच्चिन्न लभते "he takes from no one whatever".

Vocabulary XIX.

Verbs:

आस् sit; in caus. (*āsáyati*) place.

1**पा** drink; in caus. (*pāyáyati*) give to drink, water.

2**पा** protect; in caus. (*pāláyati*) protect.

प्री rejoice; in caus. (*prīṇáyati*) make rejoice, please.

भी fear; in caus. (*bhīṣáyate, bhāyáyate*) terrify, frighten.

वच् say, speak; name; in caus. (*vācáyati*) make (a written leaf) speak, i. e. read.

सह् (*sáhate*) endure.

सिध् (*sidhyati*) succeed; in caus. (*sādháyati*) perform, acquire.

हन् kill; caus. (*ghātáyati*) have killed.

ह्वा call; in caus. (*hvāyáyati*) have called.

Subst.:

कार्य n., business, concern.

कृष्ण m., *n. pr.*, a god.

कौसल्या f., *n. pr.*

गति f., gait; refuge.

चरण m., n., foot, leg.

छत्त्र n., umbrella.

दुग्ध n., milk.

देवकी f., *n. pr.*, Kṛṣṇa's mother.

पृथ्वी f., earth.

श्री, as prefix to proper names, has the meaning 'famous', 'honorable'.

सहाय m., companion, helper.

Adj.:

अन्य other.

इतर other.

विश्व all (Vedic).

सर्व all.

स्वादु sweet.

Indecl.:

अपि also, even.

विना without (*w. instr. or acc.; often postpos.*).

Exercise XIX.

सहायेन विना नैव कार्यं किमपि सिध्यति ।
एकेन चरणेनापि गतिः कस्य प्रवर्तते ॥ ७ ॥

मयि त्वयि च पितरौ स्निह्यतः । १ । यः पृथिवीं पालयति स पार्थिव उच्यते । २ । कस्यै देव्यै स्तोत्रं रचयेम । ३ । गुरवस्युष्मानाह्वाययत् । ४ ।

या वत्सान्दुग्धं पाययन्ति ता धेनूर्मा घातयत । ५ । युष्मन्मम दुःखं भवति । ६ । साधवः पुत्रैः सह स्वर्गं लभन्ते न त्वितरे जनाः । ७ । वयमेतत्पुस्तकं नेच्छामस्तदन्यस्मै कस्मैचिद्दीयताम् । ८ । त्वदन्यो* न को ऽप्यस्माभिः गृह्यते । ९ । या देवकी वसुदेवस्य पत्न्यभवत्तस्यां कृष्णो ऽजायत । १० । तव पित्रा सह नगर्या आगच्छाम । ११ । यूयं पितॄञ्छ्राद्धैः प्रीणयथ वयं अन्नेन । १२ । विश्वे देवास्त्वा पालयन्तु । १३ । अन्येषां काव्यैरिव कविः कीर्तिमसाधयत् ॥ १४ ॥

15. The husband[6] of that[5] *(gen.)* Kāusalyā[2] *(loc.)*, of whom[1] *(loc. fem.)* Rāma[3] was born[4], is called[8] Daçaratha[7]. 16. The teacher[4] rejoices[3] at thy[1] diligence[2] *(abl.)*. 17. Why (**कस्मात्**) speakest thou so? 18. Others than we could not endure this suffering. 19. The teacher teaches** us holy-writ and the law-books. 20. May all[8] those[7] kings[2] who[1] protect[6] *their* subjects[5] according to[4] (**अनु**, *post-pos.*) the law[3] *(acc.)* be victorious[9]. 21. The fruits of all these trees are sweet. 22. May the glory of all women, who honor *their* husbands, increase *(imv.)*. 23. In this kingdom the king's punishment terrifies the wicked. 24. Which of the two fruits do ye wish? 25. My father had gold given to me, cows to thee, to the other brother nothing.

Lesson XX.

237. Declension of Stems in Consonants. All noun-stems in consonants may well be classed together, since the peculiarities shown by some concern only the stems themselves, and not the endings. Masculines and feminines of the same final are inflected precisely alike; and neuters are peculiar (as usually in the other

---

* "Other than thou". With **अन्य**, as with comparatives, the ablative is used.

** "Makes us read" (**अधि-इ**, *caus.*).

declensions) only in the nom.-acc.-voc. of all numbers. But the majority of consonantal stems form a special feminine stem by adding ई (never आ) to the weak form of the masculine.

238. Variations, as between stronger and weaker forms, are very general in consonantal stems: either of strong and weak stems, or of strong, middle, and weakest. The endings are throughout the normal ones (Introd., § 90).

239. The general law concerning final consonants is as follows:

1. The more usual etymological finals are स्, र्, म्, न्, त्, क्, प्, ट्; sporadic are ङ्, ण्, ल् as finals.

2. In general, only one consonant, of whatever kind, is allowed to stand at the end of a word; if two or more would etymologically occur there, the last is dropped, and again the last, until but one remains.

3. Of the non-nasal mutes, only the first in each series, the non-aspirate surd, is allowed as final; the others — surd asp., and both sonants — are regularly converted into this, wherever they would etymologically occur.

4. A final palatal, or ह्, becomes either क्, or (less often) ट्; but ह् in a very few cases (where it represents original घ्) becomes त्.

240. According to 239. 2, the स् of the nom. sing., m. and f., is always lost; and irregularities of treatment of the stem-final, in this case, are not infrequent.

241. Before the *pada*-endings, भ्याम्, भिस्, भ्यस् and सु, a stem-final is treated as in external combination.

242. An aspirate mute is changed to its corresponding non-aspirate before another non-nasal mute or a sibilant; it stands unaltered only before a vowel or semivowel or nasal. Hence such a mute is doubled by prefixing its own corresponding non-aspirate.

243. Consonant-stems of one form in त्, द्, ध् and भ्. Before suffixal भ्, both त् and ध् as stem-finals become द्; भ् as stem-final becomes ब्. Examples: मरुत् m., 'wind'; आपद् f., 'misfortune'; जगत् n., 'the world'.

	Sing.	Plural.
N.V.	मरुत् । आपत् । जगत् ॥	मरुतस् । आपदस् । जगन्ति ॥
A.	मरुतम् । आपदम् । जगत् ॥	„ „ „
I.	मरुता । आपदा । जगता ॥	मरुद्भिस् । आपद्भिस् । जगद्भिस् ॥
D.	मरुते । आपदे । जगते ॥	मरुद्भ्यस् । आपद्भ्यस् । जगद्भ्यस् ॥
Ab.	मरुतस् । आपदस् । जगतस् ॥	„ „ „
G.	„ „ „	मरुताम् । आपदाम् । जगताम् ॥
L.	मरुति । आपदि । जगति ॥	मरुत्सु । आपत्सु । जगत्सु ॥

Dual.

N.A.V.	मरुतौ । आपदौ । जगती ॥
I.D.Ab.	मरुद्भ्याम् । आपद्भ्याम् । जगद्भ्याम् ॥
G.L.	मरुतोस् । आपदोस् । जगतोस् ॥

For the न् inserted in nom.-acc. pl. neuter, cf. *phalāni*, *madhūni*, etc.

244. In a few roots, when a final sonant aspirate (घ्, ध्, भ्; also ह्, representing घ्) loses its aspiration according to §§ **239. 3, 242**, the initial sonant consonant (ग्, द्, or ब्) becomes aspirate; thus, बुध्, nom.-voc. sing. भुत्; भुद्भ्यस्, भुत्सु.

245. Agreement of adjectives. If the same adjective qualify two or more substantives, it will be used in their combined number; if the substantives are masculine and feminine, the adj. will be masc.; but in a combination of masc. or fem. subjects with neuter, the adjective will be neuter.

Vocabulary XX.

Verbs:

रुह् grow; caus. (*roháyati* or *ropáyati*) make rise or grow; plant.

लभ्, in caus. (*lambháyati**) make receive or take; give.

Subst.:

उपनिषद् f., name of certain Vedic writings.

उपवीत n., sacred cord (worn by the three higher castes).

तडित् f., lightning.

दृषद् f., stone.

निर्वृति f., contentment, happiness.

पोषक m., supporter, maintainer.

भूभृत् m., king; mountain.

मरुत् m., wind; as pl., *n. pr.*, the Storm-gods.

वात m., wind.

विश्वास m., trust, confidence.

वृत्र m., *n. pr.*, a demon, Vṛtra.

शत n., a hundred.

शरद् f., autumn; year.

समिध् f., fagot.

सरित् f., river.

सुहृद् m., friend.

Adj.:

कुशल, f. °ला, skilled, learnèd.

त्रिवृत् m., f., n., threefold, triple.

दुर्लभ, f. °भा, hard to find or reach; difficult.

भक्त, f. °क्ता, devoted, true.

Indecl.:

अपि also; even.

पश्चात् behind (*w. gen.*).

Exercise XX.

ते पुत्रा ये पितुर्भक्ताः स पिता यस्तु पोषकः ।
**तन्मित्रं यत्र विश्वासः सा भार्या यत्र निर्वृतिः ॥ ८ ॥

हे शिष्य समिधो वनादाहर । १ । उपनिषत्सु मुक्तेर्मार्ग उपदिश्यते । २ । आपदि सुहृदो ऽस्मान्पालयेयुः । ३ । विश्वस्यां भुवि पापा

* If a nasal is ever taken in any of the strong forms of a root, it usually appears in the causal.

** See § 225; यत्र = यस्मिन् and यस्याम्; see § 235, end.

भूभृद्भिर्दह्यमानाम् । ४ । धर्मिभिरपि यतेत । ५ । पुत्रेण जगती जयेः । ६ । त्वं जीव शरदः शतम् । ७ । भूभृतः (gen.) शिखरं वयमारोहाम यूयमधस्तादतिष्ठत । ८ । काश्चित्सरितः समुद्रेण काश्चिदन्याभिः सरिद्भिः संगच्छन्ते । ९ । रात्रौ तडिददृश्यत । १० । भक्ताः सुहृदो ऽस्मान्सुखं लम्भयन्ति । ११ । अश्रुभिर्नार्यो बालाश्च मनोरथान्साधयन्ति । १२ । शरदि कासुचित्सरित्सु पद्मानि दृश्यन्ते । १३ ।

14. Indra, with the Maruts *as his* companions, killed Vṛtra. 15. Without a companion no one can perform a difficult business. 16. One (*express in pl.*) should plant trees on all the roads, for the sake of the shade. 17. Those friends who are true in misfortune are hard to find in the *three* worlds. 18. The girdle and the sacred cord of Aryans are to be made threefold (*neut. dual*). 19. Put (स्था *caus.*) this stone behind the fire. 20. The ocean is called by the poets the husband of rivers. 21. All subjects must be protected (*in.v.*) by *their* kings. 22. Some of these Brāhmans are learned in the Upaniṣads, others in the law-books.

Lesson XXI.

246. Declension of Consonant-stems, cont'd. Stems in palatals, etc. 1. Final च् of a stem reverts to the original guttural when it comes to stand as word-final, and before the *pada*-endings, becoming क् when final, and before सु, and ग् before भ्. 2. Final ज् is oftenest treated exactly like च् — for cases of other treatment, see below. 3. In the roots* दिश्, दृश् and स्पृश्, the श् is treated in the same way. 4. The स् of सु becomes ष् after क्;

* In classical Sanskrit not many root-stems are used as independent substantives; but they are frequently employed, with adjective or (present) participial value, as final element of a compound word.

thus, °ग्. E. g. वाच् f., 'speech, word'; रुज् f., 'illness'; दिश् f., 'direction, point of the compass':

	Sing.	Plural.
N.V.	वाक् । रुक् । दिक् ॥	वाचस् । रुजस् । दिशस् ॥
A.	वाचम् । रुजम् । दिशम् ॥	" " "
I.	वाचा । रुजा । दिशा ॥	वाग्भिस् । रुग्भिस् । दिग्भिस् ॥
L.	वाचि । रुजि । दिशि ॥	वाक्षु । रुक्षु । दिक्षु ॥

Dual.

वाचौ । रुजौ । दिशौ ॥
वाग्भ्याम् । रुग्भ्याम् । दिग्भ्याम् ॥
वाचोस् । रुजोस् । दिशोस् ॥

247. 1. Final श् and ष् of a stem regularly become the lingual mute (ड् or ट्) before भ् and सु, and when word-final. For exceptions, see § 246, 3. 2. The final ज् of the root-stems राज्, 'rule', यज्, 'sacrifice', and मृज्, with others; and 3. the final ह् of a number of roots, are treated like ष् above. Thus, द्विष् m., 'enemy'; विश् m. pl., 'people', the 'Vāiçya-caste'; लिह् m., f., (adj.) 'licking'.

	Sing.	Plural.
N.V.	द्विट् । लिट् ॥	द्विषस् । विशस् । । लिहस् ॥
A.	द्विषम् । लिहम् ॥	" " "
I.	द्विषा । लिहा ॥	द्विड्भिस् । विड्भिस् । लिड्भिस् ॥
L.	द्विषि । लिहि ॥	द्विट्सु । विट्सु । लिट्सु ॥

Dual.

द्विषौ । लिहौ ॥
द्विड्भ्याम् । लिड्भ्याम् ॥
द्विषोस् । लिहोस् ॥

248. But ऋत्विज् m., 'priest', though containing the root यज्,

makes ऋत्विक् etc.; and स्रज् f., 'garland', though containing √सृज्, makes स्रक् etc.

249. 1. Nouns having the roots दह्, 'burn', and दुह्, 'milk', द्रुह् 'be hostile', with others, as final element, and also उष्णिह् f. (name of a certain metre), change the final ह् into क् and ग्. Thus, काष्ठदह्, 'wood-burning', makes nom.-voc. sing. काष्ठधक्; कामदुह् f., 'granting wishes', nom.-voc. sing. कामधुक्, acc. °दुहम्, loc. pl. °धुक्षु; मित्रद्रुह् 'friend-betraying,' nom.-voc.-sing. मित्रध्रुक् etc. 2. In words with नह्, 'bind,' as final element, where ह् represents original ध्, the ह् becomes द् and त्; thus, उपानह् f., 'shoe, sandal,' nom.-voc. sing. उपानत्, acc. °नहम्, instr. du. °नद्भ्याम्, loc. pl. °नत्सु.

Vocabulary XXI.

Verbs:

दम् in caus. (*damáyati*) tame; compel.

द्रुह् (*drúhyati*) be hostile; offend.

धृ in caus. (*dhāráyati*) bear.

भृ (*bhárati, -te*) bear, support (*lit. and fig.*).

सृज् + उद् (*utsṛjáti*) let loose or out; raise (the voice).

स्वञ्ज् + परि (*pariṣvájate**) embrace.

हृ + प्र (*prahárati*) strike out; smite.

Subst.:

अन्ध्र m. pl., *n. pr.*, a people in India.

ऋच् f., verse of the Rigveda; *in pl.*, the Rigveda.

औषध n., medicine.

कौन्तेय m., *nom. pr.*

दृश् f., look, glance; eye.

द्विष् m., enemy.

बाष्प m., tears.

मधुलिह् m., bee.

माधुर्य n., sweetness.

रुज् f., sickness, disease.

सम्राज् m., great king, emperor.

* स्वञ्ज् and a few other roots, whose nasal is not constant throughout their inflection, lose it in the present-system.

सामन्त m., vassal.
स्नातक m., one who has taken a certain ceremonial bath.
स्वाध्याय m., private recitation (of sacred texts).

Adj.:

आक्रान्त, f. °**आ** (pass. part. of **क्रम्** + **आ**), attacked, smitten.
ईश्वर, f. °**आ**, rich.
कामदुह् m. f. n., granting wishes; *as f. subst.* the Wonder-cow.
दक्षिण, f. °**आ**, right hand; southern.
नीरुज् (i. e. **निस्-रुज्**) m. f. n., healthy, well.
पथ्य, f. °**आ**, wholesome (*gen.*).
बलिष्ठ, f. **आ**, strongest.
रुद्ध, f. °**आ** (pass. part. of **रुध्**), besieged, surrounded; suffused.
विद्विष्ट, f. °**आ** (pass. part. of **द्विष्** + **वि**), hated, detested.
वृद्ध, f. °**आ** (part. of **वृध्**), old.
व्याधित, f. °**आ**, sick, ill.
समेत, f. **आ**, provided with.

Adv.:

कदाचन, **कदाचित्**, **कदापि**, ever.

Exercise XXI.

दरिद्रान्भर कौन्तेय मा प्रयच्छेश्वरे धनम् ।
व्याधितस्यौषधं पथ्यं नीरुजस्तु किमौषधैः* ॥ ९ ॥

मरुतः सर्वाभ्यो दिग्भ्यो (abl.) वहन्ति ।१। सम्राजो ऽपि राज्यं द्विड्भिर्व्यनाश्यत । २ । तव वाक्षु कालिदास माधुर्यं वर्तते । ३ । यदा दिशो दहन्ति तदा शिष्यान्नाध्यापयेत् ।४। बाष्प रुद्धाभ्यां दृग्भ्यां पिता पुत्रमैक्षत पर्यष्वजत च ।५। ऋत्विजां वाक् कामधुक् सा सर्वान्नराणां मनोरथान्पूरयति ।६। सर्वासु दिक्षु द्विषो ऽदृश्यन्त ।७। परिव्राड्ग्रामं नोत्सृजेत् ।८। मित्रध्रुक् सर्वेषां विद्विष्टः । ९ । स्रग्भिरुपानद्भ्यां समेताः शिष्या गुरुं नोपतिष्ठेरन् ।१०। रुग्भिराक्रान्ता बहवो जना म्रियन्ते ।११। दक्षिणस्यां दिशि कृष्णो ऽन्ध्राणां सम्राडभवत् ।१२। मधुलिड्भिरेव बालो ऽदश्यत ॥ १३ ॥

14. In the private recitation *of the Veda* an ascetic must

---

* **किम्** (interrog.), with some other words expressing use or need, takes with it an instrumental of what is used or needed, and a genitive of the user. So here: "of what use to a well man are medicines"?

raise (*opt. or imv.*) *his* **voice. 15. That one among the priests is called** *hotṛ*, **who recites the Rigveda. 16. A** *snātaka* **must wear shoes and a garland, and** *carry* **an umbrella. 17. "Among my friends Rāma is the strongest": thus spoke Rāvaṇa. 18. Let an emperor keep** *his* **vassals in check (दम् *caus.*), and protect (पा *caus.*) the people in all the earth. 19. In the Rigveda occurs (दृश् *pass.*) the Uṣṇih. 20. The father's glance fell upon me (*loc.*). 21. Among the betrayers-of-friends is named (गणय *pass.*) Vibhīṣaṇa. 22. The seer praises Indrāṇī with verses** *of the Rigveda.* **23. The emperor smote** *his* **enemies (*acc., dat.,* or *loc.*) with the sword. 24. In the battle Kṛṣṇa was killed by his enemies. 25. "May our enemies be tormented by diseases": thus spoke the Brāhman in anger (*abl.*).**

Lesson XXII.

250. Declension of Stems in र्. The stems in इर् and उर् lengthen the vowel before consonant-endings, and in nom.-sing., and the स् of the nom. is lost. In the nom.-sing. the final र् then becomes स् (or *visarga*) under conditions requiring a surd as final (see § 95, 116). Thus, गिर् f., 'voice'; पुर् f., 'city'.

	Singular	Dual.	Plural.
N.V.	गीर् । पूर् ॥	गिरौ । पुरौ ॥	गिरस् । पुरस् ॥
A.	गिरम् । पुरम् ॥	" "	" "
I.	गिरा । पुरा ॥	गीर्भ्याम् । पूर्भ्याम् ॥	गीर्भिस् । पूर्भिस् ॥
L.	गिरि । पुरि ॥	गिरोस् । पुरोस् ॥	गीर्षु । पूर्षु

251. Stems in इन् [and in मिन् and विन्]. These are masc. and neut. only; the corresponding feminine is made by adding ई; thus, धनिनी.* They lose their final न् before consonant-endings;

* Almost any noun in अ may form a possessive derivative with

and also in the nom. sing., where the masc. lengthens the इ in compensation. Thus धनिन् m., n., 'rich'.

	Masculine.			Neuter.		
	Singular.	Dual.	Plural.	Singular.	Dual.	Plural.
N.	धनी	धनिनौ	धनिनस्	धनि	धनिनी	धनीनि
A.	धनिनम्	"	"	"	"	"
I.	धनिना	धनिभ्याम्	धनिभिस्	as in the masculine		
L.	धनिनि	धनिनोस्	धनिषु			
V.	धनिन्					

252. Derivative stems in अस्, इस्, उस्. The stems of this division are mostly neuter; but there are a few masculines and feminines. Their inflection is nearly regular (for ओ, इर्, उर् before भ् see § 241; for the loc. pl., p. 27, bottom of page). Masc. [and fem.] stems in अस् lengthen the अ in nom. sing.; and the nom.-acc. pl. neut. also lengthen अ or इ or उ before the inserted nasal (*anusvāra*). Thus, मनस् n., 'mind'; हविस् n., 'oblation'; धनुस् n., 'bow'.

	Singular.			Dual.		
N.A.V.	मनस् ।	हविस् ।	धनुस् ॥	मनसी ।	हविषी ।	धनुषी ॥
I.	मनसा ।	हविषा ।	धनुषा ॥	मनोभ्याम् ।	हविर्भ्याम् ।	धनुर्भ्याम् ॥
L.	मनसि ।	हविषि ।	धनुषि ॥	मनसोस् ।	हविषोस् ।	धनुषोस् ॥

Plural.

N.A.	मनांसि ।	हवींषि ।	धनूंषि ॥
I.	मनोभिस् ।	हविर्भिस् ।	धनुर्भिस् ॥
L.	मनस्सु ।	हविष्षु ।	धनुष्षु ॥
	or मनःसु ।	or हविःषु ।	or धनुःषु ॥

253. अङ्गिरस् m. (name of certain mythical characters): nom. sing. अङ्गिरास्, acc. अङ्गिरसम्, instr. अङ्गिरसा, voc. अङ्गिरस्; nom.-acc. pl. अङ्गिरसस्.

---

the suffix इन्; thus, from बल n., 'strength', बलिन्, 'having strength, strong'. Stems in मिन् and विन् are very rare.

254. Adjective compounds having nouns of this class as final member are very common. Thus, सुमनस् 'favorably-minded.'

	Singular.		Dual.		Plural.	
	m. f.	n.	m. f.	n.	m. f.	n.
N.	सुमनास्	°नस्	सुमनसौ	°नसी	सुमनसस्	°नांसि
A.	सुमनसम्	°नस्	"	"	"	"

दीर्घायुस् 'long-lived':

	Singular.		Dual.		Plural.	
N.	दीर्घायुस्		दीर्घायुषौ	°युषी	दीर्घायुषस्	°यूंषि
A.	दीर्घायुषम्	°युस्	"	"	"	"
I.	दीर्घायुषा etc.		दीर्घायुर्भ्याम् etc.		दीर्घायुर्भिस् etc.	

Vocabulary XXII.

Verb:

सज्ज् (*sájati*; but often pass.: *sajjáte* for *sajyáte*) hang on, be fastened on (as thoughts — *w. loc.*).

Subst.:

अप्सरस् f., heavenly nymph.

उर्वशी f., *n. pr.*, an Apsaras, Urvaçī.

क्षितिप m., king.

गिर् f., voice; song.

चक्षुस् n., eye.

चन्द्रमस् m., moon.

चार m., spy.

ज्या f., bowstring.

ज्योतिस् n., light; star; heavenly body.

तडाग m., pond.

द्वार् f., door, gate.

धनुस् n., bow.

नाली f., pipe, conduit.

पयस् n., milk.

पुर् f., city.

पुरूरवस् m., *n. pr.*, Purūravas.

प्राणिन् m., (living) creature.

भरतखण्ड m., *n.*, *pr.*, India.

मनस् *n.*, mind.

मन्त्रिन् m., minister (of state).

यजुस् n., sacrificial formula, text.

यशस् n., glory, fame.

वणिज् m., merchant.

वयस् n., age.

सुमनस् f., flower.

सूर्य m., sun.

स्थान n., place, spot, locality; stead.

स्वामिन् m., possessor, lord.

हविस् n., oblation.

Adj.:

आकृष्ट, f. °**आ** (part. of **कृष्**+**आ**), drawn, bent (as a bow).

तपस्विन् suffering, doing acts of asceticism; *as m. subst.*, ascetic.

तेजस्विन् courageous.

प्रथम, f. °**आ**, first.

मृत, f. °**आ** (part. of **मृ**), dead, fallen.

स्थित, f. °**आ** (part. of **स्था**), standing.

Indecl.:

वै to be sure, in sooth.

Exercise XXII.

गन्धेन गावः पश्यन्ति वेदैः पश्यन्ति वै द्विजाः ।
चारैः पश्यन्ति क्षितिपाश्चक्षुर्भ्यामितरे जनाः ॥ १० ॥

आ कर्णमाकृष्टेन धनुषा द्विट्सु शरान्मुञ्चन्ति क्षत्रियाः । १ । सूर्यश्च चन्द्रमाश्च जगतो ज्योतिषी । २ । धनी वणिग्द्वारि स्थितेभ्यस्तपस्विभ्यो वसु दापयेत् । ३ । यज्ञेषु य ऋत्विजो यजूंषि पठन्ति तेऽध्वर्यव उच्यन्ते । ४ । विश्वस्या भुवः सम्राट् पुरूरवा उर्वशीमप्सरसं पर्यणयत्तस्यां च पुत्रो ऽजायत । ५ । कामस्य धनुषि ज्यायाः स्थाने ऽलयः शराणां स्थाने सुमनसस्तिष्ठन्ति । ६ । प्राणिनां मनांसि जीविते सजन्ति । ७ । पुरि वारि तडागान्नाड्या पार्थिवो ऽनाययत् । ८ । मन्त्रिणः स्वामिने कदापि न द्रुह्येयुः । ९ । एतस्या धेन्वाः पयो बालान्पितरावपाययताम् । १० ।

11. Raise ye the voice in praise (*dat.*) of Hari. 12. In the cities of India dwell rich merchants and courageous warriors. 13. The praise of Purūravas was sung by Kālidāsa. 14. The king gave orders (**आ-ज्ञा** *caus.*) to have his minister called (*use or. recta*). 15. The minds of ascetics must not dwell (**सञ्ज्**) on riches (**श्री**, *loc. sing.*). 16. At night the moon gives light to all creatures. 17. One should sacrifice to the gods (*cf.* **यज्** *in Voc.* I) flowers, fruits, and milk, not living creatures. 18. The Apsarases lead into Heaven warriors fallen in battle. 19. In age (*instr.*), not in knowledge,

Çiva is the eldest among *his* brothers (*loc.*, *gen.*). **20.** The gods live by the oblation. 21. A merchant wishes wealth (श्री), a warrior fame, an ascetic deliverance. 22. The woman's eyes are suffused with tears.

Lesson XXIII.

255. Declension. Comparative Adjectives. Comparative adjectives of primary formation have a double form of stem for masculine and neuter: a stronger in यांस् (usually ईयांस्), in the strong cases, and a weaker in यस् (usually ईयस्), there being no distinction of middle and weakest cases. The voc. sing. masc. ends in यन्. The feminine-stem is made with ई from the weak stem-form. Thus, श्रेयांस्, 'better':

	Masculine.				Neuter.		
	Sing.	Dual.	Plural.		Sing.	Dual.	Plural.
N.	श्रेयान्	श्रेयांसौ	श्रेयांसस्	N.V.	श्रेयस्	श्रेयसी	श्रेयांसि
A.	श्रेयांसम्	„	श्रेयसस्		„	„	„
I.	श्रेयसा	श्रेयोभ्याम्	श्रेयोभिस्		like the masculine.		
L.	श्रेयसि	श्रेयसोस्	श्रेयस्सु, ॰यःसु				
V.	श्रेयन्						

Fem. stem श्रेयसी, declined like नदी.

256. Stems in अन्त् (or अत्) fall into two divisions: A. those made with the suffix अन्त् (अत्), being, with few exceptions, active participles, present and future; and B. those made with the possessive suffixes मन्त् (or मत्) and वन्त् (or वत्). They are masc. and neuter only, the fem. being formed with ई.

257. A. Participles in अन्त् (or अत्). E. g. जीवन्त् m., n., 'living.'

	Masculine.			Neuter.		
	Sing.	Dual.	Plural.	Sing.	Dual.	Plural.
N.V.	जीवन्	जीवन्तौ	जीवन्तस्	जीवत्	जीवन्ती	जीवन्ति
A.	जीवन्तम्	„	जीवतस्	„	„	„
I.	जीवता	जीवद्भ्याम्	जीवद्भिस्	as in masculine.		
L.	जीवति	जीवतोस्	जीवत्सु			

258. The strong form of these participles is obtained, mechanically, by cutting off the final इ from the 3rd. pl. pres. (or fut.) ind. act.; thus, नयन्ति gives strong form of pres. act. part. नयन्त्, weak नयत्; तिष्ठन्ति, तिष्ठन्त् and तिष्ठत्; — नह्यन्ति, नह्यन्त् and नह्यत्; — दण्डयन्ति, दण्डयन्त् and दण्डयत्; — भविष्यन्ति (fut.), भविष्यन्त् and भविष्यत्.

259. But those verbs which in the 3rd. pl. act. lose the न् of the usual न्ति (as e. g. the verbs following the reduplicating class in the present-system), lose it also in the present participle, and have no distinction of strong and weak stem. Thus, from √हु, 3rd pl. pres. ind. act. जुह्वति, part. (only stem-form) जुह्वत्: nom.-voc. sing. masc. जुह्वत्, acc. जुह्वतम्; nom.-voc.-acc. du. जुह्वतौ, pl. जुह्वतस्; nom.-voc.-acc. sing. neut. जुह्वत्, du. जुह्वती. pl. जुह्वति.*

260. Only the present participles of verbs of the *a*-class, the *ya*-class, and causatives, invariably insert न् in nom.-voc.-acc. du. neut. Present participles of the *á*-class, of the root-class when the root ends in आ, and *all* future participles, may either take or reject it; thus, neut.-sing. किरत्, du. किरती or किरन्ती; करिष्यत् (fut.), du. करिष्यती or करिष्यन्ती; यात् (pres. part. from या, 'go'), du. याती or यान्ती. Participles of all other verbs, and all other stems in अत्, leave out the न् in the du. neut.; thus, अदत् (अद् 'eat', root-class), du. अदती.

261. The adj. महत्, 'great', takes in strong cases the stem-

---

* The grammarians, however, allow these verbs to insert the न् in the nom.-voc.-acc. pl. neuter of the present participle.

form **महान्त्**: nom.-sing. masc. **महान्** (see § 239, 2), acc. **महान्तम्**, voc. **महन्**; du. neut. **महती**, pl. **महान्ति**. Otherwise the inflection is like that of participles.

262. The feminine of participles and adjectives in **अन्त्** (or **अत्**) is always made with **ई**, and the form is always identical with the nom. dual neuter.

Vocabulary XXIII.

Verbs:

निन्द् (*níndati*) blame.

राज् (*rā́jate*) shine; rule.

सृ + अप (*apasárati*) go away; in caus. (*apasārā́yati*) drive away.

Nouns (subst. and adj.):

आदित्य m., sun.

गरीयांस् (comp.) very honorable.

ददत् (pr. part. of **दा**) giving.

प्रकाशिन्, f. **°नी**, bright, glistening; (act.) illuminating.

भूत, f. **°आ**; become (past. pass. part. of **भू**); *as neut. subst.*, being, creature.

वत्स m., calf.

श्रेयांस् better, best; ***as neut. subst.***, salvation.

सन्त् (neut. **सत्**) being, existing; *as masc. subst.*, good man; *as fem.* (**सती**), faithful wife.*

Adv.:

श्वस् to-morrow.

हि surely, indeed.

Exercise XXIII.

सन्तो ऽपि** न हि राजन्ते दरिद्रस्येतरे गुणाः ।
आदित्य इव भूतानां श्रीर्गुणानां प्रकाशिनी ॥ ११ ॥

तिष्ठन्तं गुरुं शिष्यो ऽनुतिष्ठेद्गच्छन्तमनुगच्छेद्धावन्तमनुधावेत्*** ।१। गरीयसः (acc. pl.) श्रेयसे पूजयेत् ।२। धनिनस्तपस्विभ्यो धनं ददतः

---

* Especially a widow who immolates herself on the funeral-pile of her husband; whence Anglo-Indian *suttee*.

** "Even though they exist".

*** **अनु** in composition often conveys the idea of imitation.

शस्यन्ते । ३ । स्निह्यन्तीं भार्यां त्यजन्निन्द्यते । ४ । जीवतः पुत्रस्य मुखं पश्यन्तौ पितरौ तुष्यतः । ५ । भ्रात्रो (gen. du.) रामो यशसा गरीयान् । ६ । एतेषां वणिजां धनानि महान्ति वर्तन्ते । ७ । कुप्यते मा कुप्यत । ८ । उद्याने पतद्भ्यो विहगेभ्यो धान्यं किरतीः कन्या अपश्यम् । ९ । पित्रोर्जीवतोर्भ्रातरः स्वसारश्च तयोर्धनस्य स्वामिनो न भवेयुः । १० । धेनुं धयन्तं वत्सं मापसारय । ११ । गुरुषु पिताचार्यौ माता च गरीयांसः । १२ । त्वयि जीवति सुखेन वयं जीवामः ॥ १३ ॥

14. We blame the driver who strikes (*part.*) the horses. 15. The king who punishes (*part.*) the bad and gives (*part.*) food to the good is praised. 16. The warrior who conquers (*part.*) in battle attains great fame. 17. Among the heavenly bodies the sun and moon are the *two* great *ones*. 18. In the field I saw birds flying. 19. He who lives (*part.*) to-day is dead to-morrow. 20. The word of the good must be followed (*done*). 21. Dwell among good men. 22. A maiden, making (**सृज**) garlands, sits on a stone. 23. A husband shall punish a wife who steals (*part.*) *his* property. 24. The child (*gen.*) was afraid (*use subst.*, *no copula*) of the bees (*abl.*) flying about (**भ्रम्**) in the house.

Lesson XXIV.

263. Declension. Stems in अन्त् (or अत्), cont'd. B. Stems in मन्त् (मत्) and वन्त् (वत्). Adjectives formed with these suffixes are possessives. They are declined precisely alike*; and differ in inflection from the participles in अन्त् only by lengthening the अ in the nom. sing. masc. The feminine is made in ई; thus, श्रीमती. In the dual neut. न् is never inserted. Thus, श्रीमन्त्, 'rich', 'celebrated:'

---

* The two adjectives इयन्त्, 'so great', 'so many', and कियन्त्, 'how great?' 'how many?' are similarly declined.

	Masculine.			Neuter.		
	Singular.	Dual.	Plural.	Singular.	Dual.	Plural.
N.	श्रीमान्	श्रीमन्तौ	श्रीमन्तस्	NV. श्रीमत्	श्रीमती	श्रीमन्ति
A.	श्रीमन्तम्	"	श्रीमतस्	"	"	"
I.	श्रीमता	श्रीमद्भ्याम्	श्रीमद्भिस्	as in the masculine.		
L.	श्रीमति	श्रीमतोस्	श्रीमत्सु			
V.	श्रीमन्					

264. A stem भवन्त्* (to be carefully distinguished from भवन्त्, pres. part. act. of भू) is frequently used in respectful address as a substitute for the pronoun of the second person. It is construed with the verb in the third person. Its nom. sing. masc. is भवान् (fem. भवती); and भोस्, the contracted form of its older voc. भवस्, is a common exclamation of address: "you, sir!", "ho, there!"; and is often doubled.**

265. Derivative stems in अन्. These are made by the suffixes अन्, मन्, and वन्, and are, with one or two exceptions, masc. and neut. only. The stem has a triple form. In the strong cases of the masc. the vowel of the suffix is lengthened to आ, in the weakest cases it is in general dropped; in the middle cases the final न् is dropped, and it is also lost in the nom. sing. of all genders. In the neuter, the nom.-acc. pl., as being strong cases, lengthen the vowel of the suffix; the same cases in the dual (as weakest cases) lose अ — but this only optionally. After the म् or व् of मन् and वन्, when these are preceded by a consonant, the अ is retained in all the weakest cases, to avoid too great an accumulation of consonants. Examples: राजन् m., 'king'; नामन् n., 'name'; आत्मन् m., 'soul, self'; ब्रह्मन् n., 'devotion'.

---

* Probably contracted from भगवन्त् 'blessed'.

** भोस् loses its final स् before all vowels and all sonant consonants; thus, भो भो ऋषे.

	Masculine.			Neuter.		
	Singular.	Dual.	Plural.	Singular.	Dual.	Plural.
N.	राजा	राजानौ	राजानस्	नाम	नामनी or नाम्नी	नामानि
A.	राजानम्	„	राज्ञस्	„	„	„
I.	राज्ञा*	राजभ्याम्	राजभिस्	नाम्ना	नामभ्याम्	नामभिस्
L.	राजनि or राज्ञि	राज्ञोस्	राजसु	नामनि or नाम्नि	नाम्नोस्	नामसु
V.	राजन्			नामन् or नाम		
N.	आत्मा	आत्मानौ	आत्मानस्	ब्रह्म	ब्रह्मणी	ब्रह्माणि
A.	आत्मानम्	„	आत्मनस्	„	„	„
I.	आत्मना	आत्मभ्याम्	आत्मभिस्	ब्रह्मणा	ब्रह्मभ्याम्	ब्रह्मभिस्
V.	आत्मन्			ब्रह्मन् or ब्रह्म		

266. **Euphonic rules.** Final क्, ट् and प् remain unaltered before initial surd consonants; before sonants, whether vowel or consonant, they become respectively ग्, ड्, ब्. Before nasals they may be still further assimilated, becoming the nasals ङ्, ण्, म्. Thus, परिव्राट् न becomes either परिव्राड्न or परिव्राण्न; सम्यक् न becomes सम्यग्न or सम्यङ्न. The latter method is much more usual.

267. Before initial ह् a final mute is made sonant; and then the ह् may either remain unchanged, or be converted into the sonant aspirate corresponding to the preceding letter; thus, either सम्यग्हतः or सम्यग्घतः; either तस्माद् हस्तात् or तस्माद्धस्तात्. In practice the latter method is almost invariably followed.

---

* When a dental mute comes in contact with a lingual or palatal mute or sibilant, the dental is usually assimilated, becoming lingual or palatal respectively. Thus, *tiṣṭhati* from *ti-stha-ti; rājñā* instead of *rājnā*.

Vocabulary XXIV.

Verbs:

छिद् + **अव** out off.

मृज् in caus. (*mārjáyati*) rub, rub off, polish.

वर्णय (denom. — *varṇáyati*) describe, portray.

विज् + **उद्** in caus. (*udvejáyati*) terrify.

Subst.:

आत्मन् m., soul, self; often as simple reflexive pronoun; *in genitive*, his, etc.; one's own.

कर्मन् n., deed; ceremony; fate.

चर्मन् n., hide, skin; leather.

जन्मन् n., birth.

तीर n., bank, shore.

त्रिष्टुभ् f., name of a metre.

दिन n., day.

देवकुल n., temple.

नरक m., hell.

पक्षिन् m., bird.

पात्र n., pot, vessel.

ब्रह्मन् (*bráhman*) n., devotion; sacred word (of God); sacred knowledge; the world-spirit.

ब्रह्मन् (*brahmán* — a personification of the preceding) m., the supreme All-Soul, the creator.

भस्मन् n., ashes.

यति m., ascetic.

राजन् m., king.

लोमन् n., hair.

वर्ष n., year.

समागम m., meeting, encounter.

सीमन् f., border, boundary; outskirts.

हन्तृ m., slayer, killer.

Adj.:

आयुष्मन्त् long-lived (often used in respectful address).

इयन्त् so great, so much (263).

कियन्त् how great? how much?

कृपण, f. °**आ**, poor; niggardly.

तावन्त् so much, so many.

द्वितीय, f. °**आ**, second.

प्रियकर्मन् kind.

प्रियवाच् saying pleasant things, sociable.

बलवन्त् strong, mighty.

भगवन्त्, f. **वती**, honorable; blessed.

भास्वन्त् shining, brilliant.

मतिमन्त् shrewd, prudent.

यावन्त् how much, as many.

रूक्ष, f. °**आ**, harsh, rough.

विभु, f. °**भ्वी**, pervading, far-reaching; omnipresent; mighty.

हत, f. °**आ** (pass. part. of **हन्**) killed.

Adv.:

प्रायेण commonly.

Exercise XXIV.

नोद्विजयेज्जगद्वाचा रूक्षया प्रियवाग्भवेत् ।
प्रायेण प्रियकर्मा यः कृपणो ऽपि हि सेव्यते ॥ १२ ॥

यावन्ति हतस्य पशोश्चर्मणि लोमानि विद्यन्ते तावन्ति वर्षाणि हन्ता
नरके वसेत् । १ । भृत्या बलवन्तं राजानमायुष्मन्निति वदन्तु । २ । भा-
स्वन्तं सूर्यं दिने दिने द्विजातयः पूजयन्तु । ३ । कियतो मासान्भवान्का-
श्यां न्यवसत् । ४ । के चिद्यतयो भस्मना शरीरं मार्जयन्ति । ५ । कर्म
बलवदिति मतिमतो दरिद्रान्पश्यतो (gen.) मे मतिः । ६ । त्वयि राज्ञि
तिष्ठत्यस्माकं सर्वासां च प्रजानां सुखं न विनश्येत् । ७ । एकस्मिञ्जन्मनि
ये शूद्रा जायन्ते ते ब्राह्मणां धर्मांस्त्वनुतिष्ठन्तो द्वितीये जन्मनि
द्विजातयो भवेयुः । ८ । ग्रामे परिव्राण्न तिष्ठेद्वने परिभ्रमन्ब्रह्म ध्या-
येत् । ९ । एतस्यां पुरि श्रीमतो राज्ञोः समागमो ऽजायत । १० । ब्रह्मा
जगतः स्रष्टा वेदेषु श्रूयते । ११ । यान्पथिको नगरस्य सीमनि वृक्षादुत्प-
ततो ऽपश्यत ते सर्वे मया भ्रात्रा च पाशैर्जीवन्त एवाबध्यन्त माता चास्म-
भ्रमपश्यत ॥ १२ ॥

13. Brāhmans have *their* shoes made (*use* कृ *caus.*) of leather (*instr.*) or wood. 14. A temple of blessed Viṣṇu stands in the outskirts of this village, on the bank of the river. 15. Let him rub off the vessels diligently with ashes (*pl.*). 16. The servants announced to the king that the two celebrated poets were coming (*use or. recta with* इति). 17. O children (*du.*), tell me your (आत्मन्, *gen. du.*) names. 18. The world-spirit is described in many Upaniṣads. 19. It is said by the seers that the world-spirit is omnipresent (*use or. recta*). 20. That part of the world-spirit, which is encompassed by the body, is called the soul of man (cf. § 234). 21. Candragupta was the mighty emperor of the whole earth. 22. All the mighty warriors who fought in Kṛṣṇa's army were killed in battle by the enemy. 23. In the Rigveda (ऋच् *pl.*) occurs (विद् *pass.*) also the Triṣṭubh. 24. The king of Pāṭaliputra is by birth a Çūdra; let him not marry the beautiful daughter of the ascetic Mitrātithi.

Lesson XXV.

268. Declension. Perfect Active Participles in वांस्. The active participles of the perfect tense-system are quite peculiar as regards the modifications of the stem. In the strong cases the suffix is वांस्, which becomes वान् in the nom. sing. masc., and is shortened to वन् in the voc. sing. In the weakest cases the suffix is contracted into उष्; and in the middle cases it is changed to वत्. A union-vowel इ, if present in the strong and middle cases, disappears before उष् in the weakest. Radical इ and ई, if preceded by *one* consonant, become य् before उष्, but if preceded by more than one consonant, become इय्; whereas radical उ always becomes उव् before उष्, and radical ऋ, र्. Thus, निनीवांस्, निन्युष्; शुश्रुवांस्, शुश्रुवुष्; चकृवांस्, चक्रुष्. The feminine stem is formed with ई from the weakest stem-form; thus, निन्युषी. Examples:

1. विद्वांस् 'knowing':

	Masculine.				Neuter.	
	Singular.	Dual.	Plural.		Singular. Dual.	Plural.
N.	विद्वान्	विद्वांसौ	विद्वांसस्	N.V.	विद्वत् विदुषी	विद्वांसि
A.	विद्वांसम्	"	विदुषस्		" "	"
I.	विदुषा	विद्वद्भ्याम्	विद्वद्भिस्		as in the masculine.	
L.	विदुषि	विदुषोस्	विद्वत्सु			
V.	विद्वन्					

2. जग्मिवांस् 'having gone'*:

---

* Another form of perf. part. of this verb (गम्) makes the strong and middle stems जगन्वांस् and जगन्वत्; the weakest form is as above, जग्मुष्.

	Masculine.			Neuter.		
	Singular.	Dual.	Plural.	Singular.	Dual.	Plural.
N.	अग्निमवान्	अग्निमवांसौ	°वांसस्	अग्निमवत्	अग्मुषी	अग्निमवांसि
A.	अग्निमवांसम्	"	अग्मुषस्	"	"	"
I.	अग्मुषा	°वद्भ्याम्	°वद्भिस्	as in the masculine		
L.	अग्मुषि	अग्मुषोस्	अग्निमवत्सु			
V.	अग्निमवन्					

---

269. Stems श्वन्, युवन्. The stems श्वन् m., 'dog', and युवन् m., n., 'young', have as weakest stems शुन् and यून्; in the strong and middle cases they follow राजन्; voc. श्वन्, युवन्. Fem. शुनी and युवति.

270. The stem मघवन् m., 'generous' (in the later language almost exclusively a name of Indra), has as strong stem मघवान्, mid. °व, weakest मघोन्. Nom. sing. मघवा, voc. °वन्. Fem. मघोनी.

271. The stem अहन् n., 'day', is used only in the strong and weakest cases, the middle, with the nom. sing., coming from अहर् or अहस्. Thus:

	Singular.	Dual.	Plural.
N.A.V.	अहर् (°स्)	अहनी or अह्नी	अहानि
I.	अह्ना	अहोभ्याम्	अहोभिस्
L.	अहनि or अह्नि	अह्नोस्	अहस्सु or अहःसु

272. Compounds with √अच् or अञ्च्. The adjectives formed from this root with prepositions and other words are quite irregular. Some of them have only two stem-forms: a strong in अञ्च् and a weak in अच्; while others distinguish from the middle in अच् a weakest stem in च्, before which the अ is contracted with a preceding इ (य्) or उ (व्) into ई or ऊ. The fem. is made with ई from the weakest (or weak) stem; thus, विषूची. The principal stems of this sort are as follows:

	Strong.	Middle.	Weak (weakest).
प्राञ्च् 'forward', 'eastward'	प्राञ्च्		प्राच्
अवाञ्च् 'downward'	अवाञ्च्		अवाच्
उदञ्च् 'northward'	उदञ्च्	उदच्	उदीच्*
प्रत्यञ्च् 'backward', 'westward'	प्रत्यञ्च्	प्रत्यच्	प्रतीच्
न्यञ्च् 'low'	न्यञ्च्	न्यच्	नीच्
अन्वञ्च् 'following'	अन्वञ्च्	अन्वच्	अनूच्
तिर्यञ्च् 'going horizontally'	तिर्यञ्च्	तिर्यच्	तिरश्च्**

Vocabulary XXV.

Verbs:

गम् + अस्तम् (*astaṁgácchati*) go down, set (lit'ly "go home" — used of the heavenly bodies).

+ उद् (*udgácchati*) rise.

स्पृह् (*spṛháyati*) desire (*dat.*).

Subst.:

गौरव n., weight; dignity.

जगत् n., that which lives.

तक्षशिला f., *n. pr.*, a city (Taxila) in India.

तिर्यञ्च् m., n., animal.

त्वष्टृ m., *n. pr.*, a god, Tvaṣṭar.

परिषद् f., assembly.

भृगुकच्छ n., Baroch (a holy place in India).

मघवन् m., Indra.

युवन् m., n., young; f. युवति.

विपाक m., ripening; recompense.

श्रम m., pains, trouble.

सिंह m., lion.

स्नान n., bathing, bath.

हरिण m., gazelle.

Adj.:

अधीत, f., °आ, learned, studied.

तस्थिवांस् having stood; *as n. subst.*, the immovable.

त्रिशीर्षन् three-headed.

दष्ट, f. °आ, (part. of दंश्) bitten.

वनवासिन् forest-dwelling.

विद्वांस् knowing, wise, learnèd.

---

* ई inserted, irregularly, in weakest forms only.

** irregular (तिरस् + अञ्च्).

Exercise XXV.

विद्वान्प्रशस्यते लोके विद्वान्गच्छति गौरवम् ।
विद्यया लभ्यते सर्वं विद्या सर्वत्र पूज्यते ॥ १३ ॥

प्राच्यां दिशि ज्योतींष्युद्गच्छन्ति प्रतीच्यामस्तंगच्छन्ति । १ । विद्वद्भिरेव विदुषां श्रमो ज्ञायते । २ । त्वष्टुस्त्रिशीर्षाणं पुत्रं मघवामारयत् । ३ । अहनी एव क्षत्रियावयुध्येताम् । ४ । शुना दष्टो द्विजातिः स्नानमाचरेत् । ५ । कान्ता आजग्मुषो भ्रातॄनपश्याम । ६ । येन वेदा अधीतास्तं युवानमपि गुरुं गणयन्ति । ७ । पापाः कर्मणां विपाकेन द्वितीये जन्मनि तिर्यक्षु आयन्त इति स्मृतिः । ८ । विद्वांसो विद्वद्भिः सह समागमाय स्पृहयन्ति । ९ । कियद्भिरहोभिः कान्ताः प्रयागमगच्छत । १० । प्राचां देशे पाटलिपुत्रं नाम महन्नगरं विद्यत उदीचां तक्षशिला प्रतीचां भृगुकच्छम् ॥ ११ ॥

12. Vṛtra was killed (हन्, *caus. pass.*) by Maghavan and the Maruts. 13. Young *women* sang a song. 14. Two learned Brāhmans dispute. 15. Saramā is called in the Rigveda the dog (*f.*) of the gods. 16. Great forests are found in the west (*expr. as pred., nom. pl.*). 17. In the assembly let the best among the learned teach (उप-दिश्) the law. 18. Those who have committed evil deeds must stand by day (*acc.*) and sit by night. 19. Glory was attained by the young warrior. 20. *Turned toward the* east (*nom. sing.*) let one reverence the gods; the east (प्राची) is the quarter (दिश्) of the gods. 21. Day by day one must worship (पूज्) the sun. 22. The gazelle *has been* killed by dogs. 23. The lion is king of forest-dwelling animals.

Lesson XXVI.

Some Irregular Substantives.

273. अम्बा f., 'mother': voc. sing. अम्ब.

274. 1. सखि m., 'friend': sing. nom. सखा, acc. सखायम्, inst. सख्या, dat. सख्ये, abl.-gen. सख्युस्, loc. सख्यौ, voc. सखे; du. सखायौ,

सखिभ्याम्, सख्योस्; pl. nom. सखायस्, acc. सखीन्, instr. सखिभिस्; the rest like अग्नि. — 2. पति m., is declined regularly (like अग्नि) in composition, and when meaning 'lord, master'; when meaning 'husband', it follows सखि in the following forms: inst. sing. पत्या, dat. पत्ये, abl.-gen. पत्युस्, loc. पत्यौ.

275. The neuter stems अक्षन् 'eye', अस्थन् 'bone', दधन् 'curds', सक्थन् 'thigh', form only the weakest cases; thus, अक्ष्णा, दध्नस्, सक्थनि or सक्थ्नि, etc.; the rest of the inflection is made from corresponding stems in इ; thus, nom. sing. अक्षि etc.

276. 1. लक्ष्मी f., 'goddess of fortune', makes nom. sing. लक्ष्मीस्. — 2. स्त्री f., 'woman', follows a mixed declension; thus, nom. sing. स्त्री, acc. स्त्रियम् or स्त्रीम्, instr. स्त्रिया, dat. स्त्रियै, abl.-gen. स्त्रियास्, loc. स्त्रियाम्; du. स्त्रियौ, स्त्रीभ्याम्, स्त्रियोस्; pl. nom. स्त्रियस्, acc. स्त्रियस् or स्त्रीस्, instr. स्त्रीभिस्, etc.; gen. स्त्रीणाम्.

277. 1. अप् f., 'water', only pl.; its final is changed to द् before भ्; thus, nom. आपस्, acc. अपस्, instr. अद्भिस्, dat.-abl. अद्भ्यस्, gen. अपाम्, loc. अप्सु. — 2. दिव् f.,* 'sky', makes nom. sing. द्यौस्, du. द्यावौ, pl. (sometimes) द्यावस्; the endings are the normal ones, but the root becomes द्यु before consonant-endings: thus, acc. sing. दिवम्, nom.-acc. pl. दिवस्, instr. द्युभिस्. Not all the cases are found in use. — 3. Stem रै m. (rarely f.), 'wealth': sing. रास्, रायम्, राया etc.; du. रायौ, राभ्याम्, रायोस्; pl. रायस् (nom. and acc.), राभिस् etc.

278. 1. अनड्वह् or अनडुह् m., (from अनस् + वह् 'cart-drawing', i. e.) 'ox': strong stem अनड्वाह्, mid. अनडुद्, weakest अनडुह्; nom. sing. अनड्वान्, voc. अनड्वन्. — 2. The stem पन्थन् m., 'road', makes all the strong cases, with irregular nom. sing. पन्थास्; the corresponding middle cases are made from पथि, and the weakest from पथ्; thus, acc. sing. पन्थानम्, dat. पथे, acc. pl. पथस्,

---

* In the older language oftener masculine.

dat. पथिभ्यस्. [The stems मन्थन् m., 'stirring-stick', and ऋभुक्षन् m., an epithet of Indra, are said to follow पन्थन्.]

279. The stem पुंस् m., 'man', is very irregular. The strong stem is पुमांस्, mid. पुम्, weakest पुंस्. Thus, sing. पुमान्, पुमांसम्, पुंसा, etc., voc. पुमन्; du. पुमांसौ, पुम्भ्याम्, पुंसोस्; pl. पुमांसस्, पुंसस्, पुम्भिस् etc., पुंसु.

280. For the stem जरा f., 'age', may be substituted in the cases with vowel-endings forms from जरस् f.; thus, जरया or जरसा.

281. हृद् n., 'heart', does not make nom.-voc.-acc. of any number (except in composition), these being supplied from हृदय n.

282. The stem पद् m., 'foot', becomes पाद् in strong cases; and, in compounds, in the middle cases also; thus, nom. sing. पाद्, acc. पादम्, instr. पदा, etc. From द्विपद् 'biped', acc. sing. द्विपादम्, pl. द्विपदस्, instr. pl. द्विपाद्भिस्. [The stem पाद m., 'foot', has the complete declension of *a*-stems.]

283. The root हन् 'slay', as final member of a compound, becomes हा in nom. sing., and loses its न् in the middle cases and its अ in the weakest cases (but only optionally in loc. sing.). Further, when अ is lost, ह् in contact with न् reverts to its original घ्; thus, ब्रह्महन् m., 'killing a Brāhman', makes nom. sing. ब्रह्महा, acc. °हणम्*, instr. ब्रह्मघ्ना, etc., loc. ब्रह्मघ्नि or °हणि, voc. °हन्; du. ब्रह्महणौ, °हभ्याम् etc.; pl. nom. °हणस्, acc. °घ्नस्.

284. The stems पूषन् m., *n. pr.*, and अर्यमन् m., *n. pr.* (both personifications of the sun), make the nom. sing. in आ, but otherwise do not lengthen the अ; thus, nom. पूषा, acc. पूषणम्, instr. पूष्णा.

---

* In compound words, an altering cause in one member sometimes lingualizes a न् of the next following member. But a guttural or labial in direct combination with न् sometimes prevents the combination, as in the instr. ब्रह्मघ्ना.

Vocabulary XXVI.

Verbs:

ऋ move; in caus. (*arpáyati*) send; put; hand over, give.

गुह् (*gúhati*) in caus. (*gūháyati*) hide away, conceal.

तृप् (*tṛ́pyati*) be pleased or satisfied, satisfy or satiate oneself.

लप् + वि (*vilápati*) complain.

Subst.:

अक्षन् (अक्षि) n., eye.

अद्रोह m., faithfulness.

असुर m., demon.

चित्त n., notice, thought, mind.

देवता f., divinity, deity.

दध्यच् (weakest °धीच्) m., *n. pr.*, a Vedic saint.

पद् m., foot.

पालन n., protection.

मानव m., man (*homo*).

व्रत n., vow, obligation, duty.

Adj.:

काण f., °आ, one-eyed.

चतुष्पद् four-footed, quadruped.

द्विपद् m., biped.

नियत, f. °आ (part. of नि-यम्), ordained, fixed, permanent.

शिव, f. °आ, beneficent, gracious, blessed.

Exercise XXVI.

पत्यौ भक्तिर्व्रतं स्त्रीणामद्रोहो मन्त्रिणां व्रतम् ।
प्रजानां पालनं चैव नियतं भूभृतां व्रतम् ॥ १४ ॥

बलवन्तावनड्वाहौ लाङ्गलं वहेताम् । १ । शिवास्ते पन्थानः । २ । लक्ष्मीर्विष्णोर्भार्या । ३ । हृद्येष पुमान्परं ब्रह्म ध्यायति । ४ । बाहुभ्यां भूभृत्कृत्स्नं जगदजयत् । ५ । केन पथा भवान्सख्या सहागच्छत् । ६ । पदा मामस्पृशत्सखा । ७ । पुम्भिः सह स्त्रीरागमयद्राजा । ८ । हे युवन्पन्थानं मे दर्शय । ९ । अद्भिः पादौ क्षालयत्येष परिव्राट् । १० । स्त्री पत्ये रूपकाण्यर्पयति । ११ । एकेनाक्ष्णा यो न किंचित्पश्यति तं काणं वदन्ति । १२ । द्यौः पिता पृथिवी च माता वो रक्षताम् । १३ । एते पुमांसो हृदयेषु पापं गूहयन्ति । १४ । ब्रह्मघ्ना न संभाषेत न च तमध्यापयेद्याजयेद्वा । १५ । असुरेभ्यो भयाद्मानवा देवताः पालनं प्रार्थयन्त ताभिश्च शिवाभिः पापा असुरा अघात्यन्त । १६ । महानुदीचां राजा दरिद्रैः पथि तिष्ठद्भिः शिष्यैः संभाषमाणस्तेभ्यो भिक्षां यच्छति ॥ १७ ॥

18. The meeting of the men and women took place on the road. 19. In the Veda they call the sun Pūṣan, Mitra (*m.*), Aryaman, and Savitar. 20. Water also is named (गणय, *pass.*) among the deities in the Rik (*use* ऋचस्) and in the sacrificial formulas. 21. Be gracious, O Çiva, to biped and quadruped. 22. The seers' view is, that fire is to be found in the water (*use* वृत्, *and make a direct statement with* इति). 23. The Asura was slain by Maghavan with a bone of Dadhyañc. 24. Who knows the wind's path (*pass.*)? 25. Mother, satisfy (तृप् *caus.*) the child with curds. 26. Have food brought (*use* आ-नी, *caus.*, *pl.*) from our friend's house. 27. The Maruts are Maghavan's friends.

Lesson XXVII.

285. **Demonstrative Pronouns.** Two demonstrative-declensions are made up with particular irregularity: they are those of the pronouns अयम् and असौ (for which the natives give the stem-forms as इदम् and अदस् respectively). The first is a more indefinite demonstrative: 'this' or 'that'; the other signifies especially the remoter relation.

286. अयम् (इदम्):

	Masculine.			**Feminine.**		
	Sing.	Dual.	Plural.	Sing.	Dual.	Plural.
N.	अयम्	इमौ	इमे	इयम्	इमे	इमास्
A.	इमम्	"	इमान्	इमाम्	"	"
I.	अनेन	आभ्याम्	एभिस्	अनया	आभ्याम्	आभिस्
D.	अस्मै	"	एभ्यस्	अस्यै	"	आभ्यस्
Ab.	अस्मात्	"	"	अस्यास्	"	"
G.	अस्य	अनयोस्	एषाम्	"	अनयोस्	आसाम्
L.	अस्मिन्	"	एषु	अस्याम्	"	आसु

Neuter: Nom.-acc. sing. इदम्, du. इमे, pl. इमानि; the rest is like the masculine.

287. असौ (अदस्):

	Masculine.			Feminine.		
	Sing.	Dual.	Plural.	Sing.	Dual.	Plural.
N.	असौ	अमू	अमी	असौ	अमू	अमूस्
A.	अमुम्	"	अमून्	अमूम्	"	"
I.	अमुना	अमूभ्याम्	अमीभिस्	अमुया	अमूभ्याम्	अमूभिस्
D.	अमुष्मै	"	अमीभ्यस्	अमुष्यै	"	अमूभ्यस्
Ab.	अमुष्मात्	"	"	अमुष्यास्	"	"
G.	अमुष्य	अमुयोस्	अमीषाम्	"	अमुयोस्	अमूषाम्
L.	अमुष्मिन्	"	अमीषु	अमुष्याम्	"	अमूषु

Neuter: Nom.-acc. sing. अदस्, du. अमू, pl. अमूनि; the rest like masc. — The final ई of अमी is unchangeable (cf. § 161).

288. There is a defective pronominal stem एन, which is accentless, and hence used only in situations where no emphasis falls upon it. The only forms are the following: Sing. acc. m. एनम्, n. एनद्, f. एनाम्; instr. m., n., एनेन, f. एनया. Du. acc. m. एनौ, f., n., एने; gen.-loc. m., f., n., एनयोस्. Pl. acc. m. एनान्, n. एनानि, f. एनास्. — These forms may be used only when the person or object to which they refer has already been indicated by a form of अयम् or एष. Thus, अनेन काव्यमधीतमेनं व्याकरणमध्यापय "this one has read the art of poetry; teach him grammar".

289. Past Passive Participle in त or न. By the suffix त — or, in a comparatively small number of verbs, न — is formed, directly from the root of the verb, and unconnected with any tense-stem, a verbal adjective called the past passive participle. The fem. ends always in ॰आ. When this participle is made from transitive verbs, it qualifies something as having endured the action expressed by the verb; thus, दत्त *dattá*, 'given'; उक्त *uktá*, 'spoken'. When made from an intransitive or neuter verb, the same participle has no passive, but only an indefinite past, sense; thus, गत, 'gone', भूत, 'been'; पतित, 'fallen'.

290. This participle is often used as an adjective. Very commonly, also, it supplies the place of a finite verb, when some form of अस्, 'be', or भू is to be supplied; thus, स गतः "he is gone"; मया पत्त्रं लिखितम् "by me a letter was written". The neuter is frequently used as a substantive; thus, दत्तम् 'a gift'; दुग्धम् 'milk'; and also as *nomen actionis.* Sometimes it has a present signification, particularly when made from neuter verbs; thus, स्थित (from स्था) often 'standing'.

291. A. With suffix न [ण]. The suffix न is taken by a number of roots. Thus:

1. Certain roots in आ, and in *i* and *u*-vowels; thus, प्या or पी 'swell, be fat', पीन; हा 'abandon', हीन; म्ला 'wither', म्लान; क्षि 'destroy', क्षीण; श्वा or श्वि 'swell', शून; लू 'cut', लून.

2. The roots in variable ॠ (so-called ṝ-roots), which before the suffix becomes ईर् or ऊर्, as in the pres. pass.; thus, 2कॄ (किर्), कीर्ण; तॄ, तीर्ण; 1पॄ (पूर्) 'fill', पूर्ण.

3. A few roots ending in ज् (which becomes ग् before the न); thus, भञ्ज् 'break', भग्न; 1भुज् 'bend', भुग्न; मज्ज् 'sink', मग्न; रुज् 'be sick', रुग्ण; विज् 'fear', विग्न. Also one or two others which exhibit a guttural before the न: लग् 'attach', लग्न; व्रश्च् 'cut up', वृक्ण.

4. A number of roots, some of them very common, in द् (which becomes न् before न): सद्, सन्न; (नि—सद्, निषण्ण;) भिद् 'cut', भिन्न.*

292. Some few verbs make double forms; thus, त्वर् 'hasten', तूर्ण or त्वरित; विद् 'acquire', विन्न or वित्त.

---

* Commonest exceptions: खादित from खाद् 'eat'; मत्त from मद्; मुदित from मुद् 'rejoice'; रुदित from रुद् 'weep'; उदित from वद् 'speak'; विदित from विद् 'know'.

Vocabulary XXVII.

Verbs:

ईक्ष् + उप (*upékṣate*) neglect.

2कॄ + वि (*vikiráti*) scatter.

गणय + अव (den. — *avagaṇáyati*) despise.

चर् + उद्, in caus. (*uccāráyati*) pronounce, say.

तॄ + अव (*avatárati*) descend.

+ उद् (*uttárati*) emerge, come out.

पी or प्या (*pyā́yate*) become stout or fat.

भक्ष् (*bhakṣáyati*) eat.

भञ्ज् break.

2भुज् + उप enjoy.

भू + परि (*paribhávati*) despise.

मज्ज् (*májjati*) sink.

युज् in caus. (*yojáyati*) yoke, harness.

लग् (*lágati*) attach; hang, cling, adhere.

सद् (*sī́dati*) sit, settle down; be overcome, exhausted.

Subst.:

अश्विनौ m. du., *nom. pr.*, the Açvins (the Indian Διὸς κοῦροι).

आचार m., "walk and conversation"; conduct of life, observance.

ऋण n., debt.

कैलास m., *n. pr.* a mountain.

क्षुध् f., hunger.

ब्रह्मचर्य n., life of holiness, i. e. religious studentship.

भोजन n., meal-time, meal.

भुज्यु m., *n. pr.*, a Vedic personage.

मधुपर्क m., sweet drink.

मुक्ता f., pearl.

राक्षस m., demon.

लाभ m., acquisition, gain.

विवाह m., wedding, marriage.

व्याधि m., illness.

शकट m., car.

शय्या f., bed.

हल m., n., plough.

हार m., chain, garland.

Adj.:

क्षीण (part. of 2क्षि) reduced, decayed; ruined.

तीव्र f. °आ, great, strong, violent.

पीन (part. of पी) fat.

ब्रह्मचारिन् studying sacred knowledge; *as m. subst.*, Brāhman student.

हीन (part.) abandoned; wanting in; and so sometimes w. instr., = 'without'.

Exercise XXVII.

वर्धमानमृणं राजन्परिभूताश्च शत्रवः ।
जनयन्ति भयं तीव्रं व्याधयश्चाप्युपेक्षिताः ॥ १५ ॥

यानि कर्माण्यस्मिं लोके क्रियन्ते तेषां फलं कर्त्रामुष्मिं लोक उपभुज्यते। १। भो असावहम्* इत्युच्चारयन्गरीयसो ऽभिवादयेत् । २। अयं नः पिता रथादवतीर्णः सख्या सह संभाषमाणस्तिष्ठति। ३। आचारेण हीनं पुमांसं विद्वांसमप्यवगणयन्ति सन्तः । ४। उदधौ मग्नं म्रियमाणं भुज्युमश्विनौ नावोदहरताम् । ५। एभ्यः क्षुधा सीदद्भ्यो भिक्षुभ्यो ऽन्नं प्रयच्छ। ६। पश्यास्माकं रथो भग्नः। ७। युध्यमानानमूननडुहः पश्य। ८। भवता विकीर्णं धान्यमिमे विहगा भक्षयन्ति। ९। आभिरद्भिः पाणी प्रक्षालय। १०। इदम्** आसनमिमा आपः स्नानायायं मधुपर्क इदं भोजनमिमानि वस्त्राणीयं शय्येति गृहस्थो ऽतिथिं गृहमागच्छन्तं वदेत् ॥ ११ ॥

12. Have medicine given quickly (*use pass. part. of* त्वर्, *in nom.*) to these sick *persons*. 13. This is that mountain Kāilāsa, on which Çiva dwells. 14. In order to attain (लाभ, *dat.*) this and that *other* world (*gen.*) the priest offered sacrifice for me (यज् *caus.*). 15. The flowers in the garlands of these women are withered. 16. By that king, who *was* praised by us, we were delighted with these jewels. 17. The peasant yoked two fat oxen to the plough. 18. The learned Brāhman emerged (*pass. part.*) from the water. 19. Here comes (*pass. part.*) the queen. 20. A chain of pearls hung (*pass. part.*) on the neck of this demon. 21. What sin is not committed by *persons* reduced *in fortune*? 22. This garden is filled with men and women.

Lesson XXVIII.

293. Past Passive Participle, cont'd. B **With suffix** त.

I. **Without union-vowel** इ. Much more commonly this parti-

* "I am so-and-so; N. or M."

** Translate the pronoun-forms by 'here', and cf. § 225.

ciple is made by adding the suffix त to the bare root; thus, ज्ञात from ज्ञा; जित from जि; क्षिप्त from क्षिप्; हृत from हृ (or ह्वा); वृत्त from वृत्.

294. If the root end in a consonant other than क्, त्, प्, स्, the ordinary rules of euphonic combination apply as follows:

1. Final च् and ज् become क्; thus, सिक्त from सिच्; युक्त from युज्; त्यक्त from त्यज्.

2. Final श् becomes ष्, after which, as also after radical final ष्, त् becomes ट्; thus, दृष्ट from दृश्; द्विष्ट from द्विष्. सृष्ट and मृष्ट are made from सृज् and मृज्, and इष्ट from यज्, contrary to 1. प्रछ् makes पृष्ट; and तक्ष्, तष्ट.

3. Final ध् becomes द्, and भ्, ब्; and the following त् becomes ध्; thus, वृद्ध from वृध्, लब्ध from लभ्.

4. Final ह् is treated in various ways, according to its historical value. *a.* Sometimes ह् combines with त् to form ढ, before which short vowels (except ऋ) are lengthened; thus, गाढ from गाह्, लीढ from लिह्, रूढ from रुह्; मूढ from मुह्; but दृढ from दृह्. सह् forms सोढ. *b.* Where ह् represents original घ्, the combination is ग्ध; thus, दग्ध from दह्; दिग्ध from दिह्; दुग्ध from दुह्. The root मुह् forms also मुग्ध. *c.* नह्, where ह् represents original ध्, makes नद्ध.

295. The root before त usually has its weakest form, if there is any where in the verbal system a distinction of strong and weak forms. Thus: 1. A penultimate nasal is dropped; e. g., अक्त from अञ्ज्; बद्ध from बन्ध्; स्रस्त from स्रंस् (or स्रस्); भ्रस्त from भ्रंस्. 2. Roots which are abbreviated in the weak forms of the perfect suffer the same abbreviation here; e. g., उक्त from वच्, उप्त from वप्, सुप्त from स्वप्, ऊढ from वह्; इष्ट from यज् (the same form from इष्); विद्ध from व्यध्; पृष्ट from प्रछ्. 3. Final आ is weakened to ई in गीत from गा 'sing', पीत from 1पा 'drink'; to इ in स्थित from स्था, हित from धा 'put' (with ध् also changed to ह्), मित from

मा 'measure', and a few others. **4.** A final म् is lost after अ in गत, यत, नत, रत (from गम् etc.); and likewise final न् in घत, तत, मत, वत, हत (from घन् etc.). **5.** Isolated cases are शिष्ट from शास्; द्यूत from दीव् 'play'.

296. More irregular are the following:

1. Some roots in अम् make participles in आन्त; thus, कान्त, क्रान्त, घान्त, तान्त, दान्त, शान्त, श्रान्त, from कम् etc.

2. जन्, खन्, and सन् make जात etc.

3. The root 1दा, 'give', forms दत्त (from the derivative form दद्). The contracted form त्त is widely found in composition, especially with prepositions; thus, प्रदत्त or प्रत्त, निदत्त or नीत्त, etc.

297. II. With union-vowel इ. The suffix with इ, or in the form इत, is regularly used with the derivative verb-stems in secondary conjugation, also often with roots of derivative character (like जिन्व्, हिंस्), and not infrequently with original roots.

298. When इत is added to causative and denominative verb-stems the syllables अय are dropped; thus, चुर्, pass. part. चोरित; गणय, गणित; तड्, ताडित; मृ, caus. मारयति, caus. pass. part. मारित; हन्, caus. घातयति, घातित.

299. Among the original roots taking इत may be noticed the following:

पत् 'fall', पतित; कुप्, कुपित; वस् 'dwell', उषित; श्वस्, श्वसित; तृष् 'thirst', तृषित; लिख्, लिखित; ईच्, ईचित; वद्, उदित. ग्रह् makes गृहीत; शी 'lie' makes शयित.

300. A few roots form this participle either with or without the auxiliary इ; thus, मत्त and मदित from मद्.

301. The grammarians reckon as participles of the *na*-formation a few derivative adjectives, coming from roots which do not make a regular participle; such are क्षाम 'burnt' (क्षा); कृश 'thin', 'haggard' (कृश्); पक्व 'ripe' (पच्); शुष्क 'dry' (शुष्); फुल्ल 'expanded' (फुल्).

302. Past Active Participle in तवन्त् (or नवन्त्). From the past pass. part. is made, by adding the possessive suffix वन्त् (f. वती), a secondary derivative having the meaning and construction of a perfect active participle; thus, कृतवन्त्, प्रतिपन्नवन्त्.

303. This participle is almost always used predicatively, and generally without expressed copula, i. e., with the value of a personal perfect-form. Thus, मां न कश्चिद्दृष्टवान् "no one has seen me"; or, with copula, महत्कृच्छ्रं प्राप्तवत्यसि "thou (fem.) hast come into great misery". This participle comes to be made even from intransitives; thus, सा गतवती "she has gone".

Vocabulary XXVIII.

Verbs:

तृ + प्र in caus. (*pratārāyati*) deceive.

नह् + सम् (*saṁnáhyati*) equip oneself.

पद् + वि-आ in caus. (*vyāpādáyati*) kill.

पलाय् * (*pálāyate*) flee.

2भुज् enjoy, eat.

मन् + सम् honor.

मुह् (*múhyati*) be confused or dazed or stupid.

रुध् + अप besiege.

रुह् + प्र (*praróhati*) grow up.

विश् + प्र (*praviçáti*) penetrate, enter.

वृत् + प्र in caus. (*pravartáyati*) continue.

शिष् + अव remain over, survive.

स्तृ + उप bestrew.

Subst.:

अवसान m., end; *in loc.*, at last.

इन्द्रप्रस्थ n., *n. pr.*, Delhi.

खर m., ass.

गुहा f., cave.

चरित n., behavior, life.

पृथ्वीराज m., *nom. pr.*

पौर m., citizen.

प्रासाद m., palace.

यवन m., Greek, barbarian.

शृगाल m., jackal.

सैनिक m., soldier.

सैन्य n., army.

हस्तिन् m., elephant.

* A *quasi*-root from इ 'go' + परा 'away'.

Adj.:

भूयस् (comp.) more. *In neut. sing. as adv.*: mostly.

स्निग्ध (part. from स्निह्) affectionate.

Exercise XXVIII.

श्रीमतो (abl.) राज्ञः संमतैरेभिः कविभिरिष्टानि वसूनि लब्धानि।१।
कुतो भवानागत इति द्वारि स्थितः परिव्राड्गृहस्य पतिना पृष्टः ।२। श्व-
भिर्गृहीतो हरिणो व्याधैर्व्यापादितः ।३। मूढः खरः शृगालस्य स्निग्धा-
भिर्वाग्भिः प्रतारितः सिंहस्य गुहायामागतस्तेन हतः ।४। क्षेत्रेषु सिक्ता-
भिर्मेघानामद्भिर्धान्यं प्ररूढम् ।५। काश्यामुषितैर्भ्रातृभिः शास्त्राणि
सम्यगधीतानीति तेषामाचार्येण लिखितात्पत्त्रादवगम्यते ॥६॥ उदीच्या
दिशो (abl.) यवनेष्वागच्छत्सु पृथ्वीराज इन्द्रप्रस्थात्सैन्येन सह नि-
ष्क्रान्तः ।७। पथि संगच्छमानैर्द्विड्भिः सह महद्युद्धं संजातम् ।८।
तस्मिन्राजा पराजितः शरैर्विद्धो हस्तिनो भूमौ पतितो यवनैर्जीवन्नेव
गृहीतः पश्चाच्चासिना घातितः ॥९॥

(In the following render all finite verbs by participles.)

10. Many of the soldiers were killed; some *who* survived fled into the city. 11. The gates of the city were shut fast (दृढा अपिहिताः); the citizens equipped themselves for battle. 12. The Yavanas approached and besieged the city (*pass.*). 13. Finally the Yavanas, *proving* victorious (*past act. part.*), entered the city by force. 14. The young and old men were mostly murdered; the women made slaves; the great possessions of the citizens plundered, the palaces and houses burnt with fire. 15. The end of Pṛthvīrāja has been described by the Yavanas, and his previous life sung by the poet Caṇḍa.

Lesson XXIX.

304. **Gerund, or Absolutive.** The gerund is made in classical Sanskrit by one of the suffixes त्वा and य.

305. A. त्वा. To uncompounded roots is added the suffix त्वा. It is usually added directly to the root, but sometimes with the vowel इ interposed. With regard to the use of इ, and to the form of root before it, this formation closely agrees with that of the participle in त or न. A final root-consonant is treated as before त. Roots which make the past pass. part. in न generally reject इ before त्वा.

Examples. 1. **Without inserted इ:** ज्ञात्वा, जित्वा, नीत्वा, श्रुत्वा, भूत्वा; स्थित्वा from स्था, हित्वा from 1धा 'place' (cf. हित) and from हा, दत्त्वा from दा (cf. दत्त), गीत्वा from गा; उक्त्वा from वच्, युक्त्वा from युज्; गत्वा from गम्, मत्वा from मन्, वित्त्वा from 2विद् 'find'; तीर्त्वा from तॄ (cf. तीर्ण), पूर्त्वा from पॄ (cf. पूर्ण); दृष्ट्वा from दृश्, सृष्ट्वा from सृज्, इष्ट्वा from यज् (cf. § 295, 2), बुद्ध्वा from बुध्, लब्ध्वा from लभ्, दग्ध्वा from दह्.

2. **With inserted इ:** विदित्वा from 1विद् 'know', उषित्वा from वस् 'dwell', ग्रथित्वा from ग्रथ् (cf. ग्रथित), गृहीत्वा from ग्रह् (cf. गृहीत).

306. Some verbs make both forms; thus, from खन् either खनित्वा or खात्वा; from भ्रम् either भ्रमित्वा or भ्रान्त्वा.

307. Causatives and denominatives in अय make अयित्वा; thus, चुर्, चोरयित्वा; तड्, ताडयित्वा; स्थापयति, स्थापयित्वा.

308. B. य. Roots in composition with prepositions (or sometimes with elements of other kinds, as adverbs or nouns) take the suffix य, before which इ is never inserted. A root which ends in a short vowel adds त् before य. Thus, परिणीय, अनुभूय; — विजित्य, संस्तुत्य, अधीत्य (अधि-इ) अधिकृत्य.

309. Roots in अम् and अन् whose pass. part. ends in अत form this gerund in अत्य; thus, °गत्य, °हत्य. But such *am*-roots (not *an*-roots) may preserve the nasal; thus, °गम्य. Final changeable ॠ becomes ईर् or ऊर्; thus, °तीर्य, °पूर्य. Final आ remains unaltered; thus, आदाय. Some roots show a weak form before

this suffix; thus, प्रगृह्य, संपृच्छ्य; प्रोच्य (प्र-उच्य) from प्र-वच्; अनूद्य from अनु-वद्; व्युह्य from वि-वह्.

310. Causals and denominatives in अय reject those syllables; thus, प्रचोरयति, प्रचोर्य; प्रताड्य; प्रस्थाप्य; अवधार्य; आनाययति (आ-नी), आनाय्य. But if the root ends in a single consonant and encloses short अ which is not lengthened in the causative, then the gerund of the caus. ends in अय्य, to distinguish it from the gerund of the simple verb; thus, अव-गम्, ger. अवगम्य; caus. अवगमयति, ger. अवगमय्य.

311. The gerund or absolutive is used generally as logical adjunct to the subject of a clause. It denotes an action accompanying or (usually) preceding that which is signified by the verb of the clause. (In the later language it is not always confined to the *grammatical* subject of the clause as an adjunct.) It has thus virtually the value of an indeclinable participle, present or past, qualifying the actor whose action it describes.

Thus, तद् आकर्ण्य छागं त्यक्त्वा स्नात्वा स्वगृहं गतः "having heard this, having abandoned the goat, having bathed, he went to his own house".*

312. The gerunds of some verbs have not much more than prepositional value; thus, आदाय 'having taken', i. e. 'with', like Greek λαβών, ἔχων; मुक्त्वा 'having released', i. e. 'without', 'except'.

313. Before all gerunds may be used the privative अन् or अ; thus, अलब्ध्वा "without having received"; अनाहूय "without having summoned."

Vocabulary XXIX.

Verbs:

अस् + नि (*nyásyati*) entrust (to one's care).

आप् acquire, attain, reach.

इ + प्र go forth; die.

+ सम्-आ join.

---

* Of course the absolutives are often best rendered by relative clauses, or even by clauses coordinate with the principal clause.

कृ + अधि put at the head, appoint as ruler over (*loc.*).

चल् + प्र (*pracálati*) move on, march.

चिन्त् (*cintáyati*) consider.

च्यु (*cyávate*) totter, fall.

दा + आ take. Cf. § 312.

धा + सम्-आ lay or place on.

नी + निस् (*nirṇáyati*) bring to an end, determine, settle.

भज् + वि (*vibhájati*, *-te*) distribute.

व्रज् + प्र (*pravrájati*) wander forth; leave one's home to become a wandering ascetic.

Subst.:

अभिप्राय m., plan, design.

आहरण n., bringing.

कपि m., monkey.

करिन् m., elephant.

जय m., victory.

दुर्दशा f., misfortune.

पक्ष m., wing; side; party.

भेक m., frog.

लङ्का f., *n. pr.*, Ceylon.

शूर m., hero.

साधन n., means, device.

सेतु m., bridge, dike.

हनुमन्त् m., *n. pr.*, a monkey-king.

हुतभुज् (nom. °भुक्) m., fire.

Adj.:

अहित disagreeable.

आप्त responsible, trustworthy.

उभ du., both.

क्षुद्र, f. °आ, little, small.

नित्य, f. °आ, daily, regular.

मूर्धग on the head.

Prepos.:

प्रति (*postpos.*, *with acc.*) **against.**

Exercise XXIX.

गते हि दुर्दशां लोके क्षुद्रो ऽप्यहितमाचरेत् ।
पङ्के निमग्ने करिणि भेको भवति मूर्धगः ॥ १६ ॥

गुरावुषित्वा वेदमधीत्य स्त्रीं परिणीय पुत्रं जनयित्वा नित्यानि कर्माण्यनुष्ठाय यज्ञानिष्ट्वा दानानि च दत्त्वा प्रेत्य ब्राह्मणो न च्यवते ब्रह्मणो लोकात् । १ । भुक्त्वा पीत्वा चैते नराः सुप्ताः । २ । धीमतां मन्त्रिणामागमनं स्वामिने निवेद्य भृत्यो निष्क्रान्तः । ३ । सख्या हनुमतान्यैश्च कपिभिः समेतो ऽपां भर्तरि सेतुं बद्ध्वा लङ्कां प्रविश्य च रामो रावणं हतवान् । ४ । कृत्स्नं वनं दग्ध्वा हुतभुगधुना शान्तः । ५ । बलवतो मरुत आदाय मघवा गवामाहरणाय निर्गतः । ६ । शिष्यानाहूय गुरुस्तैः सम्यगन्वितस्तानृचो यजूंषि चाध्यापितवान् । ७ । हविर्भिर्ऋत्वि-

ग्भ्यो भूयो धनं यजमानेन दत्तम् । ८ । त्वां मुक्त्वा न केनापि तादृग्दुःखं सोढम् । ९ । गूढचारैः शत्रूणां बलं विदित्वा कार्याणि मन्त्रिषु न्यस्य सैन्य आप्तान्शूरानधिकृत्य राजा युद्धाय निर्गच्छेत् ॥ १० ॥

11. After the king had conquered the vassals of the western lands he marched (*pass. part.*) against the eastern *vassals.* 12. The merchants, in joy (*pass. part.*), took the money and gave the jewels to the king (*use ger., and pass. constr.*). 13. "After adoring the gods at twilight, and placing fagots on the fire, bring water from the cistern": thus having spoken, the teacher seated himself (*pass. part.*) on the mat. 14. The hero fought (*ger.*) with his enemies *and* gained (*part.*) great glory by the victory over them (*gen.*). 15. The Brāhman, abandoning his own (*pl.*), became an ascetic (प्र-व्रज्, *pass. part.*). 16. When the merchant had imparted (नि-विद्, *caus.*) his plan to the servant, he sent him into the village. 17. The master of the house had money brought (*ger.*) *and* distributed it to the poor. 18. Let not kings decide law-suits without hearing the arguments (वाच्) of both sides. 19. Whoever despises powerful foes, and fights with them without considering the means to victory (*gen.*), perishes. 20. Whoever becomes an ascetic without having studied the Veda, attains (*ger.*) not salvation, *but* falls into hell (*loc.*).

Lesson XXX.

314. Infinitive. The later language has a single infinitive, the ending of which is तुम् (or इतुम्). The root takes *guṇa*, when possible.

315. The ending तुम् is added directly:

1. To almost all roots ending in vowels, except those in ऊ and changeable ऋ. Thus, पा, पातुम्; दा, दातुम्; चि, चेतुम्; नी, नेतुम्; श्रु, श्रोतुम्; कृ, कर्तुम्.

2. To a number of roots ending in consonants. As root-

finals, क्, त्, प् and स् remain unchanged before तुम्; thus, शक्, शक्तुम्; मन्, मन्तुम्; आप्, आप्तुम्; क्षिप्, क्षेप्तुम्; लुप्, लोप्तुम्; शप् 'curse', शप्तुम्; 3वस् 'dwell', वस्तुम्. — Other finals are changed according to the rules given in Lesson XXVIII for the conversion of final consonants before the participial suffix त. Thus, पच्, पक्तुम्; त्यज्, त्यक्तुम्; दृश्, द्रष्टुम्*; स्पृश्, स्प्रष्टुम्*; कृष्, क्रष्टुम्*; प्रछ्, प्रष्टुम्; यज्, यष्टुम्; सृज्, स्रष्टुम्*; क्रुध्, क्रोद्धुम्; लभ्, लब्धुम्; रुह्, रोढुम्; वह्, वोढुम्; दह्, दग्धुम्; नह्, नद्धुम्. — Final द् becomes त्, and final म्, न्; thus, अद्, अत्तुम्; विद् 'know', वेत्तुम् (also वेदितुम्); गम्, गन्तुम्.

316. **The ending तुम् with इ (in the form इतुम्)** is taken by roots in final long ऊ and the root शी, with a few other vowel-roots; by the majority of roots in consonants; and by verbs of the secondary conjugations. Thus, भू, भवितुम्; शी, शयितुम्; ईक्ष्, ईक्षितुम्; वन्द्, वन्दितुम्; गुह्, गूहितुम् (cf. § 101).

317. Causatives and denominatives in अय have अयितुम्, the root being treated as in the present; thus, चुर्, चोरयितुम्; कथ्, कथयितुम्; तड्, ताडयितुम्.

318. Some roots in consonants insert or reject इ at pleasure; thus, मृज्, मार्जितुम् or मार्ष्टुम्**. The root ग्रह् makes ग्रहीतुम्.

319. The rules for the use of इ in the infinitive agree closely with those governing its use in the formation of the *s*-future and of the *nomen agentis* in तृ.

320. **Uses of the infinitive.** The chief use of the infinitive is as equivalent to an accusative, as the object of a verb, especially of the verbs शक् 'be able', and अर्ह् 'be worthy', 'have the right

---

* The increments of ऋ are sometimes र and रा instead of अर् and आर्; especially where a difficult combination of consonants is thus avoided.

** In all the tense-systems, and in derivation, the root मृज् exhibits often the *vṛddhi* instead of the *guṇa*-strengthening.

or power'; thus, कथयितुं शक्नोति "he is able to tell"; श्रोतुमर्हति कुमारः "the prince ought to hear it". अर्ह् is often thus used with the infinitive to express a respectful request or entreaty, as in the last example. The infinitive is also often found with verbs of motion, and with those meaning 'desire', 'hope', 'notice', 'know', and the like.

321. But often the infinitive has a case-value not accusative. Thus, a dative value: भवति भोक्तुमन्नम् "there is food to eat" i. e. "for eating"; a genitive value: समर्थौ गन्तुम् "capable of going". Even a construction as nominative is not unknown.

322. In certain connections the infinitive has a *quasi*-passive force. Thus, कर्तुमारब्धः "begun to be made"; श्रोतुं न युज्यते "it is not fit to be heard." This is especially frequent along with the passive forms of शक्; thus, त्यक्तुं न शक्नोति "he cannot abandon", but त्यक्तुं न शक्यते "he cannot be abandoned"; नरौ शक्याविहानेतुम् "the two men can be brought hither."

323. **Future Passive Participle, or Gerundive.** Certain derivative adjectives, mostly secondary, have acquired a value quite like that of the Latin gerundive; thus, कार्य (from कृ) 'to be done', *faciendus.* They may be made from every verb. The ordinary suffixes are three: य, तव्य, and अनीय.

324. A. **Suffix** य.* *a.* Before this suffix final radical आ becomes ए; thus, from दा, देय; गा, गेय. *b.* Other final vowels sometimes remain unchanged, sometimes have the *guṇa* or even the *vṛddhi*-strengthening; and ए often, and ओ always, are treated before य as before a vowel; thus, from जि, जेय and जय्य; from भी, भेय and भय्य; from श्रु, श्रव्य and श्राव्य; from कृ, कार्य; from धू, धूय; from भू, भाव्य. — *c.* In a few instances, a short vowel adds त् before the suffix; thus, इत्य (इ), श्रुत्य (श्रु), कृत्य (कृ). *d.* Medial अ remains

* The original value of this suffix is *ia.* Hence the conversion of ए to अय् and of ओ to अव् before it.

unchanged in one class of words, and is lengthened in another class; thus, दृश्य, वन्द्य, सद्य, but माद्य (मद्), वाच्य (वच्). *e.* Initial or medial *i*, *u*, and *ṛ*-vowels are sometimes unchanged, sometimes have the *guṇa*-strengthening; thus, ईड्य, गुह्य, तृद्य; वेद्य, योध्य, बोध्य. *f.* The root शास् makes शिष्य. A form वध्य (from the defective root वध्) is assigned to हन्. आ-लभ् makes आलभ्य and आलम्भ्य. *g.* Causatives and denominatives in अय are treated as in the present, but omit the syllables अय; thus, चुर्, चोर्य.

325. B. Suffix तव्य. This is a secondary adjective derivative from the infinitival noun in तु. Hence, both as regards the form of root and the use or omission of इ, the rules are the same as for the formation of the infinitive; thus, वक्तव्य, लब्धव्य, वन्दितव्य, शयितव्य (शी).

326. C. Suffix अनीय [अणीय]. Generally radical vowels will be found gunated before this suffix; causatives and denominatives in अय are treated as in the present-system, without the syllables अय; thus, दानीय (दा), गानीय (गा), श्रवणीय (श्रु), बोधनीय, चोरणीय, गूहनीय (गूहयति).

327. The gerundives in तव्य are common in the impersonal passive construction described in Lesson X, and not seldom have a purely future sense; thus, तेन त्वया सुखिना भवितव्यम् "with that thou shalt be happy".

Vocabulary XXX.

Verbs:

अर्ह् (*árhati*) have the right, etc. (cf. § 320.)

आप् + सम् finish, attain.

कृ + अप-आ pay.

गम् + अभि (*abhigácchati*) visit, attend.

गाह् + अव (*avagāhate*) dive under (*acc.*).

तप् (*tápati*, *-te*) burn (tr. and intr.); pain; *in pass.*, suffer, do penance.

धा + वि arrange, ordain, order.

नृत् (*nṛ́tyati*) dance.

भू + प्र be mighty, able; *valere*.

वृत् + प्र (*pravártate*) continue, go on.

Subst.:

कृषीवल m., husbandman.

गीत n., song, singing.

तपस् n., heat; self-torture.

नाटक n., drama, play.

नृत्त n., dance, dancing.

वपुस् n., body, figure.

समाज m., convention, company.

सामन् n., Vedic melody, song; pl., the Sāmaveda.

Adj.:

तरुण, f. °ई, young, delicate.

पुष्ट stout, fat.

प्रियवादिन् acceptably speaking.

फलवन्त् fruitful.

यज्ञिय destined or suitable for sacrifice.

विहित (part. of **वि-धा**) ordained.

समर्थ, f., °आ, capable, able.

स्वयम्भू self-existent; *as m. subst.*, epithet of Brahma.

Adv.:

अलम् enough, very; *w. instr.*, enough of, away with; *w. dat.*, suitable for.

स्वैरम् at pleasure.

Exercise XXX.

सर्वे पौराः कालिदासेन रचितं नाटकं द्रष्टुमागच्छन् । १ । सर्वा-
न्द्विषो बाहुभ्यां जेतुं स्वामी समर्थ इति प्रियवादिनो भृत्या राजानमु-
क्तवन्तः । २ । पापान्यपमार्ष्टुमपोऽवगाह्यर्चः पठनीयाः सामानि वा गे-
यानि । ३ । तीव्रं तपस्तप्तुं यतिर्वनाय प्रस्थितः । ४ । अश्वमारोढुमधुना
मे पथि श्रान्तस्य मतिर्जाता । ५ । पितृभ्यो दातव्यमृणमपाकर्तुं ब्राह्मणः
पुत्रं जनयेत् । ६ । स्वर्गं लब्धुं भूयसो यज्ञान्यष्टुमर्हसि । ७ । सर्वासु दिक्षु
स्वैरं चरितुं यज्ञियोऽश्वो भवद्भिर्मोक्तव्य इति राज्ञादिश्यत । ८ । भ-
वतां भाषा नावगन्तुं शक्यते (§ 322) । ९ । पुष्टावनड्वाहौ शकटे योक्तुं
कृषीवल आदेष्टव्यः । १० । स्वयंभुवा जगत्स्रष्टुं मनः कृतम् ॥ ११ ॥

(*Sentences with* must *may be rendered either with* **अर्ह्** *or with gerundives*). 12. A Brahmacārin must not visit any companies to see (**प्र-ईक्ष्**) dancing or to hear singing. 13. Remembering that works will be fruitful in the other life (*use* "thus thinking", *after* or. recta), a man must strive to perform *what is* ordained.

14. The maidens seated themselves (*pass. part.*) in the garden to bind wreaths. 15. True friends are able to save from misfortune. 16. The daughters came (*pass. part.*) to bow before their parents. 17. How is the delicate body of this fair *one* capable of enduring penance? 18. You must become a scholar (*use* भवन्त्, *and cf.* § 177). 19. You must bring a boat to cross the river. 20. Who is able to stop the mighty wind? 21. The gentlemen (*use* भवन्त्) are to read this letter. 22. Having finished the Veda, he went on to study the other sciences.

Lesson XXXI.

328. Numerals. Cardinals: एक *1*, द्व *2*, त्रि *3*, चतुर् *4*, पञ्च *5*, षष् *6*, सप्त *7*, अष्ट *8*, नव *9*, दश *10*. — एकादश *11*, द्वादश *12*, त्रयोदश *13*, चतुर्दश *14*, पञ्चदश *15*, षोडश *16*, सप्तदश *17*, अष्टादश *18*, नवदश *19*, विंशति *20*. — एकविंशति *21*, द्वाविंशति *22*, etc. — त्रिंशत् *30*, चत्वारिंशत् *40*, पञ्चाशत् *50*, षष्टि *60*, सप्तति *70*, अशीति *80*, नवति *90*, शत *100*. — द्विशत or द्वे शते *200*. — सहस्र *1000*, द्विसहस्र or द्वे सहस्रे *2000*, शतसहस्र or लक्ष *100 000*.

329. The numbers between the even tens are made by prefixing the unit-number to the ten; thus, पञ्चविंशति *25*. But note: एकादश, not एकदश, *11*. *42*, *52*, *62*, *72* and *92*, either द्विचत्वारिंशत् or द्वाच°, etc.; *43—73*, and *93*, either त्रि° or त्रयश्चत्वा° etc.; *48—78*, and *98*, either अष्ट° or अष्टाचत्वा° etc. *96* is षण्णवति.

Note also: द्वादश *12*, etc., but for *82* only द्व्यशीति; त्रयोविंशति *23*, त्रयस्त्रिंशत् *33*, for *83* only त्र्यशीति; षोडश *16*, षड्विंशति *26*, etc.; अष्टाविंशति *28*, अष्टात्रिंशत् *38*, अष्टाशीति *88*.

330. There are other ways of expressing the numbers between the tens. Thus: 1. By the use of the adj. ऊन 'deficient', in composition; e. g. एकोनविंशति '20 less 1', i. e. *19*. This usage is not common except for the nines. Sometimes एक is left off, and ऊनविंशति, etc., have the same value. 2. By the adj. अधिक or

उत्तर 'more', also in composition; e. g., अष्टाधिकनवति (also अष्टाधिका नवति) *98*.

331. The same methods are used to form the odd numbers above 100. Thus, एकशतम् *101*, अष्टाशतम् *108*, पञ्चाधिकं शतम् *105*, सप्तोत्तरं शतम् *107*.

332. Inflection of cardinals. *1.* एक is declined like सर्व, at § 231 (pl.: 'some', 'certain ones'). The dual does not occur. एक sometimes means 'a certain'; or even 'an, a', as an indefinite article.

2. द्व (dual only) is quite regular; thus, nom.-acc.-voc. m., द्वौ, f. n. द्वे; द्वाभ्याम्, द्वयोस्.

3. त्रि is in masc. and neut. nearly regular; the fem. has the stem तिसृ. Thus, nom. m. त्रयस्, acc. m. त्रीन्, nom.-acc. n. त्रीणि; instr. त्रिभिस्, dat.-abl. त्रिभ्यस्, gen. त्रयाणाम्, loc. त्रिषु. Fem.: nom.-acc. तिस्रस्, instr. तिसृभिस्, dat.-abl. तिसृभ्यस्, gen. तिसृणाम्, loc. तिसृषु.

4. चतुर् has चत्वार् in strong cases; the fem. stem is चतसृ. Thus, nom. m. चत्वारस्, acc. m. चतुरस्; nom.-acc. n. चत्वारि; instr. चतुर्भिस् etc. Fem.: nom.-acc. चतस्रस्, instr., etc., चतसृभिस्, चतसृभ्यस्, चतसृणाम्, चतसृषु.

(*5—19.*) These numbers have no distinction of gender. They are inflected with some irregularity as plurals. Thus:

5, 7, 9, 10. पञ्च, पञ्चभिस्, °भ्यस्, पञ्चानाम्, पञ्चसु. सप्त, नव, दश, and compounds of दश, are similarly declined.

6. षष् as follows: षट्, षड्भिस्, षड्भ्यस्, षण्णाम्, षट्सु.

8. अष्ट may follow पञ्च, or be declined thus: अष्टौ, अष्टाभिस्, °भ्यस्, अष्टानाम्, अष्टासु

20, 30, etc. विंशति, त्रिंशत्, etc., are declined regularly as fem. stems, in all numbers.

100, 1000. शत and सहस्र are declined regularly as neut. stems, in all numbers.

333. Construction of numerals. 1. The words from *1* to *19* are used as adjectives, agreeing in case (and in gender, if possible) with the nouns. 2. The numerals above *19* are usually treated as nouns, either taking the numbered noun as a dependent genitive, or standing in the sing. in apposition with it; thus, शतं दासीनाम् or शतं दासीः "a hundred female slaves"; षष्ट्यां शरत्सु "in sixty autumns".

334. Ordinals. प्रथम* 'first', द्वितीय, तृतीय, चतुर्थ, पञ्चम, षष्ठ, सप्तम, अष्टम, नवम, दशम, एकादश (to *19th*, the same as the cardinals, but declined like देव, etc.); विंश or विंशतितम *20th*; त्रिंश or त्रिंशत्तम *30th*, etc. Note also एकोनविंश or ऊनविंश, एकोनविंशतितम or ऊनविंशतितम, *19th*. The shorter forms (विंश etc.) are by far the commoner.

335. प्रथम, द्वितीय and तृतीय make their fem. in °आ; the rest, in ई. Occasional forms of the pronominal declension are met with from the first three; but the usual declension of nouns is the normal one for ordinals also.

336. Numeral adverbs. 1. सकृत् 'once'; द्विस् 'twice'; त्रिस् 'thrice'; चतुस् 'four times'; पञ्चकृत्वस् or पञ्चवारम् 'five times'; and so on, with °कृत्वस् or °वारम्. — 2. एकधा 'in one way'; द्विधा or द्वेधा 'in two ways'; त्रिधा or त्रेधा, चतुर्धा, पञ्चधा, षोढा or षड्धा, etc — 3. एकशस् 'one by one'; शतशस् 'by hundreds', etc.

Vocabulary XXXI.

Verbs:

कल् + सम् (*saṁkaláyati*) put together, add.

क्रम् + अति pass (of time).

जल्प् (*jálpati*) speak, chat.

भुज् in caus. (*bhojáyati*) feed.

सिच् + अभि (*abhiṣiñcáti*) anoint as king.

हृ + उद्-आ cite, mention.

Subst.:

अथर्ववेद m., the fourth Veda.

अनहिलपाटक n., *n. pr.* a city.

---

* एक forms no ordinal.

कलियुग n., the "Iron Age" of the world.

चक्र n., wheel.

ज्योतिष n., astronomy; astronomical text-book.

दर्शन n., philosophical system.

नक्षत्र n., lunar mansion.

पाण्डव m., *n. pr.*, descendant of Pāṇḍu.

पुराण n., one of a class of works on the creation of the world.

विक्रमादित्य m., *n. pr.*, a famous king.

शक m., Scythian.

शरीर n., body.

शाखा f., branch, edition, redaction.

संवत्सर m., year.

Adv.:

अनन्तरम् (*w. abl. — often postpos.*) after, immediately after.

क्वचित् sometimes (*in altern.*).

तद्यथा namely, to wit.

साम्प्रतम् at present.

Exercise XXXI.

सकृज्जल्पन्ति राजानः सकृज्जल्पन्ति साधवः ।
सकृत्कन्याः प्रदीयन्ते त्रीण्येतानि सतां सकृत् ॥ १७ ॥

सप्तानामृषीणां शरीराणि दिवि राजमानानि दृश्यन्ते* ॥ १ ॥
चत्वारो वेदा विद्यन्तेऽष्टादश पुराणानि षट्त्रिंशत्स्मृतयः षड् दर्शनानीति विदुषां मतम् । २ । चतुर्णां वेदानां तु बहवः शाखा वर्तन्ते । ३ । तद्यथा । ऋग्वेदस्य पञ्च शाखा यजुर्वेदस्य षडशीतिः सामवेदस्य सप्ताथर्ववेदस्य नवेति ।४। सर्वाः संकलय्य सप्तोत्तरं शतं शाखानां श्रूयते ॥ ५ ॥ साम्प्रतं चत्वारि सहस्राणि नव शतानि त्र्यशीतिश्च कलियुगस्य वर्षाण्यतिक्रान्तानि । ६ । श्रीविक्रमादित्यादनन्तरं पञ्चपञ्चाशाधिके शततमे संवत्सरे शकानां राजाभिषिक्तः । ७ । अधुना त्वष्टादश शतानि चत्वारि च शकानां राज्ञो वर्षाणि गतानि ॥ ८ ॥ त्रीणि लक्षाणि गवां षोडश ग्रामाश्चर्षभदत्तेन ब्राह्मणेभ्यो दत्तानि । ९ । स एव वर्षे वर्षे शतसहस्रं ब्राह्मणानामभोजयत् ॥ १० ॥

11. The wagon of the Açvins is fitted (**युज्**, *part. pass.*) with three wheels. 12. The Açvins are praised by the seer with four

*i. e., in the seven stars of the Great Bear.

Sentences 6 and 8 were true only down to 1882.

Rik-verses. 13. Kṛṣṇa is the eldest of six brothers. 14. Arjuna is the third among the five Pāṇḍavas. 15. Some think there are eight *sorts of* marriage (*pl.*); others, six (*model after 2nd sentence in Sanskrit above*). 16. Twenty-seven or twenty-eight lunar mansions are mentioned in astronomy. 17. One should consecrate a Brāhman in *his* eighth year, a Kṣatriya in *his* eleventh, a Vāiçya in *his* twelfth. 18. Two great lights shine in the sky. 19. The teacher, having taught the fifth Rik-verse, recited the sixth. 20. Çākyamuni Buddha died in the eightieth year of his age (*life*). 21. Sometimes 33 gods are reckoned in the Veda, sometimes 3333.

Lesson XXXII.

337. Comparison of Adjectives. Derivative adjectives having comparative and superlative meaning — or often, and more originally, a merely intensive value — are made either (A.) directly from roots (by primary derivation), or (B.) from other derivative or compound stems (by secondary derivation).

338. A. The suffixes of primary derivation are **ईयस्** for the comparative, and **इष्ठ** for the superlative. The root before them is accented, and usually strengthened by *guṇa* (if capable of it), or sometimes by nasalization or prolongation. — In classical Sanskrit few such formations are in use; and these attach themselves in meaning mostly to other adjectives from the same root, which seem to be their corresponding positives. In part, however, they are connected with words unrelated to them in derivation.

339. Thus **क्षेपीयस्** and **क्षेपिष्ठ** (√**क्षिप्**) attach themselves to **क्षिप्र** 'quick'; **वरीयस्** and **वरिष्ठ** (√**वृ** 'encompass'), to **उरु** 'broad'; **पापीयस्** and **पापिष्ठ**, 'worse' and 'worst', to the subst. **पाप**; **पटीयस्** and **पटिष्ठ**, to **पटु** 'skilful'; **महीयस्** and **महिष्ठ** to

महन्त्; बलीयस् and बलिष्ठ, to बलिन् or बलवन्त्; साधीयस् and साधिष्ठ to साधु.

340. The following are examples of artificial connections:

अन्तिक 'near', नेदीयस्, नेदिष्ठ; अल्प 'little', कनीयस्, कनिष्ठ (but also अल्पीयस्, अल्पिष्ठ); गुरु 'heavy', गरीयस्, गरिष्ठ; दीर्घ 'long', द्राघीयस्, द्राघिष्ठ; प्रशस्य 'praiseworthy', 'good', श्रेयस् 'better', श्रेष्ठ 'best'; प्रिय 'dear', प्रेयस्, प्रेष्ठ; बहु 'much', भूयस्, भूयिष्ठ; युवन् 'young', यवीयस्, यविष्ठ; वृद्ध 'old', वर्षीयस्, वर्षिष्ठ. ज्यायस् and ज्येष्ठ correspond sometimes to प्रशस्य or साधु, sometimes to वृद्ध.

341. The stems in इष्ठ are inflected like ordinary adjectives in अ, with the fem. in आ; those in ईयस् have a peculiar declension, with a strong stem in ईयांस्, and fem. ईयसी, for which see § 255. So also ज्यायस् and भूयस्.

342. B. The suffixes of secondary derivation are तर and तम. They are of almost unrestricted use. That form of stem is usually taken which appears before an initial consonant of a case-ending. Stems in अस् are always unchanged; final इस् and उस् become इष् and उष्, after which the त् of the suffix becomes ट्.

Thus, प्रियवाच्, प्रियवाक्तर, °क्तम; धनिन्, धनितर, °तम; विद्वांस्, विद्वत्तर, °त्तम.

343. Some stems which are substantives rather than adjectives are found to form derivatives of comparison; thus, मातृतम 'most motherly', नृतम 'most manly', गजतम 'most like an elephant.'

344. Comparison of Adverbs. Adverbs are compared by adding the suffixes in the forms तराम् and तमाम्; thus, सु 'well', सुतराम्, सुतमाम्.

345. Construction. With a comparative (and sometimes with other words used in a similar way) the ablative is the regular construction; thus, पुत्रात्कन्या तस्य प्रेयसी "a daughter is dearer to him than a son"; मतिरेव बलाद्गरीयसी "intellect alone is stronger than force". After the superlative either genitive or locative may be used. The comparative often has the force of a strengthened superlative; thus, गरीयान् 'most honorable'.

Vocabulary XXXII.

Subst.:

गन्धर्व m., one of a band of celestial singers, a Gandharva.

दक्ष m., *n. pr.*

धावन n., running, course.

परमात्मन् m., the world-spirit.

मोक्ष m., deliverance, salvation.

रोहिणी f., *n. pr.*

लोह n., metal; iron.

वायस m., crow.

वेदान्त m., a system of philosophy.

शकुन्तला f., *n. pr.*

सिन्धु m., *n. pr.*, the Indus.

सुराप m., drunkard.

हेमन्त m., winter.

Adj.:

अणु little, small; *as n. subst.*, atom.

आशु swift.

ईदृश्, f. **ईदृशी**, such.

पुराण, f. **°णा** and **°णी**, old.

वर्तिन् abiding, being.

Indecl.:

च *sometimes in sense of* if.

Exercise XXXII.

ज्येष्ठो भ्राता पिता वापि यश्च विद्यां प्रयच्छति ।
त्रयस्ते पितरो ज्ञेया धर्मे* च पथि वर्तिनः ॥ १८ ॥

मोक्षाय ज्ञानं यज्ञेभ्यः साधीय इति पुराणेषूक्तम् । १ । साम्प्रतं तु भक्त्या श्रेयो लब्धुं द्विजातयो यतन्ते ॥ २ ॥ त्रयः कनीयांसो भ्रातरो रामस्याभवन् । ३ । यवीयसीं भार्यां परिणयेत् । ४ । यदि ज्येष्ठायां भार्यायां कनिष्ठः पुत्रो जायेत तदा स एव श्रेष्ठं धनस्य भागं लभेतेत्येके । ५ । परमात्माणोरप्यणीयान्महतो ऽपि महीयान्वेदान्तेषु वर्ण्यते । ६ । पञ्चभिरेताभिर्नदीभिः सह संगतः सिन्धुर्गङ्गाया अपि वरीयान्दृश्यते । ७ । या अष्टाविंशतिर्दक्षस्य दुहितरश्चन्द्रमसा परिणीतास्तासां रोहिणी भर्तुः प्रेष्ठाभवत् । ८ । स्तेनेभ्यः सुरापाः पापीयांसः स्मर्यन्ते । ९ । पापानां पापिष्ठास्तु ब्रह्महणः । १० । प्रथीयो यशस्त्रिषु लोकेष्वर्जुनेन लब्धम् ॥ ११ ॥

---

* Translate as though genitive.

12. Of the three wives of Daçaratha, Kāusalyā was older and more honored (गुरु, *comp.*) than Kāikeyī and Sumitrā. 13. In winter the nights are very long. 14. Not very many (*express as pred.*) such jewels are found on earth. 15. Among those kings of the North Pṛthvīrāja was the mightiest. 16. The poems of Kālidāsa are sweeter than the works of Bāṇa. 17. Anāthapiṇḍika was the richest among all the merchants in Rājagṛha. 18. Iron is lighter than gold, but heavier than wood. 19. In running the horse is the swiftest of quadrupeds. 20. Çakuntalā was more beautiful than all other women of that time, and became the wife of the mightiest monarch (सम्राज्) of the whole earth. 21. The crow is called the shrewdest of birds.

Lesson XXXIII.

(Part I.)

346. Compounds. In all periods of the language the combination of stems of declension with one another, forming compounds which are treated in accent, inflection and construction as if simple words, is one of the most striking peculiarities of the Sanskrit tongue. In the Vedic period compounds of more than two elements are rare. In the later language this moderation is abandoned; and the later the period, and especially the more elaborate the style of composition, the more unwieldy and difficult do the compounds become. To such an extent is this carried that the advantages of an inflective language are often deliberately thrown away, and a clumsy aggregation of elements replaces the due syntactical union of inflected words into sentences.

347. Sanskrit compounds fall into three principal classes:

I. Copulative or Aggregative compounds, of which the members are syntactically coordinate: a joining together of words which in an uncompounded state would be connected by 'and'.* E. g. कृताकृतम् 'done and undone'; देवगन्धर्वमानुषाः 'gods and Gandharvas and men'. The members of such a compound may obviously be of any number, two or more.

II. **Determinative** compounds, of which the former member is syntactically dependent on the latter, as its determining or qualifying adjunct: being either a noun limiting it in a case-relation, or an adjective or an adverb describing it. Thus may be distinguished two sub-classes: A. **Dependent,** and B. **Descriptive,** compounds; their difference is not absolute.

Examples are: of dependents, अमित्रसेना 'army of enemies'; पादोदक 'water for the feet'; हस्तकृत 'made with hands'; — of descriptives, महाराज 'great king'; प्रियसख (§ 353, 2) 'dear friend'; दुष्कृत 'badly done'.

348. The character of compounds of classes I. and II., as parts of speech, is determined by their final member, and they are capable of being resolved into equivalent phrases by giving the proper independent form and formal means of connection to each member. But this is not true of the third class, which accordingly is more fundamentally distinct from them than they from each other.

349. III. **Secondary Adjective** compounds, the value of which is not given by a simple resolution into their component parts, but which, though having as final member a noun, are themselves adjectives. These again are of two sub-classes: A. **Possessive** compounds, which are noun-compounds of the preceding class (II. A. or B.), with the idea of 'having' added, turning them from nouns into adjectives; and B. compounds in which the second member is

* This class of compounds is of comparatively recent development; only the other two are common in others of the related tongues.

a noun syntactically dependent on the first: namely, 1. **Participial** compounds (only Vedic), of a present participle with its following object; and 2. **Prepositional** compounds, of a preposition and following noun. This whole sub-class B is comparatively small.

Examples: वीरसेन 'possessing a hero-army'; प्रजाकाम 'having desire of progeny'; अतिमात्र 'excessive'.

350. The adjective compounds are, like simple adjectives, sometimes used, especially in the neuter, as abstract and collective nouns; and in the accusative as adverbs. Out of these uses have grown apparent classes of compounds, reckoned and named as such by the Hindu grammarians.

351. A compound may, like a simple word, become a member in another compound, and so on indefinitely. The analysis of a compound (except copulatives), of whatever length, must be made by a series of bisections. Thus the dependent compound पूर्वजन्मकृत, 'done in a previous existence', is first divisible into कृत and the descriptive पूर्वजन्मन्, then this into its two elements.

352. Euphonic combination in compounds. The final of a stem is combined with the initial of another stem in composition according to the general rules for *external* combination. But:

1. Final इस् and उस् of a prior member become इष् and उष् before surd gutturals, dentals, and labials; thus, ज्योतिष्कृत्.

2. Final अस् of a prior member often remains unchanged under similar circumstances.

3. After final इ, उ, ऋ, an initial स् often becomes lingual.

4. Pronouns generally take the stem-form of the neuter; for the personal pronouns are oftenest used मद् and त्वद् in the sing., अस्मद् and युष्मद् in the pl.

5. For महन्त्, in the prior member of descriptive and possessive compounds, is used महा.

6. A case-form in the prior member is not very rare.

353. In all classes of compounds, certain changes of finals are liable to appear in the concluding member; generally they have the effect of transferring the compound as a whole to the *a*-declension. Thus: 1. A stem in अन् often drops the final न्, as in °अच, °अह, °मूर्ध, °राज. 2. An इ or ई is changed to अ, as in °भूम, °रात्र, °सख, °पथ. 3. An अ is added after a final consonant, sometimes even after an *u*-vowel or a diphthong, as in °अह्न (अहन्), गव (गो).

The separate classes of compounds will now be taken up.

(Part II.)

354. **I. Copulative compounds.** Two or more nouns — much less often adjectives, and once or twice adverbs — having a co-ordinate construction, as though joined by 'and', are sometimes combined into a compound.*

355. The noun-compounds fall, as regards their inflective form, into two classes:

A. The compound has the gender and declension of its final member, and is in number a dual or plural, according to its logical value as denoting either two, or more than two, individual things. Examples are: व्रीहियवौ 'rice and barley'; रामकृष्णौ 'Rāma and Kṛṣṇa'; अजावयः 'goats and sheep'; ब्राह्मणक्षत्रियवैश्यशूद्राः 'Brāhmans, Kṣatriyas, Vāiçyas and Çūdras'; पितापुत्रौ (§ 352, 6) 'father and son'.

B. The compound, without regard to the number denoted or to the gender of its constituents, becomes a neuter singular collective (so-called *samāhāra-dvandva*). Thus, पाणिपादम् 'hand and foot'; सर्पनकुलम् 'snake and ichneumon'; छत्त्रोपानहम् (§ 353, 3) 'umbrella and shoe'; अहोरात्रम् (§ 353, 2) 'day and night'.

356. The later language preserves several dual combinations

---

* This class is called by the Hindus *dvandva*, 'couple'; but a *dvandva* of adjectives they do not recognize.

of the names of divinities, etc., which retain their earlier forms; thus, द्यावापृथिवी and द्यावाभूमी 'Heaven and Earth'; मित्रावरुणौ 'Mitra and Varuṇa'; अग्नीषोमौ 'Agni and Soma'.

357. Adjective copulative compounds are made likewise, but are rare. Examples are: शुक्लकृष्ण 'light and dark'; वृत्तपीन 'round and plump';* स्नातानुलिप्त 'bathed and anointed'.

358. II. **Determinative compounds.** A noun or adjective is often combined into a compound with a preceding determining or qualifying word — a noun or adjective or adverb. The two principal divisions of this class are, as indicated above, A. Dependent, and B. Descriptive, compounds. Each class falls into two subdivisions, according as the final member, and therefore the whole compound, is noun or adjective.**

359. **A. Dependent compounds.** 1. Noun-compounds. The case-relation of the prior to the second member may be of any kind, but is oftenest genitive, and least often accusative. Thus, तत्पुरुष = तस्य पुरुषः; मूर्खशतानि 'hundreds of fools'; — पादोदक (= पादेभ्य उदकम्) 'water for the feet'; — विद्याधन 'money (obtained) by science'; आत्मसादृश्य (= आत्मना सादृश्यम्) 'likeness with self'; — चौरभय (= चौराद्भयम्) 'fear of a thief'; — जलक्रीडा (= जले क्री°) 'sport in the water'; — नगरगमन (= नगरं ग°) 'going to the city'; वाचस्पति 'lord of speech', *n. pr.* (§ 352, 6.).

360. 2. Dependent adjective compounds. Only a very small proportion of the compounds of this class have an ordinary adjective as final member; usually the final member is a participle, or a derivative of agency with the value of a participle (§ 204). The

* The Hindus reckon these as *karmadhārayas* (see next note).

** The whole class of determinatives is called by the natives *tatpuruṣa* (the name is a specimen of the class, meaning 'his man'); the second division, the descriptives, bears the special name *karmadhāraya*, a word of obscure meaning and application.

prior member stands in any possible case-relation. Thus, ग्रामगत 'gone to the village'; वेदविद् 'Veda-knowing'; — शिवरक्षित 'protected by Çiva'; गोहित (= गवे हितः) 'good for the cow'; — स्वर्गपतित 'fallen from the sky'; तरङ्गचञ्चलतर 'more mobile than waves'; — द्विजोत्तम (= द्विजानाम् उत्तमः) 'best of Brāhmans'; — स्थालीपक्व 'cooked in a pot'.

361. Compounds of this sort having as final member the bare root — sometimes modified in form, and, if it end originally in a short vowel, generally with an added त् — are very numerous: thus, वेदविद् above (§ 360); रथस्थ 'standing in the wagon' (or simply 'in the wagon'); मूर्धग 'on the head'; एकज 'only-born'; वनेचर (§ 352, 6) 'forest-dwelling'; मनसिज 'born in the heart' (i.e. 'love').

362. B. **Descriptive compounds.** In this division of the determinatives, the prior member stands to the other in no distinct case-relation, but qualifies it adjectively or adverbially, according as the final member is noun or adjective. Thus, प्रियसख (§ 353, 2); सुकृत 'well-done'; दुष्कृत् 'evil-doing' (adj.).

The compounds of noun-value cannot well be separated in treatment from those of adjective-value.

363. The simplest case is that in which a noun as final member is preceded by a qualifying adjective as prior member. Thus, कृष्णाश्व (= कृष्णो ऽश्वः) 'black horse'; महापुरुष 'great man'. Instead of an adjective, the prior member is in a few cases a noun used appositionally or with a *quasi*-adjective value; thus, ब्रह्मर्षि 'priest-sage'; राजर्षि 'king-sage'.

364. Sometimes compounds of this sort express a comparison; thus, घनश्याम 'black as a thunder-cloud' (cf. 'coal-black', etc.). Reversed, पुरुषव्याघ्र 'man-tiger', i. e., 'a man fierce as a tiger';*

* Literally, a tiger which is not a tiger after all, but a man. Or, perhaps better, 'tiger of (or among) men' (so Whitney).

नरसिंह 'man-lion'; पादपद्म 'foot-lotus', i. e. 'a foot lovely as a lotus'.

365. The adverbial words most commonly used as prior members of descriptive compounds, qualifying the other member, are the verbal prefixes ("prepositions"), and the words of direction related to them; likewise the inseparable prefixes अन् or अ privative, सु 'well', दुस् 'ill', etc. These are combined with nouns (in *quasi*-adjectival value) as well as with adjectives. Thus, अकृत 'not done'; अपण्डित 'not a scholar'; अनर्थ 'misfortune'; अतिदेव 'more than a god'; अतिदूर 'exceedingly far'; अतिभय 'excessive fear'; प्रतिपक्ष 'opposing side.'

Vocabulary XXXIII.

Verbs:

आप् + सम् complete.

युज् + नि station, place, appoint.

रञ्ज् + अनु (*anurájyati, -te*) be devoted to, inclined to (*loc.*).

वस् + प्र go away (on a journey).

वृत् + नि return home.

Subst.:

आकाश m., air, sky.

आश्रम m., hermitage.

कण्व m., *n. pr.*

कुमार m., boy, prince.

क्रीडा f., game, sport.

तिलक m., ornament (*often fig.*).

तीर्थ n., bathing-place; place of pilgrimage.

त्रिलोक n., °की f., the threefold world.

दुष्यन्त m., *n. pr.*

द्वीपिन् m., panther.

पद n., step; place.

पुरु m., *n. pr.*

महिषी f., queen.

मृगया f., chase.

यात्रा f., march, journey; support.

वंश m., race, family.

वृत्तान्त m., state of affairs; news.

सखी f., female friend.

सत्कार m., hospitality.

Adj.:

अनुरूप, f. °आ, suitable.

कृत्रिम, f. °आ, adopted.

गान्धर्व, f. °ई, in the manner of, or suitable for, the Gandharvas.	समीप, f. °आ, near; *as neut. subst.*, vicinity, nearness, presence.
दिव्य, f. °आ, heavenly, divine.	**Adv.:**
मानुष, f. °ई, human.	पुरा earlier, formerly.

Exercise XXXIII.

दुष्षन्तो नाम राजर्षिः पूरुवंशतिलकस्त्रिलोक्यां विश्रुतः कृत्स्नां पृथिवीमपालयत्। १। स चैकदा मन्त्रिसूतसैनिकान्वितो मृगयाक्रीडार्थं* महावनं प्रविष्टः। २। तस्मिन्वने दुष्षन्तो ऽनेकान्व्याघ्रसिंहर्क्षद्वीपिनो ऽन्यांश्च वनेचरान्प्राणिनः स्वशरैर्व्यापादयत्। ३। एकं तु हरिणं पलायमानं रथस्थो ऽनुसरन्स नदीतीरे दिव्याश्रमपदं दृष्टवान्। ४। कण्वस्य ब्रह्मर्षेरयमाश्रम इति सूतमुखाच्छ्रुत्वा सैनिकान्वने संस्थाप्यर्षिं नन्तुं राजा तत्र प्रविष्टः। ५। तदा कण्वे तीर्थयात्रार्थं प्रोषिते सति तस्य कृत्रिमा दुहिता शकुन्तला नाम सखीसमेता महाराजमतिथिसत्कारेण पूजयितुमाश्रमान्निर्गता॥ ६॥

(Form compounds of words joined by hyphens).

7. When he had seen her, brilliant (राज् *pres. part.*) with divine-beauty, as though (इव) more-than-human, the heart of the king-sage was inclined (*pass. part.*) toward her. 8. Thereupon, having learned *that* she (*acc.*) *was the* daughter-of-an-Apsaras (*acc.*), he married her by the gāndharva-ceremony (विवाह) suitable-for-Kṣatriyas. 9. Duṣṣanta, after dwelling very many days-and-nights in the hermitage, abandoned Çakuntalā and returned to his-own-city. 10. Afterwards, when Kaṇva had finished his pilgrimage, and returned to the hermitage, learning (विद्) the news[4]-of-his[1]-daughter's[2]-marriage[3], he sent her into-the-presence-of-Duṣṣanta. 11. The royal-sage at first disowned (प्रत्या-ख्या, *ger.*) Çakuntalā *when she was* come[2]-to-the-city[1]; *but* at last he put (नि-युज्, *part. in* °वन्त्) her in-the-place[3]-of-the-first[1]-queen[2]. 12. In the course of time

---

* "To engage in the sport of hunting"; cf. below, § 375, 3.

(कालेन गच्छता) a beautiful-prince, named Bharata, was born to her (*loc.*).

Lesson XXXIV.

366. III. Secondary Adjective Compounds. A compound with a noun as final member very often wins secondarily the value of an adjective, being inflected in the three genders to agree with the noun which it qualifies, and used in all the constructions of an adjective. The two divisions of this class have been given above (§ 349).

367. Certain changes are sometimes necessary in the stem of the final member to make possible the inflection in different genders. Masc. and neut. stems in अ, and fem. in आ, generally interchange; thus, from सु + हस्त comes the compound सुहस्त 'with excellent hands', nom. sing. सुहस्तस्, °स्ता, °स्तम्; so also (from त्रि + जिह्वा) त्रिजिह्वस्, °ह्वा, °ह्वम्; and (from सु + फल n.) सुफलस्, °ला, °लम्. The same holds good for masc., fem., and neut. stems in इ and उ, and stems in consonants.

368. But often a fem. in ई is used by the side of a masc. and neut. in अ; thus, द्विपर्ण 'two-leaved', f. द्विपर्णी.

369. Very frequently the suffix क (attenuated into an element of indefinite value) is added to a pure possessive compound, to help the conversion of the compounded stem into an adjective; especially to fem. stems in ई and ऊ, and to stems in ऋ; and in general, where the final of the stem is less usual or manageable in adjective inflection. Thus, बहुनदीक 'rich in rivers'; मृतभर्तृका f., 'whose husband is dead', i. e. 'widow'; महायशस् (nom. masc. and fem. °शास्) or महायशस्क.

370. Sometimes the possessive-making suffix इन् is added to secondary adjective compounds, without effect upon the meaning; thus, गर्दभनादिन् (= °नाद) 'having an ass's voice.'

371. A. Possessive compounds. The possessives are determinative compounds to which are given both an adjective inflection (as just shown), and also an adjective meaning of a kind best defined by adding 'having' to the meaning of the determinative. Thus, the dependent देवरूप n., 'beauty of a god', becomes the possessive देवरूप, °आ, m. f. n., 'having the beauty of a god'; the descriptive दीर्घबाहु m., 'long arm', becomes the possessive दीर्घबाहु m. f. n., 'having long arms'.*

372. Dependent compounds are, by comparison, not often thus turned into possessives. But possessively used descriptives are extremely frequent and various; and some kinds of combination which are rare in proper descriptives are very common as possessives.

373. An adjective as prior member takes the masculine stem-form, even though referring to a feminine noun in the final member; thus, रूपवद्भार्य (from भार्या) 'possessing a beautiful wife'.

374. As prior members are found:

1. Adjectives proper; thus, अन्यरूप 'of other form'. — 2. Participles; thus, हतमातृक 'whose mother is slain'. — 3. Numerals; thus, चतुर्मुख 'four-faced'; त्रिलोचन 'three-eyed'. — 4. Nouns with *quasi*-adjectival value; thus, हिरण्यहस्त 'gold-handed'. Especially common is the use of a noun as prior member to qualify the other appositionally, or by way of equivalence. These may well be called **appositional possessives.** Thus, कृष्णनामन् 'having "Kṛṣṇa" as name'; वीरपुरुष 'having men who are heroes'; चारचक्षुस् 'using spies as eyes'; त्वाद्दूत 'having thee as messenger'. — 5. Adverbial elements (especially inseparable prefixes);

---

* This class of compounds is called by the natives *bahuvrīhi*; the name is an example of the class, meaning 'having much rice'. — The possessive may generally, in accented texts, be distinguished from the original determinative by a difference of accent.

thus, अनन्त 'endless'; अपुत्र 'childless'; सुपुत्र 'with excellent sons'; दुर्गन्धि 'ill-savored'. The associative prefix स (less often सह) is treated like an adjective element; thus, सरूप 'of like form'; सपुत्र or सहपुत्र 'with a son', or 'having one's son along with one'; सानुकूल (स + अनुकूल n.) 'favorable'. — 6. Ordinary verbal prefixes; thus, प्रश्रवस् 'of wide fame'; व्यङ्ग 'limbless'; निर्बल 'powerless'; उन्मुख 'with uplifted face'. — 7. Ordinary adverbs; thus, इहचित्त 'with mind directed hither'.

375. Certain words, very frequent in the compounds mentioned at § 374, 4, have in part won a peculiar application.

1. Thus with आदि 'beginning' (or the derivatives आद्य or आदिक) are made compounds signifying the person or thing designated along with others — such a person or thing *et cetera*. Thus, देवा इन्द्रादयः 'the gods having Indra as first', i. e. 'the gods Indra, etc.' Often the qualifying noun is omitted; thus, अन्नपानादीनि 'food, drink, etc.' — 2. Words like पूर्व (पूर्वक) etc., are used in the same way, to denote accompaniment; chiefly adverbially. — 3. The noun अर्थ 'object', 'purpose', is used at the end of a compound, oftenest as a neut. subst. (acc. or instr. or loc.), to signify 'for the sake of', and the like; thus, दमयन्त्यर्थे 'for Damayantī's sake'; शय्यार्थे 'for a bed'. (See below, § 379). — 4. अन्तर (as neut. subst.) often means 'other' in possessives; thus, देशान्तर n., 'another region' (lit. 'that which has a difference of region').

376. In appositional possessives, the final member, if it designate a part of the body, sometimes signifies the part to which belongs what is designated by the prior member: that on or in which it is. Thus मणिग्रीव 'with necklace on neck'. Such compounds are commonest with words meaning hand; thus, असिपाणि 'with sword in hand'; लगुडहस्त 'with club in hand'.

377. The possessives are not always used with the simple

value of qualifying adjective. Often they have a pregnant sense, and become the equivalents of dependent clauses; or the 'having' implied in them becomes about equivalent to our 'having' as a sign of past action. Thus, प्राप्तयौवन 'possessing attained adolescence', i. e. 'having reached adolescence'; अनधिगतशास्त्र 'with unstudied books', i. e. 'one who has neglected study'; गतप्राण 'whose breath is gone', i. e. 'lifeless'; आसन्नमृत्यु 'to whom death is come near'.

378. **B. Compounds with governed final member.**

1. **Participial** compounds, exclusively Vedic.

2. **Prepositional** compounds. Thus may conveniently be called those compounds in which the prior member is a particle with true prepositional value, and the final member a noun governed by it. Thus, अतिरात्र 'lasting over night'; अतिमात्र 'beyond measure', 'excessive'; अधिकर्ण 'next the ear'.

---

379. **Adjective compounds as nouns and adverbs.** Compound adjectives, like simple ones, are freely used substantively as abstracts and collectives, especially in the neuter, and less often in the feminine; and they are also much used adverbially, particularly in the acc. sing. neuter.

380. The substantively used possessive compounds having a numeral as prior member, with some of the strictly adjective compounds, are treated by the Hindus as a separate class, and called *dvigu* *. Examples of such numeral abstracts and collectives are: त्रियुग n., 'the three ages'; त्रियोजन n., 'space of three leagues'. Feminines of like use occur in the later language; thus त्रिलोकी (by the side of °क n.,) 'the three worlds'.

381. Those adverbially used accusatives of secondary adjective

* The name is a sample of the class, and means 'of two cows' (said to be used in the sense of 'worth two cows').

compounds which have an indeclinable or particle as prior member are considered by the Hindus a separate class of compounds, and called *avyayībhāva* *. 1. The prepositional compounds are especially frequent in this use; thus, प्रतिदोषम् 'at evening'; समक्षम् 'in sight'; अनुगङ्गम् (= गङ्गाम् अनु) 'along the Ganges'; उपगङ्गम् 'on the G.'; प्रतिवर्षम् 'every year'. — 2. A large class of *avyayībhāvas* is made up of words having a relative adverb, especially यथा, as prior member. Thus, यथावशम्, यथाकामम्, यथेच्छम्, 'as one chooses'. And, with other adverbs: यावज्जीवम् 'as long as one lives'; यत्रकामम् 'whither one will'.

382. Occasionally quite anomalous compounds will be met with. For such, cf. Whitney, § 1314.

Vocabulary XXXIV.

Verbs:

चि + निस् determine, decide.

दृ + वि in caus. (*vidāráyati*) tear open.

पट् (*pāṭáyati*) split open.

भू + अभि overpower.

2वृ (*varáyate*) choose, select.

सद् + आ (*āsídati*) approach.

+ समा in caus. (*samāsādáyati*) meet with, encounter.

हृष् (*hárṣati*; *hṛ́ṣyati*) rejoice, be delighted.

Subst.:

अङ्ग n., limb, member, body.

आकार m., form, figure.

इन्दु m., moon.

उदर n., belly.

केतु m., banner.

कोटि f., peak; point, tip.

चूडा f., top-knot, scalp.

ज्ञान n., knowledge; insight.

तालु n., palate.

तृष्णा f., thirst, desire.

दंष्ट्रा f., tooth.

द्युति f., brilliancy.

पर्वत m., mountain.

पुलिन्द m., a tribe in India.

प्रहार m., stroke, shot; wound.

प्राण m., breath, life (*often pl.*).

मस्तक n., head.

* The word means 'conversion to an indeclinable'.

मीन m., fish.

वक्षस् n., chest, breast.

वराह m., boar.

वेदना f., pain.

स्नायु m., tendon; bowstring.

Adj.:

अनवद्य, f. °आ, blameless, faultless.

अनुकूल, f. °आ, favorable; *as neut. subst.*, favor.

अन्तर, f. °आ, inner; *as neut. subst.*, the interior, middle; interval, difference; occasion, juncture (§ 375, 4.)

पटु skilled.

बाल, f. °आ, young.

Indecl.:

अथ then, thereupon.

तद् (*adv. acc.*) therefore.

तावत् so long; often merely = *donc, doch.*

यावत् as long as, while; as soon as.

स्म asseverative particle; gives to the present the force of an historical tense.

Exercise XXXIV.

अतितृष्णा न कर्तव्या तृष्णां नैव परित्यजेत् ।
अतितृष्णाभिभूतस्य चूडा भवति मस्तके ॥ १९ ॥

कस्मिंश्चिद्वने पुलिन्दः प्रतिवसति स्म । १ । स चैकदा मृगयां कर्तुं प्रस्थितः । २ । अथ तेन प्रसर्पता (pres. part.) पर्वतशिखराकारो महावराहः समासादितः । ३ । तं दृष्ट्वा कर्णान्ताकृष्टशरेण स तेन समाहतः । ४ । तेनापि वराहेण कोपाविष्टेन बालेन्दुद्युतिना दंष्ट्राग्रेण पाटितोदरः पुलिन्दो गतप्राणो भूमावपतत् । ५ । अथ व्याधं व्यापाद्य वराहो ऽपि शरप्रहारवेदनया मृतः । ६ । एतस्मिन्नन्तरे कश्चिदासन्नमृत्युः शृगाल इतस्ततः परिभ्रमंस्तं देशमागतः । ७ । यावद्वराहपुलिन्दौ पश्यति तावत्प्रहृष्टो ऽचिन्तयत् । ८ । भोः सानुकूलो मे विधिः । ९ । तेनैतदचिन्तितं भोजनमुपस्थितम् । १० । तदहं तथा भक्षयामि यथा बहून्यहानि मे प्राणयात्रा भवति । ११ । तत्तावत्प्रथमं स्नायुपाशं धनुष्कोटिगतं भक्षयामि । १२ । एवं मनसा निश्चित्य धनुष्कोटिं मुखे क्षिप्त्वा स्नायुं भक्षयितुमारब्धः । १३ । ततश्च कर्तिते स्नायौ तालु विदार्य धनुष्कोटिर्मस्तकमध्येन निष्क्रान्ता । १४ । सो ऽपि मृतः ॥ १५ ॥

16. Those-who-have-done-evil must do penance twelve-days,

six-days, or three-days. 17. Purūravas, Indra's-friend, married the moon-faced*, faultless-limbed* Apsaras Urvaçī. 18. Bhṛgukaccha is situated (वृत्) on the Narmadā. 19. There stands the long-armed, broad-chested king-of-the-Añgas, sword-in-hand. 20. The path-of-knowledge is better than the path-of-works. 21. In-the-opinion-of-the-ancient-seers (*cpd in loc. or instr.*) one-whose-husband-is-dead may choose a second at-pleasure. 22. Love is bodiless, and *bears*-a-fish-in-his-banner; so say the poets. 23. The Brāhman's-daughter, Sītā-by-name*, *is* lotus-eyed.* 24. The king, although (अपि) many-wived, is childless. 25. The eloquent** pandit has arrived with-his-scholars. 26. With-upturned-face (उन्मुख) Cātaka prays for rain-water.

Lesson XXXV.

383. First Conjugation of Verbs. Present System.* In this conjugation the optative act., the 2nd sing. imv. act., and the 3rd pl. mid., are formed otherwise than in the *a*-conjugation.

384. Strong forms. The forms in which the stem assumes its strong form are these: the three persons sing. of the pres. and impf. indic. act., all first persons of the imv., act. and mid., and the 3rd sing. imv. act. All other forms of the present system are weak.

385. Endings. For the middle endings अन्ते, अन्त, and अन्ताम् are substituted अते, अत, and अताम्; and after reduplicated stems (and a few others) अति, अतु, and उस् are substituted for the

* Secondary adj. cpds., fem. in ई.

** Dep. cpd, "skilled in speech".

*** For a comprehensive view of the ways of forming the present-stems of verbs following this general conjugation, see Introduction, § 78.

active endings अन्ति, अन्तु, and अन् (impf.). The 2nd sing. imv. often takes the ending हि or धि. Otherwise the endings are the same as in the *a*-conjugation.

386. Optative mode-sign. The sign of the opt. act. is या *yā́*, with secondary endings; but उस् is the ending in the 3rd pl., and आ is dropped before it; thus, °युस्.

387. Present participle middle. In the first conjugation this participle is made with the suffix आन [आण], before which the stem takes the same form as before the 3rd pl. pres. ind. The fem. is always in आ.

---

388. Class IV. A: *nu*-class. The present-stem is made by adding to the root the syllable नु *nu* [णु *ṇu*], in strong forms नो *nó* [णो *ṇó*]. The उ of the class-sign may be dropped before व् and म् of the 1st du. and 1st pl. endings, except when the root ends in a consonant; and the उ before a vowel-ending becomes व् or उव्, according as it is preceded by one or by two consonants. The ending हि of the 2nd. sing. imv. is dropped if the root end in a vowel.

389. I. Roots in vowels. सु 'press'.

Indicative.

	Active.			Middle.		
1.	सुनोमि *sunómi*	सुनुवस् *sunuvás*	सुनुमस् *sunumás*	सुन्वे *sunvé*	सुनुवहे *sunuváhe*	सुनुमहे *sunumáhe*
2.	सुनोषि *sunóṣi*	सुनुथस् *sunuthás*	सुनुथ *sunuthá*	सुनुषे *sunuṣé*	सुन्वाथे *sunvā́the*	सुनुध्वे *sunudhvé*
3.	सुनोति *sunóti*	सुनुतस् *sunutás*	सुन्वन्ति *sunvánti*	सुनुते *sunuté*	सुन्वाते *sunvā́te*	सुन्वते *sunváte*

The forms सुन्वस्, सुन्मस्, सुन्वहे, सुन्महे, are alternative with those given above for 1st du. and pl., and occur oftener.

Imperfect.

1.	असुनवम्*	असुनुव	असुनुम	असुन्वि	असुनुवहि	°नुमहि
2.	असुनोस्	असुनुतम्	असुनुत	असुनुथास्	असुन्वाथाम्	°नुध्वम्
3.	असुनोत्	असुनुताम्	असुन्वन्	असुनुत	असुन्वाताम्	°न्वत

The briefer forms असुन्व, असुन्म, असुन्वहि, असुन्महि, are allowed and more usual.

Imperative.

1.	सुनवानि	सुनवाव	सुनवाम	सुनवै	सुनवावहै	सुनवामहै
	sunávāni	*sunávāva*	*sunávāma*	*sunávāi*	*sunávāvahāi*	*sunávāmahāi*
2.	सुनु	सुनुतम्	सुनुत	सुनुष्व	सुन्वाथाम्	सुनुध्वम्
	*sunú***	*sunutám*	*sunutá*	*sunuṣvá*	*sunvā́thām*	*sunudhvám*
3.	सुनोतु	सुनुताम्	सुन्वन्तु	सुनुताम्	सुन्वाताम्	सुन्वताम्
	*sunótu***	*sunutā́m*	*sunvántu*	*sunutā́m*	*sunvā́tām*	*sunvátām*

Optative.

1.	सुनुयाम्	सुनुयाव	°याम	सुन्वीय	सुन्वीवहि	सुन्वीमहि
	sunuyā́m	*sunuyā́va*	*sunuyā́ma*	*sunvīyá*	*sunvīváhi*	*sunvīmáhi*
2.	सुनुयास्	सुनुयातम्	°यात	सुन्वीथास्	सुन्वीयाथाम्	सुन्वीध्वम्
3.	सुनुयात्	सुनुयाताम्	°युस्	सुन्वीत	सुन्वीयाताम्	सुन्वीरन्

Participle.

सुन्वन्त्, f. सुन्वती   सुन्वान, f. °ना

390. **II. Roots in consonants.** आप् 'acquire'.

Indicative.

	Active.			Middle.		
1.	आप्नोमि	आप्नुवस्	आप्नुमस्	आप्नुवे	आप्नुवहे	आप्नुमहे
2.	आप्नोषि	आप्नुथस्	आप्नुथ	आप्नुषे	आप्नुवाथे	आप्नुध्वे
3.	आप्नोति	आप्नुतस्	आप्नुवन्ति	आप्नुते	आप्नुवाते	आप्नुवते

---

* The augment, without any exception in verbal conjugation, is the accented element in the verbal form of which it makes a part.

** The rare imv. in तात् (cf. § 196) would be formed thus: सुनुतात्.

Imperative.

1.	आप्नवानि	आप्नवाव	आप्नवाम	आप्नवै	आप्नवावहै	°वामहै
2.	आप्नुहि	आप्नुतम्	आप्नुत	आप्नुष्व	आप्नुवाथाम्	°ध्वम्
3.	आप्नोतु	आप्नुताम्	आप्नुवन्तु	आप्नुताम्	आप्नुवाताम्	°वताम्

Participle.

आप्नुवन्त्, f. आप्नुवती आप्नुवान, f. °आ

The other forms of this tense follow the model of सु.

391. 1. The root श्रु, 'hear', contracts to शृ before the class-sign, forming शृणो *çṛṇó* and शृणु *çṛṇu* as strong and weak stem; 2nd sing. imv. act. शृणु; 1st du. ind. act. शृणुवस् or शृण्वस्, etc.— 2. The root धू shortens its vowel in the present-system.

Vocabulary XXXV.

Verbs:

अश् (*açnuté*) acquire, obtain.
+ समुप obtain.

आप् (*āpnóti*, rarely *āpnuté*) acquire, reach.
+ अव, प्र, or सम्, reach.

चि (*cinóti, cinuté*) gather.
+ प्र or सम्, gather.
+ निस् or विनिस्, decide, conclude.

चुद् + प्र (*pracodáyati*) urge on.

दु (*dunóti*), intr., burn, feel pain or distress; tr., pain or distress (*acc.*)

धू (*dhunóti, dhunuté*) shake.

1 वृ (*vṛṇóti, vṛṇuté*) cover, surround.
+ आ cover, etc..
+ अपा open.
+ वि explain, manifest.
+ सम् shut.

शक् (*çaknóti*) be able.

श्रु (*çṛṇóti, çṛṇuté*) hear.

स्तृ (*stṛṇóti, stṛṇuté*) scatter, strew.
+ उप scatter.

हि (*hinóti*) send.

हृ + प्रत्या (*pratyāhárati*) bring back.

Subst.:

आहार m., food.

दिवस m., day.

द्वाःस्थ m., doorkeeper.

पणि m. pl., *n. pr.*, certain demons.

प्रभाव m., might, power.

भोग m., enjoyment.
मूल n., root.
रस m., taste, feeling.
वानप्रस्थ m., a Brāhman in the third period of his life.
विप्र m., Brāhman.
शब्द m., sound; noise; word.

Adj.:
नव, f. °आ, new.
पुण्य, f. °आ, meritorious, holy, auspicious.
°भाज् sharing.
मनोहर, f. °आ, entrancing, agreeable.
रसवन्त्, f. वती, tasteful.
सदृश, f. °ई, similar; worthy.

Exercise XXXV.

आचाराद्विच्युतो विप्रो न वेदफलमश्नुते ।
आचारेण तु संयुक्तः संपूर्णफलभाग्भवेत् ॥ २० ॥

बलहीना अपि बुद्धिप्रभावेन महान्तं दुःखोदधिं तरीतुं* शक्नुवन्ति । १ । वानप्रस्थः शय्यार्थं भूमिं नवपत्त्रैर्हरिणचर्मभिश्चोपास्तृणोत् । २ । स्वपितरमुद्यानादाह्वातुं बालं प्रहिणु । ३ । हे मघवन् पणिभिरपहृता अस्मद्गाः प्रत्याहर्तुं मरुतः सहायानादाय गुहाया द्वारमपावृणुया इत्यृषिभिरिन्द्रः प्रार्थ्यत । ४ । वनवृक्षान्धुन्वानस्य वायोः शब्दं पथा** गच्छन्तावशृणव । ५ । पुण्यकर्मभिर्धर्मं संचित्य मृताः स्वर्गे जन्मान्तरे च विद्यारूपादीन्गुणानाप्नवाम । ६ । यज्ञेषु होतृप्रचोदिता अध्वर्यवः सोमं सुन्वताम् । ७ । महावने चिराचं परिभ्रम्य चतुर्थदिवसस्य मध्याह्ने गिरिशिखरमवाप्नुवत । ८ । मूलफलादि वन आहारार्थं प्राचिन्वीरंस्तपस्विनः । ९ । पण्डितः शिष्येभ्यः शब्दशास्त्रं व्यवृणोत् ॥ १० ॥

11. Having entered the temple of the worshipful(भगवत्)-Viṣṇu we heard the ear-entrancing (श्रुतिमनोहर) song-of-the-young-women (*use* जन *at end of cpd*). 12. Listen to this word of a devoted (स्निह्, *pass. part.*) friend. 13. The greedy (लुभ्, *pass. part.*), *who are* always gathering riches, never attain the enjoyment of

* Infin. of तॄ.
** The instr. is sometimes used to express the medium, or space or distance or road, traversed.

them. 14. By tasteful, well-composed poems ye may attain glory in the ten regions *of the world* (दिश्). 15. Çakuntalā, mayest thou get (*imv.*) a husband worthy-of-thee. 16. My-*two*-brothers determined to travel to Benares. 17. May the king's-sword bring grief to (दु, *imv.* or *opt.*) the hearts-of-the-wives-of-his-enemies. 18. Clouds cover the sky. 19. Let the doorkeeper close the door.

Lesson XXXVI.

392. Verbs. Class IV. B. *u*-class. The few roots (only six) of this sub-class end already in न् — except one, कृ, of considerable irregularity — and so add only उ as class-sign. The inflection is quite that of the *nu*-class, the उ being gunated in the strong forms, and dropped (optionally, but in fact nearly always) before व् and म् of 1st dual and plural.

393. Thus तन्, 'stretch', makes तनोमि, तनोषि, etc.; 1st du. तन्वस् (or तनुवस्), 1st pl. तन्मस् (or तनुमस्); mid. तन्वे, तन्वहे, तन्महे, etc. — all like a vowel-root of the *nu*-class.

394. The root 1कृ 'make', makes the strong stem करो, weak कुरु; the class-sign उ is always dropped before व् and म् in 1st du. and 1st pl., and also before य् of the opt. active. Thus:

Indicative.

	Active.			Middle.		
1.	करोमि	कुर्वस्	कुर्मस्	कुर्वे	कुर्वहे	कुर्महे
2.	करोषि	कुरुथस्	कुरुथ	कुरुषे	कुर्वाथे	कुरुध्वे
3.	करोति	कुरुतस्	कुर्वन्ति	कुरुते	कुर्वाते	कुर्वते

Imperfect.

1.	अकरवम्	अकुर्व	अकुर्म	अकुर्वि	अकुर्वहि	अकुर्महि
2.	अकरोस्	अकुरुतम्	अकुरुत	अकुरुथास्	अकुर्वाथाम्	अकुरुध्वम्
3.	अकरोत्	अकुरुताम्	अकुर्वन्	अकुरुत	अकुर्वाताम्	अकुर्वत

Imperative.

1.	करवाणि	करवाव	करवाम	करवै	करवावहै	करवामहै
2.	कुरु	कुरुतम्	कुरुत	कुरुष्व	कुर्वाथाम्	कुरुध्वम्
3.	करोतु	कुरुताम्	कुर्वन्तु	कुरुताम्	कुर्वाताम्	कुर्वताम्

Optative.

1.	कुर्याम्	कुर्याव	कुर्याम	कुर्वीय	कुर्वीवहि	कुर्वीमहि
	etc.	etc.	etc.	etc.	etc.	etc.

Participle.

कुर्वन्त्, f. कुर्वती   कुर्वाण, f. °आ.

395. This root sometimes assumes (or retains from a more original condition) an initial स् after the prefix सम्*; thus, संस्करोति, संस्कुरुते, समस्कुर्वन्.

396. The adverbial prefixes आविस् and प्रादुस्, 'forth to sight', 'in view'; तिरस् 'through', 'out of sight'; पुरस् 'in front, forward'; and the purely adverbial अलम् 'enough, sufficient', are often used with कृ, and with one or two other verbs, oftenest अस् 'be' and भू 'become'.

397. Any noun or adjective-stem is liable to be compounded with verbal forms or derivatives of the roots कृ and भू, in the manner of a verbal prefix. If the final of the stem be an *a*-vowel or an *i*-vowel, it is changed to ई; if an *u*-vowel, to ऊ. Consonantal stems take the form which they have before consonant-endings — of course with observance of the usual euphonic rules; but stems in अन् change those letters to ई. Thus, स्वीकरोति 'he makes his own', 'appropriates'; भस्मीकरोति (भस्मन्) 'he changes to ashes', i. e. 'burns': स्तम्भीभवति 'becomes a post' (स्तम्भ); शुचीभवति 'becomes pure' (शुचि); साधूकरोति 'makes holy'.

398. The suffixes ता (f.) and त्व (n.) are very extensively used to form abstract nouns, denoting 'the quality of being so-

* Also sometimes after परि and उप.

and-so', from both adjectives and nouns. Thus, क्षत्रियता f., क्षत्रियत्व n., 'the rank of a Kṣatriya'.

Vocabulary XXXVI.

Verbs:

कृ (*karóti*, *kuruté*) do, make.
 + **अप** do evil to, harm (*gen.*, *loc.*, *or acc.*).
 + **अलम्** prepare, adorn.
 + **आविस्** (*āviṣkaróti*) make known, exhibit.
 + **उप** do good to, benefit (*gen.*, *loc.*).
 + **तिरस्** hide; blame, find fault with (*acc.*).
 + **पुरस्** put at the head.
 + **प्रति** pay, recompense; punish (*acc. rei*, *gen.*, *dat. or loc. pers.*).
 + **प्रादुस्** make known, or visible.
 + **सम्** (§ 395) prepare, adorn; consecrate.

क्षन् (*kṣaṇóti*, *kṣaṇuté*) wound.

तन् (*tanóti*, *tanuté*) stretch, extend (tr.); perform (a sacrifice).
 + **आ** cause, bring about.
 + **प्र** spread abroad (tr.).

दुष् (*dúṣyati*) be defiled.

मन् (*manuté*) think, consider.

Subst.:

अग्निहोत्रिन् m., priest of a certain kind.

अन्वय m., progeny, descendant.

अभिप्राय m., plan; view; opinion.

उरस् n., breast.

कलिङ्ग m., name of a tribe.

कान्ति f., charm, grace.

चमत्कार m., astonishment.

चातुर्मास्य n., a certain sacrifice.

चौलुक्य m., name of a tribe.

तिरस्करिणी f., veil.

दोष m., fault.

नीति f., conduct of life; ethics; politics.

भूभुज् m., king.

महानस n., kitchen.

मांस n., flesh.

लवण n., salt.

व्यञ्जन n., spice.

व्यवहार m., trade.

संशय m., doubt.

सूद m., cook.

Adj.:
अन्ध, f. °आ, blind.
अवश्यम्, *Adv.*, necessarily.
°ज्ञ, f. °आ, knowing.
°भुज् enjoying.
वल्लभ, f. °आ, dear.
व्यलीक, f. °आ, wrong, false.
शुभ, f. °आ, good, proper.
सज्ज, f. °आ, ready.

Exercise XXXVI.

यो ऽनधीत्य द्विजो वेदमन्यत्र कुरुते श्रमम् ।
स जीवन्नेव शूद्रत्वमाशु गच्छति सान्वयः* ॥ २१ ॥
यत्करोत्यशुभं कर्म शुभं वा यदि सत्तम ।
अवश्यं तत्समाप्नोति पुरुषो ऽत्र न संशयः ॥ २२ ॥
कुर्वन्नपि व्यलीकानि यः प्रियः प्रिय एव सः ।
अनेकदोषदुष्टो ऽपि कायः कस्य न वल्लभः ॥ २३ ॥

यो ब्रह्मणा कर्णावावृणोति तं पितरं मातरं च मन्वानो न द्रुह्येत्तस्मै कदाचन ।१। इदं ते लोभान्धस्य वृत्तं मनसि चमत्कारमातनोति ।२। भो राजन् नीतिज्ञानां मन्त्रिणामभिप्रायं श्रुत्वा यदुचितं तत्स्वीकुरुष्व ।३। अस्मद्यशांसि दिक्षु प्रतनुयुरिति मत्वा भूयसीं श्रियं भूभुजः कविभ्यो विभजन्ति ।४। मांसमूलफलादि प्रभूतव्यञ्जनैः सूदा महानसे संस्कुर्युः ।५। प्रभुषूपागतेषु शूरा युद्धाय सज्जीभूय स्वगुणानाविष्कुर्वन्तु ।६। अप्सरसस्तिरस्करिण्या वपुस्तिरस्कुर्वते ऽविज्ञाताश्च मनुष्यानुपागच्छन्ति ॥ ७ ॥

8. Every-year an Agnihotrin must perform the Cāturmāsya (*pl.*). 9. Mayest thou, O Great-King, protect thy kingdom, benefitting thy friends and harming thy enemies. 10. Brāhmans find fault with the trade-in-salt. 11. What thou didst (*mid.*), that distresses thy friends even now. 12. May I recompense him (*dat.*) who has done me a service. 13. By the command of the great-king consecrate the four princes according to the law (विधि, *instr.*). 14. The Cāulukyas held sway (राज्यं कृ) in Anahilapāṭaka 247 years. 15. By-the-charm-of-her-face the lotus-eyed eclipses (तिरस्कृ) even the moon. 16. If one consecrates a scholar, teaches him, makes

* Poss. cpd, cf. § 374, 5.

him holy, then this one becomes his child (प्रजा). 17. The king-of-the-Kaliṅgas wounded his enemy in the breast with an arrow.

Lesson XXXVII.

399. Verbs. *nā-class.* The class-sign is in the strong forms the syllable ना *nā́* [णा *ṇā́*], accented, which is added to the root; in the weak forms it is नी *nī* [णी *ṇī*]; but before an initial vowel of an ending the ई *ī* of नी *nī* [णी *ṇī*] disappears altogether.

400. Thus, क्री 'buy': strong stem क्रीणा *krīṇā́*, weak क्रीणी *krīṇī* (before a vowel, क्रीण् *krīṇ*).

Indicative.

	Active.			Middle.		
1.	क्रीणामि	क्रीणीवस्	क्रीणीमस्	क्रीणे	क्रीणीवहे	क्रीणीमहे
2.	क्रीणासि	क्रीणीथस्	क्रीणीथ	क्रीणीषे	क्रीणाथे	क्रीणीध्वे
3.	क्रीणाति	क्रीणीतस्	क्रीणन्ति	क्रीणीते	क्रीणाते	क्रीणते

Imperfect.

1.	अक्रीणाम्	अक्रीणीव	अक्रीणीम	°णि	°णीवहि	°णीमहि
2.	अक्रीणास्	अक्रीणीतम्	अक्रीणीत	°णीथास्	°णाथाम्	°णीध्वम्
3.	अक्रीणात्	अक्रीणीताम्	अक्रीणन्	°णीत	°णाताम्	°णत

Imperative.

1.	क्रीणानि	क्रीणाव	क्रीणाम	क्रीणै	क्रीणावहै	क्रीणामहै
2.	क्रीणीहि	क्रीणीतम्	क्रीणीत	क्रीणीष्व	क्रीणाथाम्	क्रीणीध्वम्
3.	क्रीणातु	क्रीणीताम्	क्रीणन्तु	क्रीणीताम्	क्रीणाताम्	क्रीणताम्

Optative.

1.	क्रीणीयाम्	क्रीणीयाव	क्रीणीयाम	क्रीणीय	क्रीणीवहि	क्रीणीमहि
	etc.	etc.	etc.	etc.	etc.	etc.

Participle.

क्रीणन्त्, f. क्रीणती   क्रीणान, f. °ना

401. The ending of the 2nd sing. imv. act. is हि, never धि; and there are no examples of its omission. But roots of this class ending in a consonant substitute for both class-sign and ending in this person the peculiar ending आन *ānā*; thus, बधान, अशान, स्तभान, गृहाण (see §§ 402, 403).

402. The roots ending in ऊ shorten that vowel before the class-sign; thus, पू, पुनाति, पुनीते. The root ग्रह् is weakened to गृह्; thus, गृह्णाति.

403. A few roots which have a nasal in some forms outside the present-system, lose it in the present; thus, ग्रथ् or ग्रन्थ्, ग्रथ्नाति; बन्ध्, बध्नाति; स्तभ् or स्तम्भ्, स्तभ्नाति. Similarly, ज्ञा makes जानाति.

---

404. **Root-class.** In this class there is no class-sign; the root itself is also present-stem, and to it are added directly the personal-endings; in the opt. (and subj.: § 60, end) of course combined with the mode-sign. The root-vowel takes *guṇa*, if capable of it, in the strong forms.

405. **Roots ending in vowels.** Roots in आ of this class are inflected only in the active. In the 3rd pl. impf. act. they may optionally take as ending उस् instead of अन्, the आ being lost before it.*

406. Thus, या 'go':

	Indicative.			Imperfect.		
1.	यामि	यावस्	यामस्	अयाम्	अयाव	अयाम
2.	यासि	याथस्	याथ	अयास्	अयातम्	अयात
3.	याति	यातस्	यान्ति	अयात्	अयाताम्	अयान् or अयुस्

---

* The same ending is also allowed and met with in a few rocts ending in consonants; viz. 1विद् 'know', चक्ष्, द्विष्, दुह्, मृज्.

	Imperative.			Optative.		
1.	यानि	याव	याम	यायाम्	यायाव	यायाम
2.	याहि	यातम्	यात	यायास्	यायातम्	यायात
3.	यातु	याताम्	यान्तु	यायात्	यायाताम्	यायुस्

Part. यान्त्, f. यान्ती or याती (260).

Vocabulary XXXVII.

Verbs:

2अश् (*açnáti*) eat.

क्री (*krīṇáti, krīṇīté*) buy.

ग्रन्थ् (*grathnáti*) string together; compose.

ग्रह् (*gṛhṇáti, gṛhṇīté*) take, seize.
 + नि hold, restrain, check.
 + प्रति take, receive.

ज्ञा (*jānáti, jānīté*) know.
 + अनु allow, permit.

2पा (*páti*) protect.

पुष् (*puṣṇáti*) make increase or grow.

पू (*punáti, punīté*) clean.

प्री (*prīṇáti, prīṇīté*), act., delight; mid., rejoice.

प्लु + आ (*āplávate*) drench.

बन्ध् (*badhnáti, badhnīté*) bind; catch; join; compose.

भा (*bháti*) gleam, glance.

मा (*máti*) measure.
 + निस् work, create.

मुष् (*muṣṇáti*) steal, rob.

2लुठ् (लुण्ठ्) + निस् steal.

2वृ (*vṛṇīté*: also *varáyati, -te*) choose.

शिष् + उद् remain over.

स्तृ (*stṛṇáti, stṛṇīté*; see also in Vocab. XXXV) strew.

स्ना (*snáti*) bathe.

हन् + अप remove.

Subst.:

अञ्जलि m., a gesture of respectful greeting.*

इच्छा f., wish.

उदय m., rise.

कला f., crescent.

कृति f., work (literary).

कोष m., treasure; treasury.

क्षण m., n., moment; time.

चामीकर n., gold.

---

* The two hands hollowed and opened, and raised to the forehead.

दानव m., demon.

नाग m., snake.

नेत्र n., leading-rope, cord.

मन्थन् (§ 278) m., stirring-stick.

मन्दर m., *n. pr.*, a mountain.

यूप m., sacrificial post.

ललाट n., forehead.

1**वर** (*vará*) m., suitor, bridegroom.

2**वर** (*vára*) m., choice, privilege, favor.

शेष m., *n. pr.*, a snake-demon who supports the earth.

समुन्नति f., height, elevation; high position.

Adj.:

अद्यतन* of to-day.

धार्मिक right, just.

प्रसन्न (part of **प्र-सद्**) kindly disposed.

°**विद्** knowing.

विवेकिन् shrewd.

Adv.:

समक्षम् before, in the preseuce of (*w. gen.*).

Exercise XXXVII.

परकाव्येन कवयः परद्रव्येण चेश्वराः ।
निर्लुण्ठितेन स्वकृतिं पुष्णन्त्यद्यतने यथा ॥ २४ ॥
विवेकिनमनुप्राप्य गुणा यान्ति समुन्नतिम् ।
सुतरां रत्नमाभाति चामीकरनियोजितम् ॥ २५ ॥

यज्ञं विधातुमिच्छन्यजमानः प्रथमं वेदविद ऋत्विजो वृणीताम् ।१। यज्ञेषु पशून्स्वलंकृतेषु यूपेषु रज्जुभिर्बध्नन्ति ॥ २ ॥ देवानां कोपाग्निं शान्तिं नेतुं तान्स्तुतिभिर्नरराजो ऽप्रीणात् ।३। प्रसन्ना वयं वरं वृणीष्वेति तैरुक्तो राजा धार्मिकत्वमवृणीत ॥ ४ ॥ सोमं दृषद्भ्यां सुत्वाध्वर्यवस्तं पुनन्तु ॥ ५ ॥ मन्दरपर्वतं मन्थानं शेषनागं च नेत्रं कृत्वा देवदानवा अमृतार्थं क्षीरोदधिममथ्नन् ॥ ६ ॥ यथा सूर्य उदये भाति तथा पापान्यपहत्य गङ्गाजलाप्लुता नरा विभान्ति ॥ ७ ॥ कुङ्कुमार्घेण गृह्णीयात्कुसुमाञ्जलिकर्मणा ॥ ८ ॥

9. Allow me to go now. 10. Take these jewels which I have

---

* With the suffix **तन** (sometimes **त्न**) are made adjectives from adverbs, especially of time; thus, **प्रत्न** 'ancient', **प्रातस्तन** 'early', **श्वस्तन** 'of the morrow'.

given you (*pass. constr.*). 11. Let the great poet weave (ग्रन्थ्, बन्ध्) a verse-wreath of word-pearls (*instr.*). 12. Every-day two thieves robbed the king's treasury. 13. He who receives (*part.*) gifts from every one is polluted (दुष्). 34. The Creator formed the world by his will (स्वेच्छया) alone. 15. Betake thyself (या) for salvation to the gods' protection. 16. Let kings restrain the wicked by punishments. 17. We saw Rāma's daughter coming out (*pres. part.*) of the house. 18. Let the bridegroom grasp the maiden's hand before the fire. 19. An Aryan must not eat another's leavings (उद्-शिष्, *pass. part.*, *neut. sing.*). 20. One must bathe daily in unconfined (*part. from* नि-रुध्) water. 21. May the three-eyed *god*, the great-lord (ईश्वर) whose-forehead-is-adorned-with-the-crescent, protect you.

Lesson XXXVIII.

407. Verbs. Root-class, cont'd.* Roots ending in an *i*-vowel or an *u*-vowel (except इ 'go') change these into इय् and उव् before vowel-endings in weak forms, when not gunated.

408. Root इ 'go' (act., but used in mid. with the prep. अधि: 'go over for oneself', i. e. 'repeat, learn, read'; the इ then becomes इय्, as above).

Indicative.

	Active.			Middle.	
1. एमि	इवस्	इमस्	अधीये	अधीवहे	अधीमहे
2. एषि	इथस्	इथ	अधीषे	अधीयाथे	अधीध्वे
3. एति	इतस्	यन्ति	अधीते	अधीयाते	अधीयते

* A number of roots belonging to this class accent the root-syllable throughout, in weak as well as in strong forms—except of course in the imperfect.

Imperfect.

(for augment cf. § 179.)

1.	आयम्	ऐव	ऐम	अध्यैयि	अध्यैवहि	अध्यैमहि
2.	ऐस्	ऐतम्	ऐत	अध्यैथास्	अध्यैयाथाम्	अध्यैध्वम्
3.	ऐत्	ऐताम्	आयन्	अध्यैत	अध्यैयाताम्	अध्यैयत

Imperative.

1.	अयानि	अयाव	अयाम	अध्ययै	अध्ययावहै	अध्ययामहै
2.	इहि	इतम्	इत	अधीष्व	अधीयाथाम्	अधीध्वम्
3.	एतु	इताम्	यन्तु	अधीताम्	अधीयाताम्	अधीयताम्

Optative.

इयाम् etc., 3rd pl. इयुस्   अधीयीय etc.

Participle.

यन्त्, f. यती   अधीयान, f. °आ

409. The root शी (mid.), 'lie', has *guṇa* throughout: thus, शये, शेषे, शेते, शेवहे etc.; impf. अशयि, अशेथास् etc.; opt. शयीय etc., part. शयान. Other irregularities are the 3rd persons pl.: indic. शेरते, imv. शेरताम्, impf. अशेरत.

410. The roots of this class ending in उ have in their strong forms the *vṛddhi* instead of the *guṇa*-strengthening before an ending beginning with a consonant.

411. Thus, स्तु 'praise':

Indicative.

	Active.			Middle.		
* 1.	स्तौमि	स्तुवस्	स्तुमस्	स्तुवे	स्तुवहे	स्तुमहे
2.	स्तौषि	स्तुथस्	स्तुथ	स्तुषे	स्तुवाथे	स्तुध्वे
3.	स्तौति	स्तुतस्	स्तुवन्ति	स्तुते	स्तुवाते	स्तुवते

Imperfect. Act.: 1. अस्तवम्, 2. अस्तौस्, 3. अस्तौत्, 3rd pl. अस्तुवन्. Mid.: 1. अस्तुवि, 3rd pl. अस्तुवत.

Imperative. Act.: स्तवानि, स्तुहि, स्तौतु, स्तवाव etc., 3rd pl. स्तुवन्तु. Mid.: स्तवै, स्तुष्व, स्तुताम्, स्तवावहै etc., 3rd pl. स्तुवताम्.

Optative. स्तुयाम् etc. स्तुवीय etc.

---

* स्तवीमि also found.

Participle. Act.: सुवन्त्, f. °वती. Mid.: सुवान.

412. The root ब्रू, 'say', takes the union-vowel ई after the root when strengthened, before the initial consonant of an ending.* Thus:

Indicative.

	Active.			Middle.		
1.	ब्रवीमि	ब्रूवस्	ब्रूमस्	ब्रुवे	ब्रूवहे	ब्रूमहे
2.	ब्रवीषि	ब्रूथस्	ब्रूथ	ब्रूषे	ब्रुवाथे	ब्रूध्वे
3.	ब्रवीति	ब्रूतस्	ब्रुवन्ति	ब्रूते	ब्रुवाते	ब्रुवते

Imperfect. Act.: अब्रवम्, अब्रवीस्, अब्रवीत्; अब्रूव etc.; 3rd pl. अब्रुवन्. Mid.: अब्रुवि, अब्रूथास् etc.; 3rd pl. अब्रुवत.

Imperative. Act.: ब्रवाणि, ब्रूहि, ब्रवीतु; ब्रवाव etc.; 3rd pl. ब्रुवन्तु. Mid.: ब्रवै, ब्रूष्व etc.

Optative. Act.: ब्रूयाम् etc. Mid.: ब्रुवीय etc.

Participle. Act.: ब्रुवन्त्. Mid.: ब्रुवाण.

413. **Emphatic Pronoun.** The uninflected pronominal word स्वयम् signifies 'self', 'own self'. It is oftenest used as a nominative, along with words of all persons and numbers; but not seldom it represents other cases also.

Vocabulary XXXVIII.

Verbs:

इ (*éti*) go.
+ अधि (*adhīté*) repeat, read.
+ अप (*apāiti*) go away, depart.
+ अभि approach.
+ अस्तम् set (of heavenly bodies).
+ उद् rise (of heavenly bodies).
+ उप approach.

ब्रू (*bravīti, brūté*) speak, say, state.
+ प्र explain, teach; announce.
+ वि explain, etc.

रु (*rāúti*) cry, scream.
+ वि scream.

शी (*çeté*) lie, sleep.
+ अधि lie asleep on (*acc.*).

सू (*sūté*) bring forth, bear.
+ प्र bring forth.

स्तु (*stāúti*) praise.

---

* Special irregularities in this verb are occasionally met with, such as ब्रूमि, ब्रवीहि. Some of the verbs in उ are allowed to be inflected like ब्रू, but forms so made are rare.

Subst.:
जिन m., *n. pr.*, a name of Buddha.
जिह्वा f., tongue.
नीलकण्ठ m., *n. pr.*
न्याय m., logic.
पुष्प n., flower.
प्रश्न m., question.
मानस n., sense, understanding.
वध m., killing, murder.
शुनःशेप m., *n. pr.*
सहचर m., companion; **°री** f., wife.
साक्षिन् m., witness.
सारस m., crane.

Adj.:
उद्यत, f. **°आ**, ready.
उद्योगिन् diligent, energetic.
करुण, f. **°आ**, lamentable
°कारिन् making, doing.

Adv.:
अधस् below, down, on the ground.

Exercise XXXVIII.

पुष्पाणीव विचिन्वन्तमन्यत्र गतमानसम् ।
अनवाप्तेषु कामेषु मृत्युरभ्येति मानवम् ॥ २६ ॥

भो दुष्कृतकारिणः । अस्माद्वनादपेतेति क्रोधादृषिराश्रमहरिण-वधोद्यतान्व्याधानब्रवीत् ॥ १ ॥ गुरुमभिवाद्य शिष्यस्तं ब्रूयादधीष्व भो (§ 264) इति ॥ २ ॥ कानि शास्त्राणि काश्यां त्वमध्येथाः । ३ । न्यायादीनि षड् दर्शनानि श्रीनीलकण्ठपण्डितस्य गृहे ऽहमध्यैयि ॥ ४ ॥ अग्नीषोमा-वष्टाभिर्ऋग्भिर्ऋषिरस्तौदिन्द्रावरुणौ च तिसृभिः ॥ ५ ॥ उद्योगिनं पुरुषसिंह स्वयमुपैति लक्ष्मीः ॥ ६ ॥ सा जिह्वा या जिनं स्तौति तच्चित्तं यज्जिने रतम् ॥ ७ ॥ आचार्याः शिष्यान्धर्मं प्रब्रुवते ॥ ८ ॥ हतसहचराः सारसाः करुणं विरुवन्ति ॥ ९ ॥ श्रीमद्भी राजभिराहूताः पण्डिताः सभां यन्ति धर्मप्रश्नांश्च विब्रुवते ॥ १० ॥

11. The three wives of Daçaratha bore four sons. 12. Rāma and Lakṣmaṇa, followed-by-Sītā, went (इ) into the forest. 13. Women whose-husbands-are-dead must sleep six months on the ground. 14. A witness stating *anything* other-*than-what-was-*seen-*or*-heard is to be punished (*fut. pass. part.*). 15. All guilt departs from one-who-has-done-penance. 16. One must not look

at (प्र-इष्) the rising or the setting sun. 17. Why hast thou come (अभि-इ) to-my-house with-wife and with-children? 18. "Praise Varuṇa": thus the gods addressed Çunaḥçepa *who was* bound to the sacrificial post. 19. Always speak the truth. 20. In a kingless land the rich do not sleep in peace (सुखेन).

Lesson XXXIX.

414. Verbs. Root-class, cont'd. Roots ending in consonants. The endings of the 2nd and 3rd sing. impf. act. are generally dropped, and the resulting root-final treated according to the usual rules for finals.* Cf. §§ 239, 242. But a root ending in a dental mute sometimes drops this final mute instead of the added स् in the second person; and, on the other hand, a root or stem ending in स् sometimes drops this स् instead of the added त् in the third person: in either case establishing the ordinary relation of स् and त् in the second and third persons.

415. Roots in च् and ज् substitute क् for those letters before त्, थ् and स् (which then becomes ष्); and ग् before ध्. Thus, वच् 'speak': वच्मि, वक्षि, वक्ति (only these three forms used).

416. Root 1विद् 'know, (act. only):

	Indicative.			Imperfect.		
1.	वेद्मि	विद्वस्	विद्मस्	अवेदम्	अविद्व	अविद्म
2.	वेत्सि	वित्थस्	वित्थ	अवेस् or अवेत्	अवित्तम्	अवित्त
3.	वेत्ति	वित्तस्	विदन्ति	अवेत्	अवित्ताम्	अविदुस्

Imv.: वेदानि, विद्धि, वेत्तु; वेदाव, वित्तम्, वित्ताम्; वेदाम, वित्त, विदन्तु. — **Opt.:** विद्याम्, etc.

* In the inflection of roots with final consonant, of this class and the reduplicating and nasal classes, euphonic rules find very frequent application. The student is therefore advised at this point to read carefully the chief rules of euphonic change in Whitney's Grammar, §§ 139–232 (the two larger sizes of print).

417. This root also makes a perfect without reduplication (but otherwise regular) which has always the value of a present. The forms of the indic. are:

Sing. 1. **वेद**, 2. **वेत्थ**, 3. **वेद**; du. 1. **विद्व**, 2. **विदथुस्**, 3. **विदतुस्**; pl. 1. **विद्म**, 2. **विद**, 3. **विदुस्**. The participle is **विद्वांस्**, f. **विदुषी** (cf. § 268).

418. The root **अद्**, 'cat' (act.), inserts **अ** before the endings of the 2nd and 3rd sing. impf.; thus, **आदस्**, **आदत्**.

419. The root **हन्**, 'kill' (act.), is treated somewhat as are noun-stems in **अन्** in declension (§ 283). Thus:

	Indicative.			**Imperfect.**		
1.	हन्मि	हन्वस्	हन्मस्	अहनम्	अहन्व	अहन्म
2.	हंसि	हथस्	हथ	अहन्	अहतम्	अहत
3.	हन्ति	हतस्	घ्नन्ति	अहन्	अहताम्	अघ्नन्

Imv.: हनानि, जहि*, हन्तु; हनाव, हतम्, हताम्; हनाम, हत, घ्नन्तु. — Opt.: हन्याम् etc. — **Part.: घ्नन्त्**, f. **घ्नती**.

420. Roots in **श्**, **ष्**, **क्ष्**, substitute **क्** before **स्** (which then becomes **ष्**), **ष्** before **त्** and **थ्** (which become **ट्** and **ठ्**), and **ड्** before **ध्** (which becomes **ढ्**). Thus, **द्विष्** 'hate' (act. and mid.):

	Indicative Act.			**Imperfect Act.**		
1.	द्वेष्मि	द्विष्वस्	द्विष्मस्	अद्वेषम्	अद्विष्व	अद्विष्म
2.	द्वेक्षि	द्विष्ठस्	द्विष्ठ	अद्वेट्	अद्विष्टम्	अद्विष्ट
3.	द्वेष्टि	द्विष्टस्	द्विषन्ति	अद्वेट्	अद्विष्टाम्	अद्विषन्

Imv. Act.: द्वेषाणि, द्विड्ढि, द्वेष्टु; द्वेषाव etc.

421. **चक्ष्**, 'see' (mid.): **Pres. Ind.: चक्षे, चक्षे, चष्टे; चक्ष्वहे, चक्षाथे, चक्षाते; चक्ष्महे, चड्ढ्वे, चक्षते. — Impf.: अचक्षि, अचष्ठास्, अचष्ट; अचक्ष्वहि, अचक्षाथाम्, अचक्षाताम्; अचक्ष्महि, अचड्ढ्वम्, अचक्षत.**

---

* **Anomalous dissimilation.**

422. 1. ईश्, 'rule' (mid.), inserts इ before endings beginning with स् and ध्; thus, 2nd sing. ईशिषे. — 2. वश्, 'wish' (act.), is in weak forms contracted to उश्; thus, 3rd. pl. उशन्ति.

423. मृज्, 'rub', 'clean' (act.), has *vṛddhi* in the strong forms, and optionally also in weak forms when the endings begin with a vowel. In the treatment of the root-final this verb follows the roots in श्. Thus, ind. 3rd sing. मार्ष्टि, du. मृष्टस्, pl. मृजन्ति or मार्जन्ति.

Vocabulary XXXIX.

Verbs:

ईश् (*īṣṭe*) rule, own (*w. gen.*).
चक्ष् (*cáṣṭe*)+आ relate; call, name.
+ व्या explain.
द्विष् (*dvéṣṭi, dviṣṭé*) hate.
+ प्र hate extremely.
मृज् (*mā́rṣṭi*) rub, wipe.
+ अप wipe away, off.
+ प्र wipe off.
राध् + अप (*aparādhnóti*) do wrong.
वश् (*váṣṭi*) wish.
1विद् (*vétti; véda*) know, consider.
हन् + अभि smite.
+ नि kill.

Subst.:

ओष्ठ m., lip.
क्षय m., decay, destruction.
चक्षुस् n., eye.
जेतृ m., conqueror.
दया f., compassion, pity.
प्रलय m., destruction.
भव m., *n. pr.*, a name of Çiva.
मन्त्र m., sacred text; spell, charm.
याम m., watch (of the night).
वृत्त n., conduct.
व्याकरण n., grammar.
व्यास m., *n. pr.*, a Rishi.
शङ्का f., hesitation.
शर्व m., *n. pr.*, a name of Çiva.
श्रुत n., learning.
सर्ग m., creation.
स्थिति f., condition, existence.

Adj.:

वाच्य, f. °आ, blameworthy, culpable.

Exercise XXXIX.

करोति पापं यो ऽज्ञानान्नात्मनो वेत्ति च क्षयम् ।
प्रद्वेष्टि साधुवृत्तांश्च स लोकस्यैति वाच्यताम् ॥ २७ ॥
पञ्च पश्वनृते हन्ति दश हन्ति गवानृते ।
शतमश्वानृते हन्ति सहस्रं पुरुषानृते* ॥ २८ ॥

सर्वं वृत्तान्तं यथावृत्तमाचड्ढ्वम् ॥ १ ॥ शर्व इति प्राञ्चः शिवमाचक्षते भव इत्युदञ्चः ॥ २ ॥ प्रद्विषतीं भार्यां किं मां द्वेक्षीत्यब्रवीत्पतिः ॥ ३ ॥ पुराणेषु त्रिभुवनसर्गस्थितिप्रलयान्व्यासो व्याचष्टे । ४ । यो ऽस्मान्द्वेष्टि यं च वयं द्विष्मस्तमेभिर्मन्त्रैर्हनाम ॥ ५ ॥ यो ब्रह्मचर्यं चरित्वा गुरुणानुज्ञातो यथाविधि स्नाति तं सर्वलोकपूज्यं स्नातकं विदुः ॥ ६ ॥ अनपराद्धं तवोपकुर्वाणं कथं भोः पापात्मंस्त्वं मां हंसि ॥ ७ ॥ अशुचिलिप्तमङ्गं मृदा प्रमृष्टमद्भिः परिमृड्ढि ॥ ८ ॥ भवो दिवो भव ईष्टे पृथिव्याः ॥ ९ ॥ गां धयन्तीं परस्मै नाचक्षीत ॥ १० ॥ बद्धमपि पृथ्वीराजं निर्दया (§ 374, 6) यवना असिनाघ्नन् ॥ ११ ॥

12. Hear the words of the learned man who explains (*pres. part.*) the-science-of-grammar. 13. Know *that* Rāma (*acc.*) *is* the son, famous in the-three-worlds, of Daçaratha, and the conqueror of Rāvaṇa, lord-of-Lañkā. 14. Having sipped (आ-चम्) water thrice, one wipes the lips twice; according to others, once.** 15. Two warriors smote (अभि-हन्) with arrows the king-of-the-Añgas, who *had* murdered their companions. 16. Kill without hesitation even (अपि) a teacher who approaches (*past. pass. part.*) in order to kill *you*. 17. Why dost thou consider (विद्) me a Çūdra, *though* knowing (ज्ञा *ger.*) my learning-and-conduct? 18. Do not hate the sons-of-Pāṇḍu. 19. The women *whose*-sons-*were*-dead, having lamented greatly, wiped the tears from their eyes. 20. Thou, O Lord, rulest over bipeds and quadrupeds (*gen.*).

---

* Refers to false witness before a court. An untruth where small beasts (sheep, etc.) are concerned, involves the destruction of five ancestors; where cattle are concerned, of ten, etc.

** सकृदित्यन्ये.

Lesson XL.

424. Verbs. Root-class, cont'd. आस् 'sit' (mid.): **Indic.** आसे, आस्से, आस्ते; आस्वहे etc.; आस्महे, आद्ध्वे*, आसते. **Impf.** आसि, आस्थास्, आस्त etc. **Imv.** आसै, आस्स्व, आस्ताम् etc. **Part.** आसीन (unique).

425. The root शास्, 'command' (act.), substitutes in the weak forms with consonant-endings the weakened stem शिष्; thus, indic. sing. शास्मि etc.; du. शिष्वस् etc.; but 3rd pl. शासति. Impf.: अशासम्, अशास्, अशात्**; अशिष्व etc.; but 3rd pl. अशासुस्. Imv. 2nd sing. शाधि; 3rd pl. शासतु.

426. The extremely common root 1अस्, 'be' (act.), loses its vowel in weak forms, except when protected by the augment. The 2nd sing. imv. is एधि; in the 2nd sing. indic. one स् is omitted; in the 2nd and 3rd sing. impf. ई is inserted before the ending. Thus:

	Indicative.			Imperfect.		
1.	अस्मि	स्वस्	स्मस्	आसम्	आस्व	आस्म
2.	असि	स्थस्	स्थ	आसीस्	आस्तम्	आस्त
3.	अस्ति	स्तस्	सन्ति	आसीत्	आस्ताम्	आसन्

Imperative.

1.	असानि	असाव	असाम
2.	एधि	स्तम्	स्त
3.	अस्तु	स्ताम्	सन्तु

Opt.: स्याम् etc.; 3rd pl. स्युस्.
Part.: सन्त्, f. सती.

427. Roots in ह् (except दिह् and दुह्) combine ह् with त्, थ् and ध् into ढ्, and then lengthen preceding अ, इ, उ; before स्, ह् becomes क्; in 2nd and 3rd sing. impf. act. (where the endings are dropped) the ह् becomes ट्. Thus, लिह् 'lick' (act. and mid.): **Impf. act.:** अलेहम्, अलेट्, अलेट्; अलिह्व, अलीढम्,

* Or आध्वे. So आद्ध्वम् or आध्वम् (imv., impf.).

** See § 414. अशात् is said to be used in 2nd pers. also.

अलीढाम्; अलिह्म, अलीढ, अलिहन्. Imv. mid.: लेहै, लिक्ष्व, लीढाम्; लेहावहै, लिहाथाम्, लिहाताम्; लेहामहै, लीढ्वम्, लिहताम्.

428. In the two roots दुह्, 'milk' (act. and mid.), and दिह्, 'smear' (act.), the final ह् represents an earlier guttural which reappears in the inflection. Thus, from दुह्:

	Indicative.			Imperfect.		
1.	दोह्मि	दुह्वस्	दुह्मस्	अदोहम्	अदुह्व	अदुह्म
2.	धोक्षि*	दुग्धस्	दुग्ध	अधोक्	अदुग्धम्	अदुग्ध
3.	दोग्धि**	दुग्धस्	दुहन्ति	अधोक्	अदुग्धाम्	अदुहन्

Ind. mid.: दुहे, धुक्षे, दुग्धे; दुह्वहे etc. Impf. mid.: अदुहि, अदुग्धास्, अदुग्ध; अदुह्वहि etc.; अदुह्महि, अधुग्ध्वम्, अदुहत. Imv. mid.: दोहै, धुक्ष्व, दुग्धाम्; दोहावहै etc.; दोहामहै, धुग्ध्वम्, दुहताम्.

429. The roots रुद्, 'weep', स्वप्, 'sleep', अन्, 'breathe', श्वस्, 'breathe' (all act.), insert इ before all endings beginning with a consonant, except स् and त् of 2nd and 3rd sing. impf., where they insert either अ or ई. Thus, रुद्: Pres. indic.: रोदिमि, रोदिषि etc., 3rd pl. रुदन्ति. Impf.: अरोदम्, अरोदस् or °दीस्, °दत् or °दीत्; अरुदिव etc.; 3rd pl. अरुदन्. Imv.: रोदानि, रुदिहि, रोदितु etc. Opt.: रुद्याम् etc. (या being mode-sign).

Vocabulary XL.

Verbs:

अन् (*ániti*) breathe.
+ प्र (*prā́ṇiti*) live.

अस् (*ásti*) be.

आस् (*ā́ste*) sit.
+ उप sit by; wait upon; attend; reverence.

---

* cf. §§ 244, 249.

** When the final sonant aspirate of a root is followed by त् or थ् of an ending, the whole group is made sonant, and the aspiration of the root-final is not lost, but is transferred to the initial of the ending.

चल् + प्र-वि (*pravicálati*) move, stir (tr.).

दिह् (*dégdhi*) smear.

दुह् (*dógdhi, dugdhé*) milk.

मील् + नि (*nimīlati*) shut (the eyes).

रुद् (*róditi*) weep.

लिह् (*léḍhi, līḍhé*) lick.

+ अव lick.

विश् + समा approach.

शास् (*çásti*) command, govern.

श्वस् (*çvásiti*) breathe.

+ आ or समा breathe gently, revive.

+ वि be confident, trust (*w. gen. or loc. of pers.*)

स्था + उद्* (*uttiṣṭhati*) arise.

Subst.:

उपभोग m., enjoyment.

केश m., hair.

दान n., gift, generosity.

बाला f., girl, maiden.

मुसल m., n., club, pestle.

रुधिर n., blood.

सत्त्र n., sacrifice.

सवितृ m., *n. pr.*, the sun-god Savitar; the sun.

स्कन्ध m., shoulder.

Adj.:

धीर, f. °आ, firm, resolute.

निपुण, f. °आ, shrewd, skilled.

न्याय्य, f. °आ, right, proper.

प्रमत्त, f. °आ, careless.

Indecl.:

प्रातर् early, in the morning.

भृशम् greatly, much.

Exercise XL.

निन्दन्तु नीतिनिपुणा यदि वा स्तुवन्तु
लक्ष्मीः समाविशतु गच्छतु वा यथेष्टम् ।
अद्यैव वा मरणमस्तु युगान्तरे वा
न्याय्यात्पथः प्रविचलन्ति पदं न धीराः ॥ २९ ॥

स्तेनो मुसलं स्कन्धे कृत्वा मुक्तकेशो राजानमुपेत्य शाधि मामिति ब्रूयात् ॥ १ ॥ स्निग्धेषु पापेषु न विश्वसिति बुद्धिमान् ॥ २ ॥ महोदधिमध्ये शेषनागमधिशयानो विष्णुः सुखं स्वपिति ॥ ३ ॥ प्रमत्तैर्ब-

---

* After उद्, the initial स् of स्था and स्तम्भ् is dropped; thus, उत्थातुम् for उत्स्थातुम्.

त्विग्भिर्भूमौ निहितानि हवींषि श्वानाववालीढाम ॥ ४ ॥ सुखमास्तां भवानिति गन्तुमनुज्ञातो ऽपयन्सखा सखायं ब्रूयात् ॥ ५ ॥ सुन्दरि समाश्वसिहि समाश्वसिहीति भयनिमीलिताक्षीमुर्वशीं पुरूरवा अब्रवीत् ॥ ६ ॥ गुरुक्रोधभीताः शिष्या रात्रिं वेदानध्यैयत ॥ ७ ॥ अस्तु यशः श्रुतवृत्ते स्तां श्रियः सन्तु न तु भक्तिं विना स्वर्गं प्राप्नुयाः ॥ ८ ॥ दानोपभोगहीनः पुमाञ्श्वसन्नपि न जीवति ॥ ९ ॥ दीर्घसत्त्रमुपासते ये ब्रह्मचर्यं चरन्ति ॥ १० ॥

11. Long may the great-king govern the earth according to law. 12. *There* was a mighty king, Nala by name (नाम), son of Vīrasena. 13. The lion, satiated-with-the-blood-of-the-slain-gazelle, licked *his* mouth with *his* tongue. 14. Let the householder say to the guest: "where didst thou sleep during the night"? 15. The cowherd milked the cows twice daily. 16. The boy, beaten by *his* father, wept bitterly (भृशम्). 17. Whose daughter art thou, girl? 18. Know *that* that by which thou livest, and the whole world lives, *is* the world-spirit. 19. Having arisen in the morning, reverence the sun (सवितृ). 20. If you do not praise Rāma, there will be no salvation for you (*use* अस्, *in pres. opt.*).

Lesson XLI.

430. Verbs. Reduplicating Class. This class forms the present-stem by prefixing a reduplication to the root.*

431. The rules governing the reduplication are as follows:

1. The consonant of the reduplicating syllable is in general the first consonant of the root; thus, दा, ददा. But, (*a*) a non-aspirate is substituted for an aspirate; and (*b*) a palatal for a guttural

* Only a small proportion of the roots of this class retain the accent on the root-syllable in the strong forms. In the great majority, the accent is on the reduplication, both in the strong forms and in those weak forms whose endings begin with vowels.

or ह्; thus, धा, दधा; खिद्, चिखिद्; ह्री, जिह्री; (*c*) if the root begin with a sibilant followed by a non-nasal mute, the latter is repeated (with observance of *a*), not the sibilant; thus, स्था, तस्था.

2. A long vowel is shortened in the reduplicating syllable; and ऋ is replaced by इ; thus, ददा and दधा above; भी, बिभी; भृ, बिभृ.

432. The present-stem gunates the root-vowel in the strong forms; thus, बिभी, strong बिभे; बिभृ, strong बिभर्.

433. The verbs of this class lose the न् from the endings of the 3rd pl. in the active as well as in the middle; and in the 3d pl. impf. act. always take उस्, before which a final radical vowel has *guṇa*; thus, अबिभरुस्.

434. Root भृ, 'bear, carry'. For 2nd and 3rd sing. impf. act., cf. §§ 122, 414.

Indicative.

	Active.			Middle.		
1.	बिभर्मि	बिभृवस्	बिभृमस्	बिभ्रे	बिभृवहे	बिभृमहे
2.	बिभर्षि	बिभृथस्	बिभृथ	बिभृषे	बिभ्राथे	बिभृध्वे
3.	बिभर्ति	बिभृतस्	बिभ्रति	बिभृते	बिभ्राते	बिभ्रते

Imperfect.

1.	अबिभरम्	अबिभृव	अबिभृम	अबिभ्रि	अबिभृवहि	°भृमहि
2.	अबिभर्	अबिभृतम्	अबिभृत	अबिभृथास्	अबिभ्राथाम्	°भृध्वम्
3.	अबिभर्	अबिभृताम्	अबिभरुस्	अबिभृत	अबिभ्राताम्	°भ्रत

Imperative.

1.	बिभराणि	बिभराव	बिभराम	बिभरै	बिभरावहै	बिभरामहै
2.	बिभृहि	बिभृतम्	बिभृत	बिभृष्व	बिभ्राथाम्	बिभृध्वम्
3.	बिभर्तु	बिभृताम्	बिभ्रतु	बिभृताम्	बिभ्राताम्	बिभ्रताम्

Opt. act.: बिभृयाम् etc.; **mid.:** बिभ्रीय etc.

Part. act.: बिभ्रत् (§ 259), f. बिभ्रती; **mid.:** बिभ्राण.

435. The roots ¹दा, 'give', and ¹धा, 'put', lose their radical vowel in the weak forms, leaving the weak stems दद् and दध्.

In the 2nd sing. imv. act. they form देहि and धेहि. The inflection of धा is as follows:*

Indicative.

	Active.			Middle.		
1.	दधामि	दध्वस्	दध्मस्	दधे	दध्वहे	दध्महे
2.	दधासि	धत्थस्	धत्थ	धत्से	दधाथे	धद्ध्वे
3.	दधाति	धत्तस्	दधति	धत्ते	दधाते	दधते

Imperfect.

1.	अदधाम्	अदध्व	अदध्म	अदधि	अदध्वहि	अदध्महि
2.	अदधास्	अधत्तम्	अधत्त	अधत्थास्	अदधाथाम्	अधद्ध्वम्
3.	अदधात्	अधत्ताम्	अदधुस्	अधत्त	अदधाताम्	अदधत

Imperative.

1.	दधानि	दधाव	दधाम	दधै	दधावहै	दधामहै
2.	धेहि	धत्तम्	धत्त	धत्स्व	दधाथाम्	धद्ध्वम्
3.	दधातु	धत्ताम्	दधतु	धत्ताम्	दधाताम्	दधताम्

Opt. act.: दध्याम् etc.; mid.: दधीय etc.

Part. act.: दधत्, *f.* दधती; mid.: दधान.

436. The root 1दा is inflected in precisely the same way, but with change everywhere of ध् to द्, except where ध् belongs to the ending.

437. The root 1हा, 'quit, abandon' (act.), drops the आ in weak forms where the ending begins with a vowel, and in the opt.; thus, indic. 3rd sing. जहाति, pl. जहति; impf. 3rd. sing. अजहात्, pl. अजहुस्; opt. जह्यात्. The 2nd sing. imv. is जहीहि or जहिहि. In the other weak forms before consonant-endings the stem is either जही or जहि; thus, जहीमस् or जहिमस्.

438. 1मा 'measure' (mid.), and 2हा, 'move, go' (mid.), form

---

* In combination with त् or थ् of an ending, the ध् of दध् does not give द्ध, but follows the general rule of aspirate and of surd and sonant combination; and the lost aspiration is thrown back upon the initial of the root.

मिमी and जिह्री before consonant-endings, मिम् and जिह् before vowel-endings; thus, 3rd persons indic. मिमीते, मिमाते, मिमते.

439. हु 'pour, sacrifice' (act. and mid.), makes the 2nd sing. imv. जुहुधि; 3rd persons impf. अजुहोत्, अजुहुताम्, अजुहवुस्.

440. 1. भी, 'fear' (act.), may shorten its vowel in weak forms; thus, बिभीमस् or बिभिमस्, बिभीयात् or बिभियात्. — 2. ह्री, 'be ashamed' (act.), changes its weak stem जिह्री to जिह्रिय् before vowel-endings; thus, indic. 3rd persons जिह्रेति, जिह्रीतस्, जिह्रियति.

Vocabulary XLI.

Verbs:

1दा (*dádāti, datté*) give.
+ प्र entrust.
1धा (*dádhāti, dhatté*) put, place.
+ अपि close, shut.
+ आ put on; (*mid.*) take, receive.
+ वि arrange, ordain.
+ सम् unite, put together; lay on.
1हा (*jáhāti*) quit, abandon, neglect.
ह्री (*jihréti*) be ashamed.

Subst.:

अभय n., safety; feeling of safety.
असुर m., demon.
आहुति f., oblation.
महिष m., *n. pr.*
मृग m., gazelle.
वित्त n., possessions, wealth.
शेष m., n., rest, remainder.
स्नातक m., one who has performed the ablution customary at the end of religious pupilage.

Adj.:

दैव, f. °ई, divine.
विशिष्ट, f. °आ, excellent, remarkable.

Adv.:

सायम् at evening.

Exercise XLI.

यद्ददासि विशिष्टेभ्यो यच्चाश्नासि दिने दिने ।
तत्ते वित्तमहं मन्ये शेषं कस्यापि रक्षसि ॥ ३० ॥

यच्च काष्ठमयो* हस्ती यच्च चर्ममयो मृगः ।
यश्च विप्रो ऽनधीयानस्त्रयस्ते नाम बिभ्रति ॥ ३१ ॥

यः सर्वभूतेभ्यो ऽभयं दत्त्वा प्रव्रजति तस्माद्यतेर्भूतानि न बिभ्यति स च तेभ्यो न बिभेति ॥ १ ॥ सायं प्रातर्ब्रह्मचारी प्रत्यहं समिधमग्नावादध्यात् ॥ २ ॥ ये द्वे कालं विधत्तस्ते महती ज्योतिषी स्तवीमि** ॥ ३ ॥ नैकं पुत्रमन्यस्मै दद्यादन्यस्मात्प्रतिगृह्णीयाद्वा ॥ ४ ॥ यस्मान्महिषासुरात्सर्वे ऽपि देवा अबिभयुस्तं शिवस्य पत्नी पार्वती न्यहन् ॥ ५ ॥ भिक्षां भवति (voc. sing. f.) देहीति क्षत्रियो भिक्षां चरन्ब्रूयात् ॥ ६ ॥ रुजा जरसा वाक्रान्तं पतिं पत्नी कदापि न जह्यात् ॥ ७ ॥ यत्र भूषणालंकृतां कन्यां पिता यज्ञभूम्यामृत्विजे ददाति स दैवो विवाह उच्यते ॥ ८ ॥ शत्रूनायातो (part., acc. pl.) दृष्ट्वा क्षत्रियाविषू धनुषोः समधत्ताम् ॥ ९ ॥ प्रायश्चित्तार्थे ऽष्टशतं घृताहुतीनां जुहुधि ॥ १० ॥

11. Let the Adhvaryus pour the sacrificial offerings into the fire. 12. The seers ordain forty sacraments in the law-books (स्मृति). 13. Daçaratha entrusted his sons to Vasiṣṭha as scholars. 14. Meeting a woman in the forest, one should say to her: "Sister, be not afraid". 15. Let a Snātaka carry (wear) a garland, and an umbrella-and-shoes. 16. One who takes (*part.*) roots-fruits-*or*-grain from a strange-field, is to be punished. 17. Let the two doorkeepers close the door. 18. Do not neglect the teacher's command. 19. The royal-sage, who wore much jewelry, shone (वि-भा) with great-brilliancy, like the sun. 20. The scholars who-have-not-learned-*their*-lessons are ashamed before their teacher (*acc. or gen.*).

Lesson XLII.

441. Verbs. Nasal class. All roots of this class end in consonants. As class-sign they insert a nasal before the final con-

---

* With the suffix मय, f. °ई, are formed adjectives signifying 'made or composed or consisting of'. — In the second line, 'bear the name' merely, i. e. are not in reality such.

** See note on § 411.

sonant, unless one be there already (as in भञ्ज्); this nasal is adapted to the consonant, except in the strong forms, where it is expanded to the syllable न [ण], which bears the accent.

442. The combination of the final radical consonants with those of the personal endings is in accordance with the rules already given for the root and reduplicating classes.

443. Thus, युज् 'join'; strong stem युनज्, weak युञ्ज्.

Indicative.

Active.			Middle.		
युनज्मि	युञ्ज्वस्	युञ्ज्मस्	युञ्जे	युञ्ज्वहे	युञ्ज्महे
युनक्षि	युङ्क्थस्*	युङ्क्थ	युङ्क्षे	युञ्जाथे	युङ्ग्ध्वे
युनक्ति	युङ्क्तस्	युञ्जन्ति	युङ्क्ते	युञ्जाते	युञ्जते

Imperfect.

अयुनजम्	अयुञ्ज्व	अयुञ्ज्म	अयुञ्जि	अयुञ्ज्वहि	अयुञ्ज्महि
अयुनक्	अयुङ्क्तम्	अयुङ्क्त	अयुङ्क्थास्	अयुञ्जाथाम्	अयुङ्ग्ध्वम्
अयुनक्	अयुङ्क्ताम्	अयुञ्जन्	अयुङ्क्त	अयुञ्जाताम्	अयुञ्जत

Imperative.

युनजानि	युनजाव	युनजाम	युनजै	युनजावहै	युनजामहै
युङ्ग्धि	युङ्क्तम्	युङ्क्त	युङ्क्ष्व	युञ्जाथाम्	युङ्ग्ध्वम्
युनक्तु	युङ्क्ताम्	युञ्जन्तु	युङ्क्ताम्	युञ्जाताम्	युञ्जताम्

Opt. act.: युञ्ज्याम् etc.; **mid.:** युञ्जीय etc.

Part. act.: युञ्जन्त्, f. युञ्जती; **mid.:** युञ्जान.

444. Root रुध् 'obstruct'; strong stem रुणध्, weak रुन्ध्.

Indicative.

Active.			Middle.		
रुणध्मि	रुन्ध्वस्	रुन्ध्मस्	रुन्धे	रुन्ध्वहे	रुन्ध्महे
रुणत्सि	रुन्द्धस्	रुन्द्ध	रुन्त्से	रुन्धाथे	रुन्द्ध्वे
रुणद्धि	रुन्द्धस्	रुन्धन्ति	रुन्द्धे	रुन्धाते	रुन्धते

* Instead of युङ्क्थस्, युङ्ग्ध्वे, and the like, it is allowed (and more usual) to write युङ्थस्, युङ्ध्वे etc.; also रुन्धस्, रुन्धे etc., instead of रुन्द्धस् etc.; in each case omitting the consonant immediately following the nasal.

Imperative.

रुणधानि	रुणधाव	रुणधाम	रुन्धै	रुणधावहै	रुणधामहै
रुन्द्धि	रुन्द्धम्	रुन्द्ध	रुन्त्स्व	रुन्धाथाम्	रुन्द्ध्वम्
रुणद्धु	रुन्द्धाम्	रुन्धन्तु	रुन्द्धाम्	रुन्धाताम्	रुन्धताम्

Imperf. act.: अरुणधम्, अरुणत्, अरुणत्; अरुन्ध्व etc.; **mid.:** अरुन्धि etc. — **Opt. act.:** रुन्ध्याम् etc.; **mid.;** रुन्धीय etc. — **Part. act.:** रुन्धन्त्, f. रुन्धती; **mid.:** रुन्धान.

445. Roots पिष्, 'grind, crush' (act.); and हिंस्, 'injure, destroy' (act.):

Imperfect.

अपिनषम्	अपिंष्व	अपिंष्म	अहिनसम्	अहिंस्व	अहिंस्म
अपिनट्	अपिंष्टम्	अपिंष्ट	अहिनस्	अहिंस्तम्	अहिंस्त
अपिनट्	अपिंष्टाम्	अपिंषन्	अहिनस् or °नत्	अहिंस्ताम्	अहिंसन्

Ind. 2nd persons: पिनक्षि, पिंष्ठस्, पिंष्ठ; — हिनस्सि, हिंस्थस्, हिंस्थ. **Imv.** 2nd persons: पिण्ड्ढि, पिंष्टम्, पिंष्ट; — हिन्धि, हिंस्तम्, हिंस्त.

446. तृह्, 'crush' (act.), combines तृणह् with ति and तु into तृणेढि and तृणेढु.

Vocabulary XLII.

Verbs:

इध् (*inddhé*) kindle, light.

छिद् (*chinátti, chintté*) cut, cut off.

+ आ take away, remove.

+ उद् exterminate.

जागरय (caus. stem) awaken.

पिष् (*pinásti*) grind, crush.

भञ्ज् (*bhanákti*) break, destroy.

भिद् (*bhinátti, bhintté*) split.

भुज् (*bhunákti, bhuñkté*) eat, enjoy.

युज् (*yunákti, yuñkté*) join; yoke, harness.

+ नि appoint, establish.

रुध् (*runáddhi, runddhé*) obstruct, check; besiege.

शिष् (*çinásti*) leave, leave remaining.

+ वि set apart, distinguish.

हन् + सम् unite.

हिंस् (*hinásti*) injure, destroy.

Subst.:

अवस्था f., condition, state.

उषस् f., dawn; also personified, Uṣas, the Dawn.

कण्टक m., thorn; enemy.

ग्रास m., bite, mouthful.

तण्डुल m., rice.

पातक n., crime.

पौत्र m., grandson.

बन्धु m., relative.

लेखन n., writing, copying.

हिमवन्त् m., the Himālaya Mts.

Adj.:

उच्छ्रित high.

क्षात्र suitable for Kṣatriyas.

गृह्य domestic.

प्रतिकूल, f. °आ, unfavorable.

शुभ, f. आ, splendid, beautiful, excellent.

Exercise XLII.

यद्ध्यायति यत्कुरुते धृतिं बध्नाति यत्र च ।
तदवाप्नोत्ययत्नेन यो* हिनस्ति न किंचन ॥ ३२ ॥
यस्यां यस्यामवस्थायां यत्करोति शुभाशुभम् ।
तस्यां तस्यामवस्थायां तत्फलं समुपाश्नुते ॥ ३३ ॥
दूत एव हि संधत्ते भिनत्त्येव च संहतान् ।
दूतस्तत्कुरुते कर्म येन भिद्यन्ते वा न वा ॥ ३४ ॥

ये गा हिंसन्ति तेषां** गरीयः प्रायश्चित्तं विदधति तस्माद्गां मा हिन्धि ॥ १ ॥ जीवत्पुत्रपौत्रो वर्षशतं निष्कण्टकं राज्यं भुङ्क्ष्वेति कवयो महाराजमब्रुवन् ॥ २ ॥ यथा वातो बलेन वृक्षान्भनक्त्येवं त्वं मे द्विषो भङ्ग्धि ॥ ३ ॥ रणे शत्रुभिर्युध्यमानः शूरः कांश्चिदिषुभिरभिनत्केषांचिन्मूर्धहस्तपादादिकमसिनाच्छिनत् ॥ ४ ॥ प्रातरश्विनावुषसा स्वस्रा सह भूतानि जागरयितुं त्रिचक्रे रथे ऽश्वौ युङ्क्त इत्यृक्षु श्रूयते ॥ ५ ॥ यो भूमिदानमाच्छिन्द्याद् आच्छिद्यमानं वानुमोदते स पञ्चभिर्महापातकैः संयुक्तः स्यात् ॥ ६ ॥ अहो प्रतिकूलो विधिर्विपिनष्टि मनोरथं मे ॥ ७ ॥ यत्र पित्रादीनां बन्धूनां शिरांसि भिन्दन्तो रुदतीं कन्यां बलाद्धरन्ति तं क्षात्रं विवाहमृषयो विदुः ॥ ८ ॥

11. After Jayasiṅha had long besieged Girinagara, he destroyed

---

* The antecedent of this relative is the subject of अवाप्नोति.

** Translate as though dative.

(भज्) it at last. 12. An ascetic shall eat only 240 mouthfuls in a month (*loc.*). 13. "Kindle the fire; cut branches for firewood (समिधर्थम्); milk the cows; grind grain": thus said one priest to another *early* in the morning. 14. The teacher entrusted (नि-युज्) the scholars with the copying of the books (*cpd., dat.*). 15. The mountain-*range* Himavant checks the course of the clouds with its exceedingly-high peaks. 16. The doers-of-right (°कृत्) are happy in Heaven, enjoying the fruits-of-*their*-works. 17. A king who has conquered a foreign realm must not exterminate the royal-family. 18. Aryans must kindle the domestic-fire at the time-of-the-wedding. 19. Women pounded the rice with pestles.

Lesson XLIII.

447. Verbs. Perfect-System. In the later language the perfect-system comprises only an indicative mode and a participle, each both active and middle. Its formation is essentially alike in all verbs; its characteristics are: 1. reduplication; 2. distinction of strong and weak forms; 3. endings in some respects peculiar; 4. the frequent use of the union-vowel *i*.

448. Reduplication. 1. Initial consonants are reduplicated according to the rules given in Less. XLI for the reduplicated present-stem.

2. Medial and final vowels, short and long, are represented by the corresponding short vowel, diphthongs by their second element; but ऋ (or अर्) is represented always by अ, never by इ as in the reduplicated present-stem. Thus, क्रम्, चक्रम्; स्था, तस्था; सिच्, सिषिच्; सेव्, सिषेव्; गा, जगा; कृ, चकृ.

3. Initial अ, followed by a single consonant, becomes आ (through अ-अ); thus, अद्, आद्.

4. Initial इ and उ follow the same analogy; but in the strong

forms, where the root-vowel is gunated, the reduplicating vowel is protected from combination by the insertion of य् or व्; thus, इष्, strong perfect-stem इयेष् (*i-y-eṣ*) weak ईष् (i.e. *i-iṣ*); उच्, strong उवोच् (*u-v oc*), weak ऊच् (*u-uc*).

5. Roots beginning with vowels long by nature or position do not in general make the ordinary perfect-system, but use instead a periphrastic formation (see below). But आप् is an exception, making the constant perfect-stem आप्; and a few roots with initial अ or ऋ show the anomalous reduplication आन् in the perfect.*

449. Strong and weak forms. In the three persons sing. act. the root-syllable is accented, and exhibits usually a stronger form. As regards the strengthening:

1. In roots with medial vowels long by nature or position, and in those with initial आ, the difference of strong and weak forms does not appear, except in accented texts.

2. Medial and initial vowels are gunated, if possible, in the strong forms; thus, भिद्, w. बिभिद्, s. बिभेद्; इष्, w. ईष्, s. इयेष्; उच्, w. ऊच्, s. उवोच् (§ 448, 4).

3. Medial अ before a single final consonant is vriddhied in the 3rd pers., and optionally in the 1st; thus, from पच्, in 1st sing. either पपच् or पपाच्, in 2nd पपच्, in 3rd पपाच्.

4. A final vowel takes either *guṇa* or *vṛddhi* in the 1st person, *guṇa* in the 2nd, *vṛddhi* in the 3rd; thus, from नी, in 1st निने or निनै, 2nd निने, 3rd निनै.

450. The root भू makes, irregularly, the perfect-stem बभू, and adds व् before a vowel-ending.

451. Some roots, instead of strengthening the vowel in the

---

* The grammarians prescribe (doubtless falsely) this reduplication for all verbs beginning with अ or ऋ followed by more than one consonant.

strong forms, weaken it in the weak forms; some few even do both. See below.

452. Personal Endings. The perfect-endings are these:

	Active.			Middle.		
1.	*a*	*vá*	*má*	*é*	*váhe*	*máhe*
2.	*tha*	*áthus*	*á*	*sé*	*ā́the*	*dhvé*
3.	*a*	*átus*	*ús*	*é*	*ā́te*	*ré*

But roots ending in *ā* take *āu* in 1st and 3rd sing. act.; thus, स्था, तस्थौ.

453. Union-vowel. The endings beginning with consonants are in classical Sanskrit usually joined to the base by the union-vowel इ. The most important rules for the use of इ are as follows:

1. The रे of 3rd pl. mid. always has इ before it.

2. The other endings beginning with consonants, except थ, take it in nearly all verbs. But it is rejected throughout (except from रे) by eight verbs: viz. 1कृ 'make', भृ 'bear', सृ 'go', 2वृ 'choose', द्रु 'run', श्रु 'hear', स्तु 'praise', स्रु 'flow'.

3. For its use or omission in 2nd sing. act. the rules are too complicated to be given here.

454. With the union-vowel इ a final radical इ or ई is not combined into ई, but becomes य् or (if more than one consonant precede) इय्; thus, from नी, निन्यिव *ni-ny-i-va.*

Examples of inflection. A. Roots in final vowels.

455. I. Roots in इ or ई. The ए and ऐ of gunated and vriddhied vowels become अय् and आय् before the vowel beginning an ending. See also § 454.

Thus, 1. नी: **Act.:** Sing. 1. निनय or निनाय, 2. निनयिथ or निनेथ, 3. निनाय; du. 1. निन्यिव, 2. निन्यथुस्, 3. निन्यतुस्; pl. 1. निन्यिम, 2. निन्य, 3. निन्युस्. —**Mid.:** Sing. 1. निन्ये, 2. निन्यिषे, 3. निन्ये;

du. 1. निन्यिवहे, 2. निन्याथे, 3. निन्याते; pl. 1. निन्यिमहे, 2. निन्यिध्वे, 3. निन्यिरे.

2. क्री: **Act.:** Sing. 1. चिक्रय or चिक्राय, 2. चिक्रयिथ or चिक्रेथ, 3. चिक्राय; du. 1. चिक्रियिव, 2. चिक्रियथुस्, 3. ०यतुस्; pl. 1. चिक्रियिम, 2. चिक्रिय, 3. चिक्रियुस्.

456. II. Roots in उ or ऊ follow the model of the last-mentioned. Thus, स्तु: **Act.:** Sing. 1. तुष्टव or तुष्टाव, 2. तुष्टोथ (not तुष्टविथ — see § 453, 2), 3. तुष्टाव; du. 1. तुष्टुव, 2. तुष्टुवथुस्, 3. तुष्टुवतुस्. — लू: **Act.:** du. लुलुविव etc.

457. भू is irregular in the perfect. (Cf. § 450):

	Active.			Middle.		
1.	बभूव	बभूविव	बभूविम	बभूवे	बभूविवहे	बभूविमहे
2.	बभूविथ	बभूवथुस्	बभूव	बभूविषे	बभूवाथे	बभूविध्वे
3.	बभूव	बभूवतुस्	बभूवुस्	बभूवे	बभूवाते	बभूविरे

458. III. Roots in ऋ. 1. 1कृ (see § 453, 2):

1.	चकर, चकार	चकृव	चकृम	चक्रे	चकृवहे	चकृमहे
2.	चकर्थ	चक्रथुस्	चक्र	चकृषे	चक्राथे	चकृध्वे
3.	चकार	चक्रतुस्	चक्रुस्	चक्रे	चक्राते	चक्रिरे

So also भृ, सृ, 2वृ 'choose'. 2. The other roots in ऋ make the first persons thus: from धृ, दधर or दधार, दध्रिव, दध्रिम; दध्रे, दध्रिवहे, दध्रिमहे.

459. If the final ऋ be preceded by more than one consonant, the formation is as follows: स्मृ, 1. सस्मर or सस्मार, 2. सस्मर्थ, 3. सस्मार; du. सस्मरिव, सस्मरथुस्, etc. — the ऋ being gunated.

460. IV. Roots in आ (including those written by the natives with ए or ऐ or ओ). These take औ in 1st and 3rd sing. act.; and the आ is lost before vowel-endings and इ. 1. 1धा:

1.	दधौ	दधिव	दधिम	दधे	दधिवहे	दधिमहे
2.	दधाथ, दधिथ	दधथुस्	दध	दधिषे	दधाथे	दधिध्वे
3.	दधौ	दधतुस्	दधुस्	दधे	दधाते	दधिरे

2. प्या, ह्वा, and similar roots, make their weak forms from the

simpler root-forms पी, ह्व etc.; and ह्वा makes its strong forms also from हू; thus, जुहव or जुहाव etc.

B. Roots in final consonants.

461. I. With medial vowel capable of *guṇa*.

1. भिद्: **Act:** Sing. 1. बिभेद, 2. बिभेदिथ, 3. बिभेद; du. बिभिदिव etc.; pl. बिभिदिम etc. **Mid.:** बिभिदे etc. 2. So from तुद्: तुतोद etc.; 3. from दृश्: 1. ददर्श, 2. ददर्शिथ or दद्रष्ठ, 3. ददर्श; du. ददृशिव etc.

462. II. With initial vowel capable of *guṇa*.

1. इष्: Sing. 1. इयेष, 2. इयेषिथ, 3. इयेष; du. 1. ईषिव, 2. ईषथुस्, 3. ईषतुस्; pl. 1. ईषिम, 2. ईष, 3. ईषुस्. 2. उच्: उवोच etc. 3. The root इ, 'go', also follows this rule, forming इयाय etc., 3rd. pl. ईयुस्. 4. ऋच् makes (see § 448, 5) आनर्च, आनर्चिथ etc.

463. III. With initial अ.

अस्, आस etc.; अद्, आद etc. But अश् (originally अंश्) makes आनंश etc. (§ 448, 5).

464. IV. With medial अ.

1. क्रम्: **Act.:** sing. 1. चक्रम or चक्राम, 2. चक्रमिथ, 3. चक्राम; du. चक्रमिव etc. **Mid.:** चक्रमे etc.

Thus all such roots beginning with more than one consonant, or with an aspirate, a guttural mute, or ह्.

465. 2. Roots in general having medial अ before a single final consonant, and beginning also with a single consonant which is repeated unchanged in the reduplication — i. e. not an aspirate, a guttural, or ह् — contract with the reduplication into one syllable, with ए as its vowel, in the weak forms; and this is allowed also in 2nd sing act. when the union-vowel इ is taken.* Thus, पच्, s. पपच् and पपाच्, w. पेच्:

---

* Several roots not having the form here defined are said to undergo the same contraction, most of them optionally.

पपच, पपाच	पेचिव	पेचिम	पेचे	पेचिवहे	पेचिमहे
पपक्थ, पेचिथ	पेचथुस्	पेच	पेचिषे	पेचाथे	पेचिध्वे
पपाच	पेचतुस्	पेचुस्	पेचे	पेचाते	पेचिरे

466. 3. Certain roots beginning with व *va* (also one with य *ya*) and ending in one consonant, reduplicate with the syllable उ (the one root just mentioned, with इ), and abbreviate the व (य) of the root to उ (इ) in weak forms. They are treated like roots with initial उ (इ: § 462) but retain the full root form in the strong persons. These roots are वच्, वद्, वप्, वश्, वस् 'dwell', and वह्; also यज्. Thus, वच्: Act. sing. 1. उवच or उवाच, 2. उवक्थ or उवचिथ. 3. उवाच; du. ऊचिव (*u-uc-i-va*) etc. Mid. ऊचे etc. — यज्: Act. sing. 1. इयज or इयाज, 2. इयष्ठ or इयजिथ, 3. इयाज; du. ईजिव etc. Mid. ईजे etc.

467. 4. Several roots which have medial अ between single consonants, but cannot follow the rule of § 465, drop out the अ from the weak forms. These roots are, in the classical language, खन्, गम्, घस्, हन्; and also जन्, which might be expected to follow § 465. They form the weak stems चख्न्, जग्म्, जक्ष्, जघ्न्; and जज्ञ्. Thus, चखन or चखान etc., चख्निव etc. हन् makes its strong stem जघन् and जघान्.

468. 5. The roots व्यध्, स्वप्, and one or two others, reduplicate from the semivowel, and contract य and व to इ and उ in weak forms. Thus, strong सुष्वप् or सुष्वाप्, weak सुषुप्.

469. 1. The root अह्, 'speak', is found only in this tense, and only in the following forms: sing. 2. आत्थ, 3. आह; du. 2. आहथुस्, 3. आहतुस्; pl. 3. आहुस्. These forms have only the value of the present.—2. The root 1विद्, 'know', makes a perfect without reduplication, but otherwise regular, which has only present-value; see § 417. 2विद्, 'find', forms the regular विवेद्.

470. The roots चि, चित्, जि, and हि, form as perfect-stems चिकि, चिकित्, जिगि, and जिघि.

471. Perfect participle. 1. **Active.** The ending of the pf. part. active is वांस् (mid. वत्, w. उष्), which is added to the weak perfect-stem.* When this is monosyllabic the union-vowel इ is inserted (but not in the weakest cases, before उष्). Thus, *a.* from इष्, strong stem of part. ईषिवांस्, mid. ईषिवत्, w. ईषुष्; from पच्, पेचिवांस्, पेचिवत्, पेचुष्; from वच्, ऊचिवांस्, ऊचिवत्, ऊचुष्; from दा, ददिवांस्, ददिवत्, ददुष्. But, from नी, निनीवांस्, निनीवत्, निन्युष्; from स्तु, तुष्टुवांस्, तुष्टुवत्, तुष्टुवुष्; from भिद्, बिभिद्वांस्, बिभिद्वत्, बिभिदुष्. — *b.* The root गम् makes as its strong stem of pf. part. जगिमवांस् or जगन्वांस्, mid. जगिमवत् or जगन्वत्, weakest only जग्मुष्. Similarly, from हन्, जघ्निवांस् or जघन्वांस्, जघ्निवत् or जघन्वत्, जघ्नुष्. — *c.* 1विद्, 'know', makes विद्वांस् etc.; 2विद्, 'find', विविद्वांस् etc.

2. **Middle.** The pf. part. middle is made with the suffix आन, which is added to the weak stem as this appears in the middle voice; thus, बुध्, बुबुधान; धा, दधान; कृ, चक्राण; नी, निन्यान; तन्, तेनान.

Periphrastic Perfect.

472. Most roots beginning with a vowel long by nature or position adopt a periphrastic formation in the perfect tense; the same is also taken by the secondary conjugations, and optionally by a few primary roots not falling in the above category. It is made as follows:

473. To the accusative of a derivative noun-stem in आ, made from the present-stem which is the general basis of each conjugation, are added, for the active, the perfect active forms of कृ or अस् (or, very rarely, of भू); for the middle, only the perfect middle forms

---

* Mechanically, the weakest participle-stem is identical with the 3rd pl. act. (of course, ष् instead of स्).

of कृ. Thus, from चोरयति, pf. चोरयामास or चोरयांचकार; from ईष्, ईषांचक्रे.

---

474. Force of the Perfect. In classical Sanskrit the perfect coincides in meaning with the imperfect, as a tense of narration, but is less often met with.

Lesson XLIV.

475. Verbs. Future-System (and Conditional). The verb has two futures: I. The simple, or *s*-future, which is by far the older, and much more common, than the other; and II. the periphrastic future.

476. I. Simple Future. This tense contains an indicative mode and a participle, active and middle. It may be made from all verbs. The tense-sign is the syllable स्य, added to the root either directly, or by the union-vowel इ (in the latter case becoming इष्य). The root has the *guṇa*-strengthening when possible; and some roots with medial ऋ gunate with र instead of अर्. The inflection is precisely like that of the present indicative of a verb of the *a*-conjugation; thus, from भू, भविष्यति, °ते.

477. When इ is not taken, final radical consonants suffer the same changes before स्य as before स् in the inflection of the root-class or reduplicating or nasal class. Thus, from दुह्, धोक्ष्यति; मुच्, मोक्ष्यति; भिद्, भेत्स्यति; रुध्, रोत्स्यति; नम्, नंस्यति; लिह्, लेक्ष्यति; द्विष्, द्वेक्ष्यति; दृश्, द्रक्ष्यति. The root वस् 'dwell', makes वत्स्यति.

478. 1. Most roots ending in vowels reject इ; thus, दा, दास्यति; गा, गास्यति; जि, जेष्यति; श्रु, श्रोष्यति. 2. But all roots in ऋ take इ; thus, कृ, करिष्यति; तॄ, तरिष्यति; and also the roots श्री (श्रयिष्यति) and भू (भविष्यति). 3. ग्रह् makes ग्रहीष्यति.

479. In general, the verbs which take इ in the infinitive and periphrastic future (see below), take it also in this tense. But the accordance is far from complete; and these parts should be learned, as a matter of usage, for any given verb.

480. Stems of causative inflection, and denominatives in अय, make their future-stems in अयिष्य; thus, चुर्, चोरयिष्यति.

481. Participle. The participles, act. and mid., are made from the future-stem precisely as from the present-stem; thus, दा, दास्यन्त् (f. °स्यती), दास्यमान; कृ, करिष्यन्त्, करिष्यमाण. Cf. §§ 260, 262.

---

482. Conditional. A tense called the conditional (indic. only) is made from the stem of the simple future precisely as the imperfect is made from the present-stem, and similarly inflected. Thus, अदास्यम्, अकरिष्यम्; अदास्ये, अकरिष्ये. It is of extremely rare occurrence.

---

483. II. Periphrastic Future. This tense, which is allowed to be made from all verbs, contains a single indicative tense, active,* It is formed by the *nomen agentis* in तृ, having the value of a future active participle, to the nom. sing. of which (ता) are added, in the 1st and 2nd persons of all numbers, the corresponding inflected forms of the pres. of 1अस् 'be'. In the 3rd persons the *nomen agentis* is used alone, in the proper number, without the auxiliary.

484. The root has in most cases the same form before the suffix तृ which it takes before the तुम् of the infinitive. Thus, गातृ; जि, जेतृ; स्तु, स्तोतृ; भू, भवितृ; कृ, कर्तृ; कथय, कथयितृ.

485. The inflection is then as follows:

---

* The Hindus also prescribe a middle formation; it has, however, practically no existence.

1.	कर्तास्मि	कर्तास्वस्	कर्तास्मस्
2.	कर्तासि	कर्तास्थस्	कर्तास्थ
3.	कर्ता	कर्तारौ	कर्तारस्

Aorist-System.

486. The aorist comprises three quite distinct formations, each with certain sub-varieties; but all are bound together into one complex system by certain correspondences of form and meaning. In classical Sanskrit aorists are comparatively rare. Their value is quite that of impf. or pf. as tenses of narration. But they are used also (though not nearly so often as the prohibitive opt.) with the particle मा, in prohibitions, the augment being then omitted; thus, मा दाः 'do not give'; मा भैषीः 'do not fear'. With this exception the aorist always has the augment in classical Sanskrit. The tense comprises, in the later language, only an indicative mode.* The main varieties of aorist are three: I. Simple Aorist; II. Reduplicated Aorist; III. Sibilant Aorist.

487. I. **Simple aorist. (1) Root aorist.** This aorist is precisely like an imperfect of the root-class. It is limited to the active voice of a few roots in आ, and of भू. E. g.

	1दा			भू		
1.	अदाम्	अदाव	अदाम	अभूवम्	अभूव	अभूम
2.	अदास्	अदातम्	अदात	अभूस्	अभूतम्	अभूत
3.	अदात्	अदाताम्	अदुस्	अभूत्	अभूताम्	अभूवन्

Like दा: धा, अधात्; स्था, अस्थात्; पा, अपात्; गा 'go', अगात्.

488. (2) The *a*-aorist. This is like an imperfect of the *a*-class, active and middle. Thus, from सिच्, 1st persons असिचम्, असिचाव, असिचाम; असिचे, असिचावहि, असिचामहि. In general the root

---

* The **precative** is strictly a peculiar aor. optative; **but it is so rare** that its formation need not be explained here.

assumes a weak form; but three or four roots in final ऋ take *guṇa*. Thus, आप्, आपत्; गम्, अगमत्; भ्रंश्, अभ्रशत्; मुच्, अमुचत्; सद्, असदत्; शक्, अशकत्; स्रंस्, अस्रसत्. — **Irregular:** ख्या, अख्यत्; ह्वा, अह्वत्; श्वा, अश्वत्; शास्, अशिषत्; 2अस् 'throw', आस्थत् (anomalous). वच् makes अवोचत्, and पत्, अपप्तत्, which, with one or two others, were doubtless originally reduplicated aorists.

489. II. Reduplicated Aorist (3). This aorist differs from all others in that it has come to be attached nearly always to the derivative (caus., etc.) conjugation in अय, as its aorist. The connection is not formal, as the aorist is not made from the stem in अय, but from the root. Its characteristic is a reduplication, of quite peculiar character.

490. The reduplicated aorist is very unusual in classical Sanskrit, and it will be sufficient for the present to give an example or two of its formation. Thus, जन् makes अजीजनत्; स्पृश्, अपिस्पृशत्; स्था, अतिष्ठिपत्. The inflection is the usual one of imperfects of the *a*-conjugation.

491. III. Sibilant Aorist, of four varieties. **(4) The *s*-aorist.** The tense-stem is made by adding स् to the augmented root, which usually has its vowel strengthened. E. g. नी: **Act.:** sing. 1. अनैषम्, 2. अनैषीस्, 3. अनैषीत्; du. 1. अनैष्व, 2. अनैष्टम्, 3. अनैष्टाम्; pl. 1. अनैष्म, 2. अनैष्ट, 3. अनैषुस्. **Mid.:** sing. 1. अनेषि, 2. अनेष्ठास्, 3. अनेष्ट; du. 1. अनेष्वहि, 2. अनेषाथाम्, 3. अनेषाताम्; pl. 1. अनेष्महि, 2. अनेढ्वम्, 3. अनेषत. — लभ् (mid.only): sing. 1. अलप्सि, 2. अलब्धास्, 3. अलब्ध etc.

492. (5) The *iṣ*-aorist. The tense-stem is made by adding स् by means of an inserted इ. The root is generally strengthened. E. g. पू 'purify': **Act.:** sing. 1. अपाविषम्, 2. अपावीस्, 3. अपावीत्; du. 1. अपाविष्व, 2. अपाविष्टम्, 3. °ष्टाम्; pl. 1. °विष्म, 2. °विष्ट, 3.° विषुस्. — Mid. sing. 1. अपविषि, 2. अपविष्ठास्, 3. अ-

पविष्ट; du. 1. °**विष्वहि**, 2. °**विषाथाम्**, 3. °**ताम्**; pl. 1. °**विष्महि**, 2. °**विढ्वम्**, 3. °**विषत**. — This is the only aorist of which forms are made in the secondary and denominative conjugations (but for causatives and denominatives in **अय**, cf. § 489).

493. (6) The *siṣ*-**aorist** is active only, the corresponding middle being of the *s*-form. An example will suffice here. **या**: sing. 1. **अयासिषम्** etc., quite like the inflection of the *iṣ*-aorist.

494. (7) The *sa*-**aorist.** **दिश्**: Act. sing. 1. **अदिक्षम्**, 2. °**क्षस्**, 3. °**क्षत्**; and so on, like an impf. of the *a*-conjugation. But in the mid. the grammarians prescribe the 1st. sing. **अदिक्षि**, and 2nd and 3rd du. **अदिक्षाथाम्** and °**ताम्**.

---

495. Aorist Passive. Generally the middle forms of aorists **4**, **5**, or **7**, are used also for the passive. Roots which do not ordinarily take aorists of these forms, may make them like **4** or **5** especially for the passive.

496. But a 3rd pers. sing., of peculiar formation, has become a recognized part of the passive conjugation. It is formed by adding **इ** to the root, which takes also the augment, and is usually strengthened, in some cases by *guṇa*, in others by *vṛddhi*. After final **आ** is added **य्**. Thus, **नी**, **अनायि**; **श्रु**, **अश्रावि**; **कृ**, **अकारि**; **वच्**, **अवाचि**; — but **दम्**, **अदमि**; **दृश्**, **अदर्शि**; **दा**, **अदायि**.

Lesson XLV.

Derivative or Secondary Conjugations.

497. Secondary conjugations are those in which a whole system of forms, more or less complete, is made from a derivative conjugation-stem, this whole system being usually connected with a certain definite modification of the original radical sense. These conjugations are: I. Passive. II. Intensive. III. Desiderative. IV. Causative. V. Denominative.

498. I. Passive. The present-system of the passive has been described; as also the peculiar 3rd pers. sing. used as aor. pass., the past pass. participle in त or न, and the fut. pass. participles or gerundives. In all other parts of the verb middle forms are used, if necessary, with passive meaning.

499. II. Intensive. The intensive conjugation signifies the intensification or the repetition of the action expressed by the primary conjugation of a root. Forms outside the present-system are too rare to need notice here; indeed, even within that system they are by no means common in the later language. Intensives fall into two classes.

500. 1. The verbs of the first class (only act.) form their intensive-stem by reduplication, and the reduplicating syllable is strengthened. *a.* Radical अ and आ are reduplicated with आ, इ and ई with ए, उ and ऊ with ओ; thus, वावद्, दाधृ, नेनी, शोशुच्. *b.* Sometimes the reduplicating syllable has a final consonant, taken from the end of the root; thus, चर्चर्, मर्मृज्. *c.* Sometimes the reduplication is dissyllabic, an *i*-vowel being inserted after the final consonant of the reduplicating syllable; thus, वरीवृत्. — The model of inflection is the present-system of the reduplicating-class, but deviations are not rare; in particular, an ई is sometimes inserted between stem and ending.

501. 2. From the intensive-stem as just described may be formed another, formally identical with a passive-stem, by the suffix य. It takes middle inflection, but has no passive value, being used precisely as is the intensive just mentioned. Thus, मृज्, मर्मृज्यते.

502. A few intensives, having lost their value as such, come to be used as presents, and are treated by the native grammarians as simple roots. Thus जागृ, really intensive of गृ 'wake', is assigned to the root-class: pres. जागर्मि etc., du. जागृवस् etc.; impf. 1. अजागरम्, 2. अजागर्, 3. अजागर्; du. अजागृव etc. So also दरिद्रा, intens. of द्रा 'run', used as a present with the sense 'be poor'. निज् 'wash', and some others, use the intensive present-system in the same way, and are assigned to the reduplicating class; thus, 3rd sing. नेनेक्ति, 3rd pl. नेनिजति.

Intensive forms outside the present-system are very rare.

503. III. Desiderative. By this conjugation is denoted a desire for the action or condition denoted by the simple root; thus, पिबामि 'I drink', desid. पिपासामि 'I wish to drink'.

504. To form the desiderative-stem the root is reduplicated, and adds स, sometimes इष. The consonant of the reduplication is determined by the usual rules; the vowel of reduplication is इ if the root has an *a*-vowel, an *i*-vowel, or ऋ, and उ if the root has an *u*-vowel. Thus, या, यियासति; नी, निनीषति; भू, बुभूषति; कृ, चिकीर्षति; भिद्, बिभित्सति; तिज्, तितिक्षते.

505. A number of roots form an abbreviated desiderative-stem; thus, आप्, ईप्सति; दा, दित्सति.

506. The conjugation in the present-system is like that of other *a*-stems. Outside of that desiderative forms are quite infrequent. The perfect is the periphrastic. The aorist is of the *iṣ*-form; thus, ईप्स, ऐप्सीत्; अतितिक्षिष्ट. The futures are made with the auxiliary vowel इ; thus, ईप्सिष्यति, ईप्सितास्मि. The verbal nouns are made with इ in all forms where that vowel is ever taken. A passive may be made; thus, ईप्स्यते 'it is desired to be obtained'; part. ईप्सित.

507. IV. Causative. 1. The present-system of the causative has been treated of already. 2. The perfect is the periphrastic, the derivative noun in आ being formed from the causative-stem; thus, धारयां चकार. 3. The aorist is the reduplicated, made in general directly from the root, and formally unconnected with the causative-stem; thus, धृ, अदीधरम्, अबूभुवम्. In a few instances, where the root has assumed a peculiar form before the causative-sign, the reduplicated aorist is made from this form, not from the simple root; thus, स्ना, स्नापयति, असिष्णपत्. 4. Both futures are made from the causative-stem, the auxiliary इ replacing the final अ; thus, धारयिष्यति, धारयितास्मि. 5. The verbal nouns and adjectives are in part formed from the causative-stem in the same manner as the futures, in part from the causatively strengthened root-form; thus, pass. part. श्रावित; fut. pass. part. (gerundive) तर्पयितव्य, स्नाप्य; inf. जोषयितुम्; gerund सादयित्वा, °स्नाप्य, °गमय्य (§ 310).

508. Causative passive and desiderative. These may be made from the causative-stem as follows. 1. The passive-stem is formed by adding the usual passive sign य to the causatively strengthened root, the syllables अय being omitted; thus, धार्यते. 2. The desiderative-stem is made by reduplication and addition of the syllables इष, of which the इ replaces the final अ of the causative-stem; thus, दिधारयिषति, बिभावयिषति. This is a rare formation.

509. V. Denominative. A denominative conjugation is one that has as basis a noun-stem. In general, the base is made from the noun-stem by means of the conjugation-sign य, which has the accent. Intermediate between the denominative and causative conjugations stands a class of verbs plainly denominative in origin but having the causative accent. Thus, from मन्त्र, मन्त्रयते *mantráyate*; from कीर्ति, कीर्तयति *kīrtáyati*. See § 76.

510. The denominative meaning is of the greatest variety; e. g. 'be like', 'act as', 'regard or treat as', 'make into', 'desire, crave' — that which is signified by the noun-stem. Examples: from तपस् 'penance, asceticism', तपस्यति 'practise ascetism'; from नमस्, नमस्यति 'honor'; कृष्णायते 'blacken'; अश्वायति 'seek horses'; गोपायति 'play the herdsman, protect'; वसूयति 'desire wealth'; भिषज्यति 'play the physician, cure'; पुत्रकाम्यति 'desire a son', from the poss. cpd. पुत्रकाम 'desiring a son'.

Glossary to the Exercises.

For the alphabetic order of Sanskrit words see p. xii.

I. Sanskrit-English.

Adjectives in *-a* form their feminine in *-ā*, unless otherwise stated.

akṣa m., die, dice.
akṣan (*akṣi*: **275**) n., eye.
agni m., fire; as *n. pr.*, Agni, the god of fire.
agnihotrin m., a kind of priest.
agra n., front; tip, end.
aṅga n., limb; body.
aṅgiras (**253**) m., certain mythical characters.
añjali m., a gesture (Voc. 37).
aṇu a., small; as n., atom.
atas adv., hence.
ati adv., across, past; in cpds, to excess.
atithi m., guest.
atra adv., here, hither.
atha adv., then; thereupon.
atharvaveda m., the fourth Veda.
adas (*asāu*: **287**) pron., that one; so-and-so.
adya adv., to-day.
adyatana adj., of to-day.
adroha m., faithfulness.
adharma m., injustice, wrong.
adhas adv., below, down.
adhastāt adv., below; prep., w. gen., underneath.
adhi adv., over, above, on.
adhika a., additional; superior.
adhīta part. of *adhi-i*.
adhunā adv., now.
adhvaryu m., priest who recites the Yajurveda.
√ *an* (*ániti*: **429**) breathe; — + *pra* breathe; live.
an, before cons. *a*, negative prefix.
anaḍuh (**278**) m., ox.
anantaram adv., after, immediately afterward; as prep., w. abl., right after.
anartha m., misfortune.
anavadya a., faultless.
anahilapāṭaka n., *n. pr.*, a city.
anu adv., after, along, toward.
anukūla a., favorable; as n., favor.
anujñā f., permission.
anurūpa a., suitable.
aneka a., several.

anṛta n., untruth.
anta m., end; in loc., at last.
antara a., inner; as n., interior, middle; interval, difference; occasion, juncture. Cf. **375, 4.**
andha a., blind.
andhra m., *n. pr.*, a people.
anna n., food, fodder.
anya (**231**) pron. adj., other.
anyatra adv., elsewhere.
anvañc (**272**) a., following.
anvaya m., descendant, progeny.
ap (**277**) f. pl., water.
apara (**233**) pron. adj., hinder; other.
api (**190**) adv., unto; further; as conj., also, even.
apsaras f., heavenly nymph.
abhaya n., feeling of safety; safety.
abhi adv., to, unto.
abhiprāya m., plan, design; view.
abhyāsa m., study, recitation.
amṛta a., immortal; as n., nectar.
ambā (**273**) f., mother.
ayam same as *idam.*
ari m., enemy.
artha m., purpose; meaning; wealth.
√ *arthaya* (den.: *artháyate*) ask for (w. two acc.); + *pra* idem.
aryaman (**284**) m., *n. pr.*
√ *arh* (*árhati*) deserve; have a right to; w. inf. (**320**), be able.
alam adv., enough; very; w. instr., enough of, away with; w. dat., suitable for.
ali m., bee.
ava adv., down, off.

avaçyam adv., necessarily.
avasthā f., condition, state.
avāñc (**272**) a., downward.
√ 1*aç* (*açnuté*) acquire, obtain; — + *sam-upa* idem.
√ 2*aç* (*açnā́ti*) eat; caus. (*ācáyati*) make eat, give to eat.
açīti (**332**) num., eighty.
açru n., tear.
açva m., horse.
açvin m. du., *n. pr.*, the Açvins (the Indian Διὸς κοῦροι).
aṣṭa (**332**) num., eight.
aṣṭādaça (**332**) num., eighteen.
aṣṭāviṅçati (**329,332**) num., twenty-eight.
√1*as* (*ásti*: **426**) be, exist.
√2*as* (*ásyati*) throw, hurl; — + *abhi* repeat, study, learn; — + *ni* entrust; — + *pra* throw forward or into.
asi m., sword.
asura m., demon.
asāu same as *adas.*
asthan (*asthi*: **275**) n., bone.
asmad same as *vayam;* as stem in cpds, cf. **352, 4.**
ahan (*ahar, ahas*: **271**) n., day.
aham (**223**) pron., I.
ahita a., disagreeable.
aho excl., oh! ah!
ahorātra n., a day and a night.

ā (**130**) adv., hither, unto; as prep., w. abl., hither from; until.
ākāra m., form, figure.
ākāça m., air, sky.
ākṛṣṭa part. of *ā-kṛṣ.*
ākrānta part. of *ā-kram.*

āgamana n., arrival.
ācāra m., "walk and conversation"; conduct; observance.
ācārya m., teacher.
ājñā f., command.
ātman m., soul, self; often simple reflexive pronoun.
ādi m., beginning; in cpds, cf. 375, 1.
āditya m., sun.
ādeça m., command, prescription.
√ *āp* (*āpnóti*, *āpnuté*) acquire, reach; — + *ava*, *pra*, or *anu-pra*, idem; + *sam* idem; finish.
āpad f., calamity.
āpta part. of *āp*, trustworthy; fit.
āyuṣmant (263) a., long-lived.
āviṣṭa, part. of *viç* + *ā*, entered (by), i. e. filled (with).
āçā f., hope.
āçu a., swift.
āçrama m., hermitage.
√ *ās* (*áste*: 424) sit; caus. (*āsáyati*) place; — + *upa* sit by; wait upon; reverence.
āsana n., seat, chair.
āharaṇa n., bringing.
āhāra m., food.
āhuti f., oblation, offering.

√ *i* (*éti* [-*ité*: 408]) go: — + *adhi* mid., go over, repeat, read; caus. (*adhyāpáyati*) teach; — + *anu* follow; — + *apa* go away; — + *abhi* approach; — + *astam* (lit'ly go home) set (of the sun, etc.); — + *ud* rise; + *upa* approach; — + *pra* go forth; die; — + *sam-ā* come together, join.
icchā f., wish.
itara (231) pron. adj., other.
itas adv., hence.
iti adv., thus, so.
ittham adv., in this way, so.
idam (285-286) pron., this, this here.
√ *idh*, *indh* (*inddhé*: 444) kindle, light.
indu m., moon.
indra m., *n. pr.*, the god Indra.
indraprastha n., *n. pr.*, Delhi.
indrāṇī f., *n. pr.*, a goddess.
iyant (263) a., so great; so much.
iyam fem. of *idam*.
iva adv., postpos., as; like.
√ *iṣ* (*icchati*: 109) wish, desire.
iṣu m., arrow.
iha adv., here, hither.

√ *īkṣ* (*īkṣate*) see, behold; — + *upa* neglect; — + *prati* expect.
īdṛç, f. -*ī*, a., such.
√ *īç* (*īṣṭe*: 422) rule, own (gen.).
īçvara m., master; lord; rich man.

---

ucchrita part. of *ud-çri*, high.
ud adv., up, up forth or out.
udañc (272) a., northward.
udadhi m., ocean.
udaya m., rise.
udara n., belly.
udyata part. of *ud-yam*, ready.
udyāna n., garden.
udyoga m., diligence.
udyogin a., diligent, energetic.
upa adv., to, toward.
upanayana n., initiation.
upaniṣad f., certain Vedic works.
upabhoga m., enjoyment.

upavīta n., sacred cord of the three higher castes.

upānah (249) f., sandal, shoe.

ubha a., du., both.

uras n., breast.

uru, f. *urvī*, a., wide.

urvaçī f., *n. pr.*, an Apsaras.

uṣas f., dawn; as n. pr., Uṣas, goddess of the dawn.

√*ṛ* (*ṛcchāti*: 109) move; go to; fall to one's lot, fall upon; caus. (*arpáyati*) send; put; give.

ṛkṣa m., bear.

ṛgveda m., the Rigveda.

ṛc f., verse of the Rigveda; in pl., the Rigveda.

ṛṇa n., debt.

ṛtvij m., priest.

ṛṣabhadatta m., *n. pr.*

ṛṣi m., seer.

eka (231) num., one; pl., some; *eke · · eke*, some · · others.

ekadā adv., once upon a time.

ekādaça (332) num., eleven.

ekādaça (334) a. eleventh.

etad (231) pron., this, this here.

eva adv., just, exactly.

evam adv., so, thus.

eṣa same as *etad*.

---

oṣṭha m., lip.

āuṣadha n., medicine.

---

ka (232) pron. 1. interrogative, who, what; *kim* w. instr., cf. note on p. 89. — 2. indefinite, adj. and subst., chiefly w. particles *ca, cana, cid, api*, some one or other; so also w. relatives; oftenest in neg. clauses: no one whatever (236).

kaṭa m., mat.

kaṇṭaka m., thorn, enemy.

kaṇṭha m., neck.

kaṇva m., *n. pr.*

katham adv., how?

√*kathaya* (den.: *katháyati*) relate, tell.

kadā adv., when? — + *cana, cid, api*, at some time, ever; often w. neg.

kaniṣṭha a., youngest.

kanīyas a., younger.

kanyā f., daughter, maiden.

kapi m., monkey.

kapota m., dove.

√*kamp* (*kámpate*) tremble.

kara m., hand; trunk (of elephant); ray; toll, tax.

karin m., elephant.

karuṇa a., lamentable.

karṇa m., ear.

kartṛ m., doer, maker (202); author.

karman n., deed; ceremony; fate

√*kal* + *sam* (*saṁkaláyati*) put together, add.

kalaha m., quarrel.

kalā f., crescent.

kaliṅga m., *n. pr.*, a people.

kaliyuga n., the "Iron Age" of the world.

kalyāṇa n., advantage; salvation.

kavi m., poet.

kāṇa a., one-eyed.

kānti f., charm; grace.

kāma m., desire, love; as *n. pr.*, the god of love.

kāmadugha a., granting wishes; as f. subst., sc. *dhenu*, the fabulous Wonder-cow.

kāmaduh a., idem.

kāya m., body.

kāraṇa n., reason, cause.

-kārin a., causing, making.

kārya n., business, concern.

kāla m., time.

kālidāsa m., *n. pr.*, a poet.

kāvya n., poem.

kāçī f., *n. pr.*, a city, Benares.

kāṣṭha n., fagot; wood.

kāṣṭhamaya a., made of wood.

kim neut. of *ka*; w. *tu*, however.

kiyant (263) pron. adj., how great?

kīrti f., glory.

kutas adv., whence? why?

kutra adv., where? whither?

kunta m., spear.

√ *kup* (*kúpyati*) be angry (gen. or dat.).

kumāra m., boy, prince.

kuçala a., able; clever; learnèd.

√ 1*kṛ* (*karóti*, *kurutė́*: 394-5) make, do, perform; — + *adhi* put at the head, make ruler over (loc.); — + *apa* do evil to, harm (gen., loc., acc.); — + *apa-ā* pay; — + *alam* prepare, adorn; — + *āvis* (*āviṣkaroti*) make known, exhibit; — + *upa* do good to, benefit (gen., loc.); — + *tiras* (*tirask.*) hide; blame; — + *puras* put at the head; — + *prati* pay, recompense, punish (acc. rei, gen., dat., or loc. pers.); — + *prādus* make known or visible; — + *sam* (395) prepare, adorn.

√ 2*kṛ* (*kiráti*) strew, scatter; — + *vi*, idem.

√ *kṛt* (*kṛntáti*: 110) cut, cut off; — + *ava* idem.

kṛti f., work (literary).

kṛtrima a., adopted.

kṛtsna a., whole, entire.

kṛpaṇa a., poor; niggardly.

kṛpā f., graciousness, pity.

√ *kṛṣ* (*kárṣati*) draw; — + *ā* draw on or up; — (*kṛṣáti*) plough.

kṛṣi f., agriculture.

kṛṣīvala m., husbandman, peasant.

kṛṣṇa a., black; as m., *n. pr.*, the god Kṛṣṇa.

√ *kḷp* (*kálpate*) be in order; tend or conduce to (dat.); caus. (*kalpáyati*, *-te*) ordain, appoint.

ketu m., banner

keça m., hair.

kāilāsa m., *n. pr.*, a mountain.

koṭi f., peak; point, tip.

kopa m., anger.

koṣa m., treasure; treasury.

kāunteya m., *n. pr.*

kāusalyā f., *n. pr.*

√ *kram* (*krāmati*, *krámate*: 134) step; — + *ati* pass beyond; transgress; pass (of time); — + *ā* stride up to, attack; — + *nis* go out.

√ *krī* (*krīṇā́ti*, *krīṇītė́*) buy.

krīḍā f., game, sport.

√ *krudh* (*krúdhyati*) be angry (gen. or dat.).

krodha m., anger.

kva adv., where? whither? + *cit* sometimes, ever.

kṣaṇa m. n., moment; time.

kṣatriya m., warrior, man of the second caste.

kṣaya m., decay, destruction.

√*kṣan* (*kṣaṇóti*, *kṣaṇuté*) hurt, wound.

√*kṣal* (*kṣāláyati*) wash; — + *pra* idem.

kṣātra a., suitable for Kṣatriyas.

√ 2*kṣi* (*kṣiṇóti*) destroy.

kṣitipa m., king.

√*kṣip* (*kṣipáti*) hurl, throw.

kṣīṇa part. of 2*kṣi*, reduced, decayed, ruined.

kṣīra n., milk.

kṣudra a., little, small.

kṣudh f., hunger.

kṣetra n., field.

√*khan* (*khánati*) dig.

khara m., ass.

---

gaṅgā f., *n. pr.*, the Ganges.

gaja m., elephant.

√*gaṇaya* (den.: *gaṇáyati*) number, count; — + *ava* despise.

gati f., gait; course.

gandha m., odor, perfume.

gandharva m., a Gandharva, one of a band of celestial singers.

√*gam* (*gácchati*: **100**) go; — + *anu* follow; — + *abhi* visit, attend; — + *ava* understand; — + *astam* go down, set (cf. *i* + *astam*); — + *ā* come; — + *upa-ā* come near; — + *ud* rise; — + *nis* come forth; proceed from; — + *sam* (mid.) come together, meet (instr.).

garīyas comp., very honorable.

√2*gā* (*gā́yati*) sing.

gāndharva, f. -*ī*, a., in the manner of Gandharvas.

√*gāh* (*gā́hate*) plunge; — + *ava* dive or plunge under (acc.).

gir f., voice, song.

giri m., mountain.

gīta n., song; singing.

guṇa m., quality, excellence.

guru m., teacher.

√*guh* (*gū́hati*: **101**) hide, conceal; caus. (*gūháyati*) idem.

guhā f., cave.

gṛha n., house.

gṛhastha m., householder, head of family.

gṛhya a., domestic.

go (**209**) m., f., bull, steer, cow; as f., fig., speech.

gotva n., ox-nature, stupidity.

gopa m., cowherd, shepherd; guardian.

√*gopāya* (den.: *gopā́yati*) be keeper; guard.

gāurava n., weight; dignity.

√ *granth* (*grathnā́ti*) string together; compose.

grantha m., literary work, book.

√*grah* (*gṛhṇā́ti*, *gṛhṇīté*) receive, seize; — + *ni* hold, restrain, check; — + *prati* take.

grāma m., village.

grāsa m., bite, mouthful.

---

ghaṭa m., pot, vessel.

ghāsa m., fodder, hay.
ghṛta n., clarified butter; *ghee.*
√*ghrā* (*jighrati*: 102) smell.

---

ca encl. conj., and, also, *τε*, *-que*; sometimes = if.
cakra n., wheel.
√*cakṣ* (*cáṣṭe*: 421) see, behold; — + *ā* relate; call, name; — + *vi-ā* explain.
cakṣus n., eye.
catur (332) num., four.
caturtha, f. *-ī*, a., fourth.
caturdaça (332) num., fourteen.
catuṣpad (282) a., quadruped.
catvāriṅçat (332) num., forty.
candra m., moon.
candramas m., moon.
√*cam*, used only with *ā* (*ācā́mati*), sip; rinse the mouth.
camatkāra m., astonishment.
√*car* (*cárati*) go, wander; graze (of cattle); tr., perform, commit; — + *ā* perform, complete, do; — + *sam-ā* idem; — + *ud* caus. (*uccārāyati*) pronounce, say.
-cara a., moving, going.
caraṇa m., n., foot, leg.
carita n., behavior, life.
carman n., hide, skin; leather.
carmamaya a., leathern.
√*cal* (*cálati*) stir; — + *pra* move on, march; — + *pra-vi*, tr., move, stir.
cāturmāsya n., a certain sacrifice.
cāmīkara n., gold.
cāra m., spy.
cāru a., beautiful.
√*ci* (*cinóti, cinuté*) gather; — + *nis* or *vi-nis* decide, conclude; + *pra* gather; — + *vi* idem; — + *sam* collect.
citta n., notice; thought; mind.
√*cint* (*cintáyati*) consider.
ciram adv., long, a long time.
√*cud* + *pra* in caus. (*pracodáyati*), impel.
√*cur* (*coráyati*) steal.
cūḍā f., top-knot, scalp.
ced adv., postpos. if.
√*ceṣṭ* (*céṣṭati, -te*) stir, be alive.
cāulukya m., *n. pr.*, a people.
√*cyu* (*cyávate*) totter, fall; — + *vi* fall away.

---

chattra n., umbrella.
chāyā f., shade.
√*chid* (*chinátti, chinddhé*) cut, cut off; — + *ava* idem; — + *ā* take away, remove; — + *ud* exterminate.

---

jagat n., that which moves; men and beasts; the world.
√*jan* (*jā́yate*: 155; *janáyati*) trans. (*janáyati* and active forms) beget, produce; intrans. (*jā́yate* and middle forms) be born (mother in loc.), arise, spring up; — + *ud* (*ujjāyate*) be born, arise (abl.); — + *pra* or *sam* idem.
jana m., man; pl., and coll. in sing., people, folks.
janaka m., father.
jananī f., mother.
janman n., birth, existence.
jaya m., victory.
jaras (280) f., old age.

jarā (280) f., old age.
jala n., water.
√ *jalp* (*jálpati*) speak; chat.
√ *jāgaraya* (caus.) awaken.
jāti f., birth; caste; kind.
jāmātṛ m., son-in-law.
jāyā f., woman, wife.
jāla n., net.
√ *ji* (*jáyati*) trans. and intrans., conquer, win; — + *parā*, mid., be conquered (cf. in Voc. 9).
jina m., *n. pr.*, a name of Buddha.
jihvā f., tongue.
√ *jīv* (*jívati*) live.
jīvita n., life.
juhū f., spoon, esp. sacrificial spoon.
jetṛ m., conqueror, victor.
-jña a., knowing.
√ *jñā* (*jānáti*, *jānīté*: 403) know; — + *anu* permit; — + *ā* caus. (*ājñāpáyati*) command; — + *vi* recognize.
jñāna n., knowledge; insight.
jyā f., bowstring.
jyeṣṭha (340) a., best; oldest.
jyotiṣa n., astronomy; astronomical text-book.
jyotis n., light; star; heavenly body.

---

ta (228–230) pron., he, etc.; that, both subst. and adj.; also as def. article.
takṣaçilā f., *n. pr.*, Taxila, a city.
√ *taḍ* (*tāḍáyati*) strike, beat.
taḍāga m., pond.
taḍit f., lightning.
taṇḍula m., rice.
tatas adv., thence, therefore; thereupon.
tatra adv., there, thither.
tathā adv., in that way, so.
tad nom. and acc. s. n. to *ta*; as adv., therefore.
tadā adv., then.
tadyathā adv., namely, to wit.
√ *tan* (*tanóti*, *tanuté*), tr., stretch, extend; perform (a sacrifice); — + *ā* cause, bring about; — + *pra* extend.
√ *tap* (*tápati*, *-te*), tr. and intr., burn; pain; in pass., suffer, do penance.
tapas n., heat; self-torture.
tapasvin a., practising asceticism; as m., ascetic.
√ *tam* (*tā́myati*: 131) be sad.
taru m., tree.
taruṇa, f. *-ī*, a., young, delicate.
tasthivāṅs pf. part. of *sthā*; as n., the immovable.
tādṛç a., such.
tālu n., palate.
tāvant adj., so great, so much; *tāvat* as adv., so long, so much; often concessive, like *donc*, *doch*.
tiraskariṇī f., veil.
tir‿añc (272) a., going horizontally; as subst., animal.
tilaka m., ornament (often fig.).
tīra n., bank, shore.
tīrtha n., bathing-place; place of pilgrimage.
tīvra a., great, strong, violent.
tu conj., but, however.
√ *tud* (*tudáti*) push; strike.
√ *tul* (*toláyati*) weigh.

√*tuṣ* (*túṣyati*) rejoice, take pleasure in (w. instr.).

√*tṛ* (*tárati*) cross over; — + *ava* descend; + *ud* emerge; — + *pra* in caus. (*pratāráyati*), deceive.

tṛtīya, f. -*ā* (335), a., third.

√*tṛp* (*tṛ́pyati*) satisfy oneself.

tṛṣṇā f., thirst, desire.

tejasvin a., courageous.

√*tyaj* (*tyájati*) leave, abandon; + *pari* leave off, give up.

trayodaça (332) num., thirteen.

tri (332) num., three.

triṅçat (332) num., thirty.

triloka n., -*kī* f., the threefold world.

trivṛt a., triple, threefold.

triçīrṣan a., three-headed.

triṣṭubh f., name of a metre.

tryaçīti num., eighty three.

tva stem of pron. of 2d pers. (226; cf. 352, 4).

tvad so-called stem of pron. *tva*.

tvaṣṭṛ m., *n. pr.*, a god, Tvaṣṭar.

√*daṅç* (*dáçati*) bite.

daṅṣṭrā f., tooth.

dakṣa m., *n. pr.*

dakṣiṇa a., right-hand; southern.

daṇḍa m., stick; punishment.

√*daṇḍaya* (den.: *daṇḍáyati*) punish.

dadhan (*dadhi*: 275) n., curds.

dadhyañc (weakest -*dhīc*) m., *n. pr.*

√*dam* (*dā́myati*: 131) control; caus. (*damáyati*) tame; compel.

dayā f., compassion, pity.

daridra a., poor.

darçana n., philosophical system.

daça (332) num., ten.

daçaratha m., *n. pr.*

daṣṭa part. of *daṅç*.

√*dah* (*dáhati*) burn.

√1*dā* (*dádāti*, *datté*: 436) give; in caus. (*dāpáyati*) make give or pay; — + *ā* take (312); — + *pra* entrust; give in marriage.

√2*dā* (*dyáti*: 132) cut.

dātṛ m., giver; as adj. (204), generous.

dāna n., gift, present; generosity.

dānava m., demon.

dāsa m., slave, groom.

dāsī f., female slave, servant.

dina n., day.

div (277) f. (rarely m.), sky.

divasa m., day.

divya a., heavenly, divine.

√*diç* (*diçáti*) show, point out; — + *ā* command; — + *upa* teach, instruct.

diç f., point, cardinal point; quarter, region; direction.

√*dih* (*dégdhi*: 428) smear.

dīrgha a., long; — *am* adv., afar.

dīrghāyus a., long-lived.

√*dīv* (*dī́vyati*) play.

√*du* (*dunóti*), intr., burn, feel distressed; tr., distress (acc.).

duḥkha n., misery; misfortune.

dugdha n., milk.

durjana m., scamp, rogue.

durdaçā f., misfortune.

durlabha a., hard to find or reach; difficult.

√*duṣ* (*dúṣyati*) be defiled.

duṣprayukta a., badly arranged.

duṣṣanta m., *n. pr.*

dus insep. prefix, bad; hard.
√*duh* (*dógdhi*, *dugdhé*: **428**) milk.
duhitṛ f., daughter.
dūta m., messenger, envoy.
√*dṛ* in caus. (*dāráyati*) + *vi* tear open.
√*dṛç* (**127**) see; caus. (*darçáyati*) show; pass. (*dṛçyáte*) seem, look.
dṛç f., look, glance; eye.
dṛṣad f., stone (in Vocab. XX).
deva m., god; f. -*ī*, goddess; queen.
devakī f., *n. pr.*
devakula n., temple.
devatā f., divinity, deity.
deça m., region, land.
dāiva, f. -*ī*, divine.
doṣa m., fault.
dyuti f., brilliancy.
dravya n., property; object.
draṣṭṛ m., seer; author (of Vedic hymns, etc.).
√*dru* (*drávati*) run.
√*druh* (*drúhyati*) be hostile, offend.
dva (**332**) num., two.
dvāḥstha m., doorkeeper.
dvār f., door, gate.
dvija m., Aryan.
dvijāti m., Aryan.
dvitīya (**335**) a., second.
dvipad (**282**) a., biped.
√*dviṣ* (*dvéṣṭi*, *dviṣṭé*) hate; — + *pra* hate extremely.
dviṣ m., enemy.
dvis adv., twice.
dvīpin m., panther.
dhana n., money, riches.
dhanin a., wealthy.
dhanus n., bow.
dharma m., right; law; virtue.
√1*dhā* (*dádhāti*, *dhatté*: **435**) put, place; — + *api* close, cover, keep shut; — + *ā* put on; mid., receive; — + *sam-ā* lay or place on; — + *ni* lay down; — + *pari* in caus. (-*dhāpáyati*), make put on, clothe in (two acc.); — + *vi* arrange, ordain; — + *sam* put together, unite; lay on.
√2*dhā* (*dháyati*: **126**) suck.
dhātṛ m., creator.
dhānya n., grain.
dhārmika a., right, just.
√*dhāv* (*dhávati*) run; — + *anu* run after.
dhāvana n., running; course.
dhī f., understanding, insight.
dhīmant a., wise, prudent.
dhīra a., steadfast, firm, brave.
√*dhū* (*dhunóti*, *dhunuté*: **391**), shake.
√*dhṛ* in caus. (*dhāráyati*) bear.
dhṛti f., firmness; courage.
dhenu f., cow.
dhāirya n., steadfastness.
√*dhyā* (*dhyā́yati*) think, ponder.

---

na adv., not; with opt., cf. **207**.
nakṣatra n., lunar mansion.
nagara n., -*ī* f., city.
nadī f., river.
√*nand* (*nándati*, -*te*) + *abhi* rejoice in, greet joyfully (acc.).
√*nam* (*námati*), intr., bow, bend; tr., honor, reverence (acc.).
namas n., honor, glory.
nara m., man (*vir* and *homo*).

naraka m., hell.
narmadā f., *n.pr.*, a river in India.
nala m., *n. pr.*
nava a., new.
nava (**332**) num., nine.
navati (**332**) num., ninety.
navadaça (**332**) num., nineteen.
navīna a., new.
√*naç* (*náçyati*) perish; — + *vi* perish; disappear.
√*nah* (*náhyati*) bind; — + *sam* gird, equip oneself.
nāga m., snake.
nāṭaka n., drama, play.
nāman n., name; *nāma* adv., by name.
nārī f., woman, wife.
nālī f., pipe, conduit.
nāça m., destruction.
ni adv., down; in, into.
nitya a., constant; daily; *-am* as adv., always, daily.
nideça m., command.
√*nind* (*nindati*) blame.
nipuṇa a., shrewd, skilled.
niyata, part. of *ni-yam*, ordained, fixed, permanent.
nirdaya a., pitiless.
nirvṛti f., contentment, happiness.
nis adv., out, forth.
niçcaya m., decision, certainty.
√*nī* (*náyati*; caus. *nāyáyati*) lead, guide; — + *apa* lead away; — + *ā* bring; — + *upa* introduce, consecrate, initiate; — + *nis* bring to an end, determine, settle; — + *pari* lead about; marry.
nīca a., low.
nīti f., conduct of life; ethics, politics.
nīruj a., healthy, well.
nīlakaṇṭha m., *n. pr.*
√*nṛt* (*nṛtyati*) dance.
nṛtta n., dance, dancing.
nṛpa m., king.
nṛpati m., king.
netṛ m., leader.
netra n., leading-rope, cord; eye.
nāu f., ship.
nyañc (**272**) a., low.
nyāya m., logic.
nyāyya a., right, proper.

---

pakṣa m., wing, side; party.
pakṣin m., bird.
paṅka n., mud, bog.
√*pac* (*pácati*) cook.
pañca (**332**) num., five.
pañcadaça (**332**) num., fifteen.
pañcapañcāça (**334**) a., fifty-fifth.
pañcāçat (**332**) num., fifty.
√*paṭ* (*pāṭáyati*) split open.
paṭu a., skilled.
√*paṭh* (*páṭhati*) recite, read.
paṇi m. pl., *n. pr.*, certain demons.
paṇḍita m., learned man: pandit.
√*pat* (*pátati*) fall, fly; — + *ud* fly up.
pati (**274**) m., lord, master; husband.
pattra n., leaf, letter.
patnī f., wife, consort.
pathi same as *panthan*.
pathya a., wholesome.
pad (**282**) m., foot.
√*pad* (*pádyate*) go; — + *vi-ā* in caus. (*vyāpādáyati*) kill; — +

nis (*niṣpádyate*) grow, arise from (abl.); — + *pra* flee for refuge to (acc.).

pada n., step; place.

padma m. n., lotus.

panthan (**278**) m., road, path.

payas n., milk.

para (**233**) a., chief, highest; other.

paramātman m., the world-spirit.

paraçu m., axe.

parā adv., to a distance, away.

pari adv., round about, around.

parivrāj (**247**, 2) m., wandering ascetic.

pariṣad f., assembly.

parvata m., mountain.

√*palāy* (*pálāyate*: cf. p. 116, note) flee.

√*paç* (*páçyati*: **127**) see.

paçu m., beast.

paçcāt adv., behind (w. gen.).

√1*pā* (*píbati*: **102**) drink; caus. (*pāyáyati*) give to drink, water.

√2*pā* (*páti*) protect; caus. *pālá-yati*) idem.

pāṭaliputra n., n. pr., the city Patnā.

pāṭha m., lecture, lesson.

pāṇi m., hand.

pāṇini m., n. pr.

pāṇḍava m., descendant of Pāṇḍu.

pātaka n., crime, sin.

pātra n., pot, vessel.

pāda m., foot; quarter; ray, beam.

pāpa a., bad; as n. subst., sin.

pārthiva m., prince.

pārvatī f., *n. pr.*

pālana n., protection.

pāça m., noose, cord, snare.

pāçupālya n., cattle-raising.

pitṛ m., father; du., parents; pl., Manes.

√*piṣ* (*pináṣṭi*) grind, crush.

√*pī* same as *pyā*.

pīna part. of *pī*, fat.

√*pīḍ* (*pīḍáyati*) torment, vex.

puṁs same as *pumāṅs*.

puṇya a., meritorious, holy, auspicious; as n., merit.

putra m., son; *-trī* f., daughter.

punar adv., again, but.

pumāṅs (**279**) m., man, male.

pur f., city.

purā adv., earlier, formerly.

purāṇa, f. *-ā* and *-ī*, a., former, ancient; as n., one of a class of works on the creation, etc.

puruṣa m., man (*homo*).

purūravas m., *n. pr.*, Purūravas.

purohita m., domestic priest.

pulinda m., *n. pr.*, a tribe in India.

√*puṣ* (*puṣṇāti*) make increase or grow.

puṣṭa part. of *puṣ*, stout, fat.

puṣpa n., flower.

pustaka n., book (manuscript).

√*pū* (*punāti*, *punīté*) clean.

√*pūj* (*pūjáyati*) honor.

pūra m., flood, high-water.

pūru m., *n. pr.*

pūṣan (**284**) m., *n. pr.*, Pūṣan, the Sun-god.

pṛthivī f., earth, ground.

pṛthu a., broad, wide.

pṛthvī f., earth.

pṛthvīrāja m., *n. pr.*

√1*pṛ* (*pipárti*; caus. *pūráyati*) fill.

√2 *pṛ* (*pāráyati*) overcome (evils); prevail.

poṣaka m., supporter, maintainer.

pāutra m., grandson.

pāura m., citizen.

√*pyā* (*pyā́yate*) swell, get stout.

pra adv., forward, forth.

prakāçin a., bright, glistening; act., illuminating.

√*prach* (*pṛccháti*) ask, ask about.

prajā f., creature, subject.

prati adv. and prep., back, back again; towards (postpos., w. acc.).

pratikūla a., unfavorable.

pratyañc (272) a., backward, westward.

pratyaham adv., daily.

√*prath* in caus. (*pratháyati*), spread; proclaim.

prathama (335) a., first.

prabhāva m., might, power.

prabhūta a., much; many.

pramatta a., careless.

prayāga m., *n. pr.*, Allahābād.

prayukta part. of *pra-yuj*.

prayoktṛ m., arranger, user.

pralaya m., destruction.

praçna m., question.

prasanna, part. of *pra-sad*, well-disposed.

prahāra m., stroke, shot; wound.

prāñc (272) forward, eastward.

prāṇa m., often pl., breath, life.

prāṇin m., living creature.

prātar adv., early, in the morning.

prāyaçcitta n., penance, expiation.

prāyeṇa adv., commonly.

prāsāda m., palace.

priya a., dear.

priyakarman a., kind.

priyavāc a., saying pleasant things, sociable.

priyavādin a., idem.

√*prī* (*prīṇā́ti*, *prīṇīté*), act., delight; mid., rejoice; caus. (*prīṇáyati*), make glad, please.

√*plu* (*plávate*) + *ā* drench.

---

phala n., fruit, reward.

phalavant a., fruitful.

√*bandh* (*badhnā́ti*, *badhnīté*) bind; entangle, catch; join; compose.

bandhu m., relative.

bala n., strength, might.

balavant a., strong, mighty.

baliṣṭha a., strongest.

bahu a., much, many.

bāla a., young; as m., child, boy; f. -*ā*, girl.

bāṣpa m., tear, tears.

bāhu m., arm.

bindu m., drop.

buddha part. of *budh*, awakened; enlightened.

buddhi f., prudence, intelligence.

buddhimant a., prudent.

√*budh* (*bódhati*, -*te*; *búdhyati*, -*te*), wake; know.

budha m., wise man, sage.

brahmacarya n., life of holiness, esp. religious studentship.

brahmacārin a., studying sacred knowledge; as m., Brāhman student.

bráhman n., devotion; sacred word (of God); sacred knowledge; world-spirit.

brahmán (a personification of *bráhman*) m., the supreme All-Soul; Brahma, the Creator.

brahmahan (283) m., killing a Brāhman.

brāhmaṇa m., priest, Brāhman.

√*brū* (*bravī́ti*, *brūté*), speak, say; — +*pra* explain, teach, announce; — +*vi* explain, announce.

---

bhakta a., devoted, true.

bhakti f., devotion; honor.

√*bhakṣ* (*bhakṣáyati*) eat.

bhakṣaṇa n., eating.

bhagavant a., honorable, blessed.

√*bhaj* (*bhájati*, *-te*) divide; — +*vi* distribute.

√*bhañj* (*bhanákti*) break, destroy.

bhadra a., good, pleasant; as n., fortune.

bhaya n., fear.

bharatakhaṇḍa m., *n. pr.*, India.

bhartṛ m., supporter; preserver; lord, master; husband.

bhava m., *n. pr.*, a name of Çiva.

bhavant, f. *bhavatī;* in voc. *bhos*, f. *bhavati;* used in respectful address instead of pronoun of 2nd person. Cf. § 264.

bhasman n., ashes.

√*bhā* (*bhā́ti*) gleam, glance; — + *ā* or *vi* idem.

bhāga m., part, piece, share.

-*bhāj* a., sharing.

bhānu m., sun.

bhāra m., burden.

bhāryā f., wife, woman.

√*bhāṣ* (*bhā́ṣate*) speak; — +*prati* answer (acc. of pers.); — +*sam* converse.

bhāṣā f., speech, language.

bhāsvant a., shining, brilliant.

√*bhikṣ* (*bhikṣate*) beg, get by begging.

bhikṣā f., begging, alms.

bhikṣu m., beggar; ascetic.

√*bhid* (*bhinátti*, *bhinddhé*) split.

√*bhī* (*bibhéti*) fear; in caus. (*bhīṣáyate*, *bhāyáyate*) terrify.

√2*bhuj* (*bhunákti*, *bhuñkté*) eat, enjoy; caus. (*bhojáyati*) feed; — + *upa* enjoy.

-*bhuj* a., enjoying.

bhujyu m., *n. pr.*, a Vedic person.

bhuvana n., world.

√*bhū* (*bhávati*, *-te*) become; be, exist; — + *abhi* overpower; — + *pari* despise; — + *pra* arise; be mighty, rule; *valere*.

bhū f., earth, ground.

bhūta part. of *bhū;* as n. subst., being, creature.

bhūti f., prosperity, blessing.

bhūbhuj m., king.

bhūbhṛt m., king; mountain.

bhūmi f., earth, ground, land.

bhūyas (340) comp. adj., more; -*yas* adv., mostly.

bhūṣaṇa n., ornament.

√*bhṛ* (*bhárati*, *-te*) support (lit. and fig.).

bhṛgukaccha n., *n. pr.*, Baroch, a holy place in India.

bhṛtaka m., servant.

bhṛtya m., servant.

bhṛçam adv., greatly, much.

bheka m., frog.

bhoga m., enjoyment.

bhojana n., meal.

bhos see *bhavant*.

√ *bhram* (*bhrámati, -te; bhrā́myati*: 131) wander about, flit; — + *pari* idem.

bhrātṛ m., brother.

bhrū f., eyebrow.

---

makṣikā f., fly, gnat.

maghavan (270) m., Indra.

√ *majj* (*májjati*) sink; — + *ni* idem.

maṇi m., jewel.

mati f., mind.

matimant a., shrewd, prudent.

matsya m., fish.

mathi same as *manthan*.

mad called stem of *aham*; cf. 352, 4.

√ *mad* (*mádyati*) get drunk; — + *pra* be careless.

madhu n., honey.

madhuparka m., sweet drink.

madhulih m., bee.

madhya a., middle; as n., middle; waist.

√ *man* (*mányate; manuté*) think, suppose; — + *sam* honor.

manas n., mind.

manuṣya m., man (*homo*).

manoratha m., wish.

manohara a., agreeable; entrancing.

mantra m., sacred text; spell, charm.

mantrin m., minister; councillor.

√ *manth* (*mathnā́ti*) stir.

manthan (278) m., stirring-stick.

mandara m., *n. pr.*, a mountain.

maraṇa n., death.

marut m., wind; pl., *n. pr.*, the Storm-gods.

mastaka n., head.

mahant (261) a., great.

mahānasa n., kitchen.

mahārāja m., great king.

mahiṣa m., *n. pr.*

mahiṣī f., queen.

√ 1*mā* (*mā́ti; mimīté*: 438) measure; — + *nis* work, create.

mā adv. and conj., not; used in prohibitions, etc., like Lat. *ne*, Greek μή; cf. 195, 486.

māṅsa n., flesh.

mātṛ f., mother.

mādhurya n., sweetness.

mānava m., man (*homo*).

mānasa n., sense; understanding.

mānuṣa, f. *-ī*, human.

mārga m., road, way, street.

mālā f., garland.

māsa m., month.

mitra n., friend.

mitradruh (249) a., friend-betraying.

mīna m., fish.

√ *mīl* (*mī́lati*) wink; + *ni* close the eyes.

muktā f., pearl.

mukti f., salvation, deliverance.

mukha n., mouth, face.

mukhya a., principal, first.

√ *muc* (*muñcáti*: 110) free, release, let fly, shoot; *muktvā*, without (312).

√ *mud* (*módate*) rejoice; — + *anu* allow.

muni m., sage; ascetic.

√ *muṣ* (*muṣṇā́ti*) steal, rob.

musala m. n., club, pestle.

√ *muh* (*múhyati*) be confused or dazed or stupid.

mūrdhaga a., on the head.

mūrdhan m., head.
mūla n., root.
√*mṛ* (*mriyáte*: **155**) die; caus. (*mā-ráyati*) kill.
mṛga m., wild animal; gazelle.
√*mṛgaya* (den.: *mṛgáyate*) hunt for, seek.
mṛgayā f., chase. hunting.
√*mṛj* (*mā́rṣṭi*: **423**) rub, wipe; caus. (*mārjáyati*) rub off, polish; — + *apa*, *pari* or *pra*, wipe off.
mṛta, part. of *mṛ*, dead, fallen.
mṛtyu m., death.
mṛd f., earth, dirt.
mekhalā f., girdle.
megha m., cloud.
mokṣa m., deliverance; salvation.
moha m., infatuation.

---

ya (**231**) rel. pron., used as subst. and adj., who, which, what; cf. **234** ff.
√*yaj* (*yájati*, -*te*) sacrifice (acc. pers., instr. rei); caus. (*yājáyati*) make to sacrifice, offer sacrifice for (acc.).
yajus n., sacrificial formula, text.
yajña m., sacrifice.
yajñiya a., suitable for sacrificing.
√*yat* (*yátate*) strive after (dat.).
yatas adv., whence; wherefore.
yati m., ascetic.
yatna m., exertion.
yatra adv., where, whither.
yathā adv., in which way; as.
yadā adv., when, if.
yadi adv., if.
√*yam* (*yácchati*: **100**) furnish, give; — + *ud* undertake; — + *ni* ordain, fix, appoint; + *pra* give, give in marriage.
yamunā f., *n. pr.*, the river Jumna.
yavana m., Greek, barbarian.
yaças n., glory, fame.
yaṣṭi f., stick, staff.
√*yā* (*yā́ti*) go; with abstracts, come into such and such a state; — + *ā* approach.
yātrā f., march, journey; support.
yāma m., watch of the night.
yāvant a., how much or many; *yāvat* as adv., as long as, while; as soon as.
yuga n., age of the world.
yugma n., pair.
√*yuj* (*yunákti*, *yuñkté*) join, yoke, harness; caus. (*yojáyati*) idem; — + *ni* place, appoint, establish, caus. set (as jewels); — + *pra* arrange; use.
yuddha n., battle.
√*yudh* (*yúdhyate*) fight (instr.).
yuvati f. to *yuvan*.
yuvan (**269**) a., young; f. *yuvati*.
yuṣmad called stem of *yūyam*; as stem in cpds. (**352**, **4**.), you.
yūpa m., sacrificial post.
yūyam (**226**) pron., you.

√***rakṣ*** (*rákṣati*) protect.
rakṣaṇa n., protection.
rakṣitṛ m., protector.
√*rac* (*racáyati*) arrange, compose (a literary work).
rajju f., cord.
√*rañj* + *anu* (*anurájyati*, -*te*) be inclined or devoted to (loc.).
raṇa m. n., battle.
ratna n., jewel.

ratha m., wagon.
rathyā f., street.
√*rabh* (*rábhate*) grasp; — + *ā* take hold on, begin.
√*ram* (*rámate*) amuse oneself; — + *vi* (*virámati*) cease (abl.).
raçmi m., ray; rein.
rasa m., taste, feeling.
rasavant a., tasteful.
rākṣasa m., demon.
√*rāj* (*rā́jati*, *-te*) direct, rule; shine; be illustrious.
rājan m., king.
rājya n., kingdom.
rātri f., night.
√*rādh* (*rādhnóti*) succeed; — + *apa* do wrong.
rāma m., *n. pr.*, a hero.
rāmāyaṇa n., a noted poem.
rāvaṇa m., *n. pr.*, a demon.
rāçi m., heap.
√*ru* (*rāúti*: 410) cry, scream; — + *vi* idem.
√*ruc* (*rócate*) please (dat., gen.).
ruj f., sickness, disease.
√*rud* (*róditi*: 429) weep.
ruddha, part. of *rudh*, besieged, surrounded; suffused.
√*rudh* (*ruṇáddhi*, *runddhé*) obstruct, check, besiege; — + *upa* besiege.
rudhira n., blood.
√*ruh* (*róhati*) rise, spring up, grow; caus. (*roháyati*, *ropáyati*) make rise or grow, plant; — + *ava* descend; — + *ā* climb, mount, ascend; — + *pra* grow up.
rūkṣa a., harsh, rough.
rūpa n., form, beauty.
rūpaka n., gold-piece.
rāi (277) m., rarely f., possessions, wealth.
rohiṇī f., *n. pr.*

---

lakṣa n., a hundred thousand.
lakṣmī (276) f., goddess of fortune.
√*lag* (*lágati*) attach, hang, cling.
laghu, f. *-ghu* or *-ghvī*, a., light; small, little.
laṅkā f., *n. pr.*, Ceylon.
√*lap* (*lápati*) prate; — + *vi* complain.
√*labh* (*lábhate*) receive, take; caus. (*lambháyati*) make receive, give.
lalāṭa n., forehead.
lavaṇa n., salt.
lāṅgala n., plough.
lābha m., acquisition, gain.
√*likh* (*likháti*) scratch, write.
√*lip* (*limpáti*) smear.
√*lih* (*léḍhi*, *līḍhé*: 427) lick; — + *ava* idem.
√*luṇṭh* (*luṇṭháyati*) + *nis* rob.
√*lup* (*lumpáti*) break to pieces; devastate; plunder.
√*lubh* (*lúbhyati*) covet (dat., loc.).
lekhana n., writing, copying.
loka m., world; sing. and pl., people.
lobha m., desire, avarice.
loman n., hair.
loha n., metal; iron.

---

vañça m., race, family.
vakra a., crooked, bent.

vakṣas n., chest, breast.
√*vac* (*vákti*: 415) speak, say; name; caus. (*vācáyati*) make (a written leaf) speak, *i. e.* read.
vaṇij m., merchant.
vatsa m., calf.
√*vad* (*vádati*) speak, say; — + *abhi* in caus. (*abhivādáyati*) greet; — + *vi* (mid.) dispute, argue.
vadha m., killing, murder.
vadhū f., woman; wife.
vana n., woods, forest.
vanavāsin a., forest-dwelling.
√*vand* (*vándate*) greet, honor.
√*vap* (*vápati*) scatter; sow.
vapus n., body; figure.
vayam (223) pron., we.
vayas n., age.
1*vará* m., suitor, bridegroom.
2*vára* m., choice, privilege; favor.
3*vara* a., best; better (w. abl.: than).
varāha m., boar.
varuṇa m., *n. pr.*, a god.
varṇa m., color; caste.
√*varṇaya* (*varṇáyati*) describe, portray.
vartin a., abiding, being.
varṣa n., year.
vallabha a., dear.
√*vaç* (*váṣṭi*) wish.
√*vas* (*vásati*) dwell; — + *ni* inhabit, dwell; — + *pra* go away on a journey; — + *prati* inhabit.
vasati f., dwelling.
vasu n., wealth, money.
vasudeva m., *n. pr.*
vastra n., garment.
√*vah* (*váhati*) tr., carry, bear; intr., proceed; flow; blow.
vā encl., or.
vāc f., voice; word.
vācya a., blameworthy, culpable.
vāṇijya n., trade.
vāta m., wind.
vānaprastha m., a Brāhman in the third stage of his life.
vāpī f., cistern.
vāyasa m., crow.
vāyu m., wind.
vāri n., water.
vi adv., apart, away, out.
viṅça (334) a., twentieth.
viṅçati (332) num., twenty.
viṅçatitama (334) a., twentieth.
vikramāditya a., *n. pr.*, a king.
√*vij* (*vijáti*) tremble; — + *ud* in caus. (*udvejáyati*) terrify.
vitta n., possessions; wealth.
√*vid* (*vétti*; *véda*: 416—417) know, consider; caus. (*vedáyati*) inform (dat.); — + *ni* caus., idem.
√2*vid* (*vindáti*, *-te*) find, acquire.
-vid a., knowing.
vidyā f., knowledge, learning.
vidvāṅs a., knowing, wise.
vidviṣṭa pass. part. of *vi-dviṣ*, detested.
vidhi m., rule, fate; Brahma.
vidheya a., obedient.
vinaya m., obedience.
vinā prep., without (with instr. or acc., often postpos).
vipāka m., ripening; recompense.
vipra m., Brāhman.

vibhu, f. *-bhvī*, a. pervading, far-reaching; omnipresent, mighty.
vivāha m., wedding, marriage.
vivekin a., shrewd.
√*viç* (*viçáti*) enter; — + *sam-ā* approach; — + *upa* seat oneself; — + *pra* enter, penetrate.
viç m. pl., people; the Vāiçya-caste.
viçiṣṭa part. of *vi-çis*, excellent, remarkable.
viçruta part. of *vi-çru*, famous.
viçva (231) a., all (Vedic).
viçvāsa m., trust, confidence.
viṣa n., poison.
viṣṇu m., *n. pr.*, a god.
vihaga m., bird.
vihita part. of *vi-dhā*, ordained.
√1*vṛ* (*vṛṇóti, vṛṇuté*) cover, surround; — + *ā* cover; — + *apa-ā* open; — + *vi* explain; manifest; — + *sam* shut.
√2*vṛ* (*vṛṇīté; varáyati, -te*) choose, select.
vṛka m., wolf.
vṛkṣa m., tree.
√*vṛt* (*vártate*) turn; exist, subsist, be, become; — + *ni* return home; — + *pra* get a-going, break out, arise; continue; caus. (act.) continue (trans.).
vṛtta n., conduct.
vṛttānta m., state of affairs; news.
vṛtra m., *n. pr.*, a demon.
vṛddha part. of *vṛdh*, old.
√*vṛdh* (*várdhate*) grow; caus. (*vardháyati, -te*) make grow; bring up.
√*vṛṣ* (*várṣati*) rain, give rain; fig., shower down; overwhelm.
veda m., science, knowledge; esp. sacred knowledge, holy writ.
vedanā f., pain.
vedānta m., a system of philosophy.
vedi f., altar.
vāi assev. particle, to be sure, in sooth; often untranslated.
vāiçya m., man of the third caste.
vyañjana n., spice.
√*vyath* in caus. (*vyatháyati*) torment.
√*vyadh* (*vidhyati*) hit, pierce.
vyalīka a., false, wrong.
vyavahāra m., trial, law-suit; trade.
vyākaraṇa n., grammar.
vyāghra m., tiger.
vyādha m., hunter.
vyādhi m., disease, illness.
vyādhita a., sick, ill.
vyāsa m., *n. pr.*
√*vraj* (*vrájati, -te*) proceed; — + wander forth; become an ascetic.
vraṇa m., wound.
vrata n., vow, obligation; duty.

√*çaṅs* (*çáṅsati*) praise; proclaim; — + *pra* proclaim.
√*çak* (*çaknóti*) be able; sometimes pass., cf. 322.
çaka m., Scythian.
çakaṭa m., car.
çakuntalā f., *n. pr.*
çaṅkā f., hesitation.
çata (332–333) n., a hundred.
çatatama a., hundredth.

çatru m., enemy.
çabda m., sound, noise, word.
√*çam* (*çámyati*) become quiet, be extinguished, go out.
çayyā f., bed, couch.
çara m., arrow.
çaraṇa n., protection.
çarad f., autumn; year.
çarīra n., body.
çarva m., *n. pr.*, a name of Çiva.
çākhā f., branch; edition, redaction.
çānti f., repose.
√*çās* (*çāste*) command; rule; punish.
çāstṛ m., governor, punisher.
çāstra n., science; text-book.
√*çikṣ* (*çíkṣate*) learn.
çikhara m., summit.
çiras n., head.
çiva a., beneficent, gracious; blessed; as m., *n. pr.*, a god.
çiçu m., child.
√*çiṣ* (*çinásṭi*) leave, leave remaining; — + *ava* remain over, survive; — + *ud* idem; — + *vi* set apart, distinguish.
çiṣya m., pupil, scholar.
√*çī* (*çéte*: 409) lie; sleep; — + *adhi* lie asleep on (acc.).
çīta a., cold.
√*çuc* (*çócati*) grieve, sorrow.
çuci a., pure, clean.
çunaḥçepa m., *n. pr.*
√*çubh* (*çóbhate*) be brilliant, shine.
çubha a., good; splendid.
√*çuṣ* (*çúsyati*) dry up.
çūdra m., man of the fourth caste.
çūdratva n., condition of a Çūdra.
çūra m., hero.
çṛgāla m., jackal
çeṣa m. n., rest, remainder.
çeṣa m., a fabulous snake supporting the earth.
√*çram* (*çrámyati*: 131) become weary.
çrama m., pains, trouble.
çrāddha n., oblation to the Manes (cf. in Voc. 16).
√*çri* + *ā* (*āçráyate*) go for protection, take refuge with (acc.).
çrī f., luck, fortune, riches; as *n. pr.*, goddess of fortune; as prefix to proper names, famous, honorable, etc.
çrīmant a., rich; famous.
√*çru* (*çṛṇóti, çṛṇuté*: 391) hear; in caus. (*çrāváyati*) make hear, i. e. recite, proclaim (acc. pers.).
çruta part. of *çru*; as n., learning.
çruti f., hearing; holy writ.
çreyas a., better; best; *çreyas* as n., salvation.
çvan (269) m., dog.
çvaçura m., father-in-law.
çvaçrū f., mother-in-law.
çvas adv., to-morrow.
√*çvas* (*çvásiti*: 429) breathe; — + *sam-ā* breathe gently: revive; — + *vi* be confident; trust (gen. or loc.).
çveta a., white.

ṣaṭtriṅçat (329) num., thirty-six.
ṣaḍaçīti (329) num., eighty-six.
ṣaṣ (332) num., six.
ṣaṣṭi (332) num., sixty.
ṣaṣṭha, f. *-ī* (334), a., sixth.

ṣoḍaça (332) num., sixteen.

---

saṁyukta part. of *sam-yuj*, provided with.

saṁvatsara m., year.

saṁçaya m., doubt.

sakṛt adv., once.

sakthan (*sakthi*: 275) n., thigh.

sakhi (274) m., friend.

sakhī f., female companion, friend.

sajja a., ready.

√*sañj* (*sájati*; *sajjáte*: cf. in Voc. 22) hang on, be fastened on (loc.).

satkāra m., hospitality.

sattra n., sacrifice.

satya n., truth, righteousness.

√*sad* (*sī́dati*) sit; settle down; be overcome or exhausted; — + *ā* approach; — + *sam-ā* seat oneself; caus. (-*sādáyati*) meet, encounter; — + *ni* sit down; — + *pra* be favorable.

sadā adv., always.

sadṛça, f. -*ī*, a., similar; worthy.

saṁdigdha a., doubtful; unsteady.

saṁdhyā f., twilight.

sant, part. of 1*as*, being, existing; good; as m., good man; as f. *satī*, good woman, especially a widow who immolates herself.

sapta (332) num., seven.

saptati (332) num., seventy.

saptadaça (332) num., seventeen.

sabhā f., council, meeting, court.

sam adv., along with; completely.

samakṣam adv., before, in the presence of (gen.).

samartha a., capable, able.

samāgama m., meeting, encounter.

samāja m., convention, company.

samidh f., fagot.

samīpa a., near; as n., vicinity, nearness, presence.

samudra m., ocean.

samunnati f., height, elevation; high position.

sameta a., provided with.

sampūrṇa part. of 1*pṛ* + *sam*, full.

samyak adv., well, properly.

samrāj m., great king; emperor.

sarit f., river.

sarga m., creation.

sarpa m., snake.

sarva (231) a., all.

sarvatra a., everywhere.

savitṛ m., *n. pr.*, the Sun-god Savitar; sun.

√*sah* (*sáhate*) endure.

saha adv., together; prep., often postpos., with, along with, (instr.).

sahacara m., companion; -*ī* f., wife.

sahasā adv., suddenly, quickly.

sahasra n., a., thousand.

sahāya m., companion, helper.

sākṣin m., witness.

sādhana n., means, device.

sādhu m., holy man, saint.

sāman n., Vedic melody, song; pl., the Sāmaveda.

sāmanta m., vassal.

sāmpratam adv., at present.

sāyam adv., at evening.

sārasa m., crane.

siṅha m., lion.

√*sic* (*siñcáti*) drip, drop, moisten; — +*abhi* anoint as king.

√1*sidh* (*sédhati*) repel; — +*prati* hold back; forbid.

√2*sidh* (*sidhyati*) succeed; in caus. (*sādháyati*) perform; acquire.

sindhu m., *n. pr.*, the Indus.

sīman f., border, boundary; outskirts.

su adv., well; easy; very.

√*su* (*sunóti*, *sunuté*) press.

sukha n., fortune, luck, happiness.

sundara, f. -ī, a., beautiful.

sumanas a., favorably-minded; as f., flower.

surāpa m., drunkard.

suvarṇa n., gold.

suhṛd m., friend.

√*sū* (*sūté*) generate, bring forth; — +*pra* generate.

sūkta n., Vedic hymn.

sūta m., driver, charioteer.

sūda m., cook.

sūrya m., sun.

√*sṛ* (*sárati*) flow; — +*anu* follow up; — +*apa* go away; in caus. (-*sāráyati*) drive away.

√*sṛj* (*sṛjáti*) let go, create; — +*ud* let loose or out; raise (the voice).

√*sṛp* (*sárpati*) move; — +*pra* idem.

sṛṣṭi f., creation.

setu m., bridge, dike.

senā f., army.

√*sev* (*sévate*) serve, honor; — +*ni* dwell; devote oneself to; attend.

sāinika m., soldier.

sāinya n., army.

soma m., the intoxicating fermented juice of the Soma-plant.

skandha m., shoulder.

√*stu* (*stāúti*: 411) praise.

stuti f., song of praise; praise.

√*stṛ* (*stṛṇóti*, *stṛṇuté*; *stṛṇā́ti*, *stṛṇīté*) scatter, strew; — +*upa* scatter, bestrew.

stena m., thief.

stotra n., song of praise.

strī (276) f., woman.

√*sthā* (*tíṣṭhati*) stand, intr.; be in or on, etc., be situated; caus. (*sthāpáyati*) put, place; appoint; stop; — +*adhi* mount, stand over; rule, govern; — +*anu* follow out, accomplish; (cf. also p. 96, last note); — +*ud* arise, rise (cf. Voc. 40); — +*upa* approach, reach; — +*pra* mid., start off; in caus. (act.), send; — +*sam* in caus., cause to remain

sthāna n., place, locality; stead.

sthita part. of *sthā*; cf. 290, end.

sthiti f., condition.

√*snā* (*snā́ti*) bathe.

snātaka m., one who has performed the ablutions customary at the end of religious pupilage.

snāna n., bathing, bath.

snāyu m., tendon, bowstring.

snigdha part. of *snih*, affectionate.

√*snih* (*snihyati*) feel inclined to, love (gen., loc.).

snuṣā f., daughter-in-law.

√*spṛç* (*spṛçáti*) touch.

√*spṛh* (*spṛháyati*) desire (dat.).

sma encl., slightly assev.; often accompanies a present tense, giving it the force of an historical tense.

√*smṛ* (*smárati*) remember; think on; call to mind; teach; esp. in pass. *smaryate* 'it is taught, i. e. traditional'.

smṛti f., tradition; law-book.

sraj f., garland.

sraṣṭṛ m., creator.

sva a., own; one's own.

√*svañj* (*svájate*) embrace; — + *pari* (Cf. Voc. 21) idem.

svadṛç a., similar.

√*svap* (*svápiti*: **429**) sleep.

svapna m., sleep, dream.

svayam pron., own self, self.

svayambhū a., self-existent; as m., epithet of Brahma.

svarga m., heaven.

svasṛ f., sister.

svādu a., sweet.

svādhyāya m., private recitation of sacred texts.

svāmin m., possessor, lord.

svāiram adv., at pleasure.

---

hata part. of *han*.

√*han* (*hánti*: **419**) kill; caus. (*ghātáyati*), have killed; — + *apa* remove; — + *abhi* smite; — + *sam-ā* wound; — + *ni* kill; — + *prati* hinder; injure, offend; — + *sam* write.

-han (233) a., killing.

hanu f., jaw.

hanumant m., *n. pr.*, a monkey-king.

hantṛ m., killer, slayer.

hari m., *n. pr.*, a god.

hariṇa m., gazelle.

hala m. n., plough.

havis n., oblation.

hasta m., hand.

hastin m., elephant.

√1*hā* (*jáhāti*) abandon, give up; neglect.

√2*hā* (*jihīte*: **438**) move.

√*hi* (*hinóti*) send; — + *pra* idem.

hi assev. particle, surely; causal, for, because.

√*hiṅs* (*hinásti*) injure, destroy.

hita part. of 1*dhā*; as adj., advantageous; as n., advantage.

himavant a., snowy; as m., the Himālaya Mts.

hīna part. of 1*hā*, abandoned; wanting in; w. instr., without.

√*hu* (*juhóti*, *juhuté*) sacrifice.

hutabhuj (nom. *-bhuk*) m., fire.

√*hū* see *hvā*.

√*hṛ* (*hárati*) take away; steal; plunder; — + *apa* idem; — + *ā* act. and mid., fetch, bring; — + *ud-ā* cite, mention; — + *praty-ā* bring back; — + *ud* save, rescue.

hṛd (**281**) n., heart.

hṛdaya n., heart.

√*hṛṣ* (*hárṣati*, *hṛṣyati*) rejoice, be delighted; — + *pra* idem.

he interj., O, ho.

hemanta m., winter.

hrasvam adv., near by.

√*hrī* (*jihréti*) be ashamed.

hrī f., modesty, bashfulness.

√*hvā* (*hváyati*) call; in caus. (*hvāyáyati*) have called; — + *ā* call, summon.

II. English - Sanskrit.

abandon, to: *tyaj; 1hā.*
able: *samartha; çakya.*
able, to be: *çak.*
according to: *anu*, postpos.
acquire, to: *labh; āp.*
Açvins: *açvināu*, du.
address, to: *brū.*
adore, to: *nam+pra.*
adorn, to: *1kṛ + alam.*
advantage: *hita* n.; *kalyāṇa* n.
adversity; *duḥkha* n.
afraid, to be: *bhī.*
afterward: *tatas.*
again: *punar.*
against: *prati.*
age: *vayas* n.
all: *sarva;* (entire) *viçva.*
all protecting: *viçvapā.*
allow, to: *jñā+anu.*
alms: *bhikṣā* f.
alone (adv.): *eva.*
also: *api.*
altar: *vedi* f.
although: *api.*
always: *sadā, nityam.*
amuse oneself, to: *ram.*
ancient: *purāṇa.*
and: *ca*, postpos.; *tathā.*
anger: *kopa* m.; *krodha* m.
animal: *tiryañc* m.
announce, to: 1*vid+ni*, caus.
answer, to: *bhāṣ+prati.*
appoint, to: *kḷp*, caus.; *yuj + ni.*
approach, to: *gam + ā; yā + ā.*
argument (reason): *vāc* f.
arise, to: *bhū;* (get up) *sthā + ud.*
arm: *bāhu* m.
army: *senā* f.
arrive, to: *gam + ā.*
arrow: *çara* m.; *iṣu* m.
Aryan: *dvija* m.; *dvijāti* m.
ascetic: *muni* m.; *yati* m.; *parivrāj* m.; *tapasvin* m.; — to become an a., *vraj+pra.*
ashamed, to be: *hrī.*
ashes: *bhasman* n.
ask, to (inquire): *prach.*
ask for, to: *arthaya.*
assembly: *sabhā* f.; *pariṣad* f.
astronomy: *jyotiṣa* n.
attain, to: *labh; 2vid; 1aç; āp; āp +ava* or *pra.*
attainment: *lābha* m.
author: *kartṛ* m.; (of Vedic hymnns, etc.) *draṣṭṛ* m.
axe; *paraçu* m.

---

bad: *pāpa.*
bank: *tīra* n.
banner: *ketu* m.
barbarian: *yavana* m.
bathe, to: *snā.*

battle: *raṇa* m. n.; *yuddha* n.
be, to: *bhū; vṛt;* (be situated) *sthā.*
bear, to: *bhṛ*; (bring forth) *sū; sū+pra.*
bear: *ṛkṣa* m.
beat, to: *taḍ.*
beautiful: *sundara; rūpavant.*
beauty: *rūpa* n.
become, to: *bhū; vṛt.*
bee: *ali* m.; *madhulih* m.
beg, to: *bhikṣ.*
begin, to: *rabh+ā.*
behind: *paçcāt* (w. gen.).
behold, to: *īkṣ.*
Benares: *kāçī* f.
bend, to: *nam.*
benefit, to; 1*kṛ+upa.*
beseech, to: *pad+pra.*
besiege, to: *rudh; rudh+upa.*
best: *çreṣṭha; jyeṣṭha.*
betake oneself, to: *yā; çri+ā.*
better: *çreyas; jyāyas.*
bind, to: *bandh.*
biped: *dvipad.*
bird: *vihaga* m.; *pakṣin* m.
birth: *jāti* f.; *janman* n.
black: *kṛṣṇa.*
blame, to: *nind;* 1*kṛ+tiras.*
blessed: *bhagavant;* (as prefix) *çrī.*
blood: *rudhira* n.
blow, to (intr.): *vah.*
boat: *nāu* f.
body: *çarīra* n.; *vapus* n.; *kāya* m.; (heavenly: sun, etc.): *jyotis* n.
bone: *asthan* n.
book: (manuscript) *pustaka* n.; (work) *grantha* m.
born, to be: *jan; jan+ud.*
both: *ubha* du.
bow, to: *nam.*
boy: *bāla* m.; *kumāra* m.
Brāhman: *brāhmaṇa* m.; *dvija* m.; *dvijāti* m.; *vipra* m.
branch: *çākhā* f.
brave: *dhīra.*
breast: *uras* n.; *vakṣas* n.
bridegroom: *vará* m.
brilliancy: *tejas* n.
bring, to: *nī+ā; hṛ+ā.*
broad: *pṛthu; uru.*
brother: *bhrātṛ* m.
burn, to: *dah.*
business: *kārya* n.
but: *tu; kiṁtu; punar.*
call, to: *hvā;* (name) *vac; vad.*
capable: *samartha.*
caste: *jāti f.*
cattle: *go* m. pl.
cease, to: *çam; ram+vi.*
celebrated: *viçruta; çrīmant.*
chain: *hāra* m.
charioteer; *sūta* m.
charm: *kānti* f..
check, to: *dam,* caus.; *rudh.*
chest: *vakṣas* n.; *uras* n.
child: *bāla* m.; *çiçu* m.
choose, to: 2*vṛ.*
cistern: *vāpī* f.
citizen: *pāura* m.
city: *nagara* n.; *-ī* f.; *pur* f.
cleverness: *buddhi* f.
climb, to: *ruh + ā.*
close, to: 1*vṛ + sam*; 1*dhā + api.*
cloud: *megha* m.
coachman: *sūta* m.
come, to: *gam + ā; yā + ā; i +*

abhi or *ā*; come out: *gam* + *nis*; *yā* + *nis*.
command, to: *diç+ā*; *jñā+ā* caus.
command: *ajñā* f.; *nideça* m.
commit, to: *car* + *ā*; 1*kṛ*.
companion: *sahāya* m.; *sahacara* m.
company: *samāja* m.
compose, to: *rac*.
conduct: *vṛtta* n.
confine, to: *rudh* + *ni*.
conquer, to: *ji*.
consecrate, to: *nī* + *upa*.
consider, to: *cint*; 1*vid*.
consort: *patnī* f.
cook, to: *pac*.
copying: *lekhana* n.
cord, sacred: *upavīta* n.
count, to: *gaṇaya*.
courageous: *tejasvin*.
course: *gati* f.
cover, to: 1*vṛ* (mid.); 1*vṛ* + *sam* (mid.).
cow: *dhenu* f.; *go* f.
cowherd: *gopa* m.
create, to: *sṛj*.
creator: *dhātṛ* m.; *sraṣṭṛ* m.
creature: *prāṇin* m.; *jagat* n.
crescent: *kalā* f.
cross, to: *tṛ*.
crow: *vāyasa* m.
curds: *dadhan* n.
cut, to: *kṛt*; *chid*.
cut off, to: *kṛt* + *ava*; *chid* + *ava*.

---

daily: *nitya*; (adv.) *nityam*; *pratyaham*.
dancing: *nṛtta* n.
daughter: *kanyā* f.; *putrī* f.; *duhitṛ* f.
day: *divasa* m.; *dina* n.; *ahan* n.;
d. by d.: *dine dine*; *pratyaham*;
a day and a night: *ahorātra* n.
dead: *mṛta*; *vipanna*.
decide, to (settle): *nī* + *nis*.
deed: *karman* n.
deity: *devatā* f.
delicate: *taruṇa*.
delight, to (tr.): *tuṣ*, caus.
deliverance: *mukti* f.
demon: *rākṣasa* m.
depart, to: *i* + *apa*.
describe, to: *varṇaya*.
desire, to: *lubh*.
destroy, to: *bhañj*.
despise, to: *man* + *ava*; *bhū* + *pari*.
determine, to: *ci* + *nis* or *vi-nis*.
devoted: *bhakta*; *snigdha*.
devotion: *bhakti* f.
die: *akṣa* m.
die, to: *mṛ*; *i* + *pra*; *pad* + *vi*.
difficult: *durlabha*; *duṣkara*.
dig, to: *khan*.
diligence: *udyoga* m.
diligently: *bhṛçam*.
disappear, to: *naç* + *vi*.
disease: *ruj* f.; *vyādhi* m.
dismount, to: *ruh* + *ava*.
disown, to: *khyā* + *prati-ā*.
dispute, to: *vad* + *vi*.
distress, to: *du*.
distribute, to: *bhaj* + *vi*.
divine: *divya*.
do, to: 1*kṛ*; *car* + *sam-ā*.
domestic: *gṛhya*.
dog: *çvan* m.; *çunī* f.
door: *dvār* f.

doorkeeper: *dvāḥstha* m.
dove: *kapota* m.
draw, to: *vah.*
drink, to: 1*pā.*
driver: *sūta* m.
drop, to: *sic.*
drop: *bindu* m.
dwell, to: 3*vas; vas + ni;* dwell on (fig.): *sañj.*

---

ear: *karṇa* m.
earth: *pṛthivī* f.; *bhū* f.; *bhūmi* f.
east, eastern: *prāñc*; the E.: *prācī* f., sc. *diç.*
eat, to; *ad;* 2*aç; bhakṣ; bhuj.*
eating: *bhakṣaṇa* n.
eclipse, to: 1*kṛ + tiras.*
eight: *aṣṭa.*
eighth: *aṣṭama.*
eighty: *açīti* f.
eightieth: *açītitama.*
eldest: *jyeṣṭha.*
elephant: *gaja* m.; *hastin* m.
eleventh: *ekādaça.*
emerge, to: *tṛ + ud.*
eminent, to be: *çubh.*
emperor: *samrāj* m.
encompass, to: 1*vṛ; chid + ava.*
end: *anta* m.
endure, to: *sah.*
enemy: *ari* m.; *çatru* m.; *dviṣ* m.
enjoy, to: *bhuj.*
enjoyment: *bhoga* m.
enter, to: *viç + pra.*
entrancing: *manohara.*
envoy: *dūta* m.
entrust, to: 1*dā + pra.*
equip, to: *nah + sam.*
eulogy: *stotra* n.
even (adv.): *api.*
every: *sarva.*
evil (adj.): *pāpa*; (subst.) *pāpa* n.
exceedingly: *ati.*
explain, to: *brū + vi;* 1*vṛ + vi; cakṣ + vi-ā.*
exterminate, to: *chid + ud.*
eye: *netra* n.; *cakṣus* n.; *akṣan* n.; *locana* n.

---

face: *mukha* n.
fagot: *samidh* f.
fair: *sundara.*
fall, to: *pat; pat + ni;* fall to one's lot: *ṛ;* fallen (killed): *patita; mṛta.*
fame: *kīrti* f.; *yaças* n.
family: *vaṅça* m.
famous: *viçruta.*
fast (firm): *dṛḍha.*
fasten, to: *bandh.*
fat: *pīna; puṣṭa.*
father: *janaka* m.; *pitṛ* m.
fault, to find: 1*kṛ + tiras.*
faultless: *anavadya.*
fear: *bhaya* n.
field: *kṣetra* n.
fifth: *pañcama.*
fight, to: *yudh.*
filled: *pūrṇa; sampūrṇa.*
finally: *ante.*
find, to: 2*vid.*
finish, to: *āp + sam.*
fire: *agni* m.; *hutabhuj* m.
firewood: *samidh* f.
first: *prathama;* at first: *prathamam.*
fish: *matsya* m.; *mīna* m.
fit, to: *yuj.*

five: *pañca*.
flee, to: *palāy*.
flit, to: *bhram*.
flock: *paçu* m. pl.
flower: *puṣpa* n.; *sumanas* f.
fly, to: *pat*; fly up: *pat* + *ud*.
fodder: *ghāsa* m.
foe: *ari* m.; *çatru* m.
follow, to: *gam* + *anu*; *i* + *anu*.
fond, to be: *tuṣ*.
food: *anna* n.
foot: *pāda* m.; *pad* m.
force: *bala* n.
foreign: *para*.
forehead: *lalāṭa* n.
forest: *vana* n.
forest-dwelling: *vanavāsin*.
form, to: 1*mā* + *nis*.
formula (sacrificial): *yajus* n.
fortune: *çrī* f., often pl.; goddess of f.: *çrī* f.
forty: *catvāriṅçat* f.
four: *catur*.
free, to: *muc*.
friend: *mitra* n.; *sakhi* m.; *suhṛd* m.
friend-betrayer: *mitradruh*.
front: *agra* n.; in f. of: *agre*, *samakṣam* (gen.).
fruit: *phala* n.
fruitful: *phalavant*.
full: *pūrṇa*; *sampūrṇa*.

---

gain, to: *labh*.
garden: *udyāna* n.
garland: *mālā* f.; *sraj* f.
gate: *dvār* f.
gather, to: *ci* + *sam*.
gazelle: *hariṇa* m.; *mṛga* m.
generous: *dātṛ*.
get, to: *labh*; 1*aç*; *āp*.
gift: *dāna* n.
gird, to: *nah* + *sam*.
girdle: *mekhalā* f.
girl: *kanyā* f.; *bālā* f.
give, to: *yam*; 1*dā*.
giver: *dātṛ* m.
glance: *dṛç* f.
glory: *kīrti* f.; *yaças* n.
go, to: *car*: *yā*; *gam*; *i*; go on (continue): *vṛt* + *pra*.
god: *deva* m.; goddess: *devī* f.
gold: *suvarṇa* n.
govern, to: *çās*; *rājyaṁ kṛ*.
good: *sādhu*; *sant*.
gracious: *çiva*.
graciousness: *kṛpā* f.
grain: *dhānya* n.
grammar: *vyākaraṇa* n.
grasp, to: *grah*.
graze, to: *car*.
great: *mahant*.
great king: *mahārāja* m.
greater: *mahīyas*; *adhika*.
greatly: *bahu*; *bhṛçam*.
greedy: *lubdha*.
Greek: *yavana* m.
greet, to: *vand*; *vad* + *abhi*, caus.
grieve, to: *du*.
ground: *bhūmi* f.; on the g.: *adhas*.
grind, to: *piṣ*.
guard, to: *rakṣ*; *gopāya*.
guest: *athiti* m.
guilt: *pāpa* n.; *enas* n.

---

hand: *kara* m.; *pāṇi* m.; *hasta* m.
hang, to: *sañj*; *lag*.
happiness: *sukha* n.

happy, to be: *mud.*
hard to find: *durlabha.*
harm, to: 1*kṛ* + *apa.*
hate, to: *dviṣ*; *dviṣ* + *pra.*
hear, to: *çru.*
heart: *hṛdaya* n.; *hṛd* n.
heaven: *svarga* m.
heavy: *guru.*
hell: *naraka* m.
here: *atra*; *iha.*
hero: *çūra* m.; *vīra* m.
hesitation: *çaṅkā* f.
high: *ucchrita.*
high water: *pūra* m.
hold shut, to: 1*dhā* + *api.*
holy: *sādhu.*
holy writ: *çruti* f.
home (adv.); *gṛham.*
honey: *madhu* n.
honor, to: *pūj*; *nam*; *sev.*
hope: *āçā* f.
horse: *açva* m.
house: *gṛha* n.: master of the h., *gṛhastha* m.
householder: *gṛhastha* m.
house-priest: *purohita* m.
how?: *katham.*
human: *mānuṣa.*
hunter: *vyādha* m.
hurl, to: 2*as*; *kṣip.*
husband: *pati* m.; *bhartṛ* m.
hymn: *sūkta* n.

I: *aham.*
impart, to: 1*vid* + *ni*, caus.
inclined, to be: *snih.*
increase, to: *vṛdh.*
India: *bharatakhaṇḍa* m.
initiate, to: *nī* + *upa.*
injustice: *adharma* m.
intelligence: *buddhi* f.
iron: *loha* n.

---

jaw: *hanu* f.
jewel: *maṇi* m.; *ratna* n.; *bhūṣaṇa* n.

---

kill, to: *mṛ*, caus.; *han*; *han*, caus.
kindle, to: *idh.*
king: *nṛpa* m.; *nṛpati* m.; *pārthiva* m.; *rājan* m.; *bhūbhuj* m.; *bhūbhṛt* m.
kingdom: *rājya* n.
know, to: 1*vid*; *jñā.*
knowledge: *vidyā* f.; *jñāna* n.

---

lament, to: *lap* + *vi.*
land: *deça* m.
language: *bhāṣā* f.
last, at: *ante.*
law: *dharma* m.; *vidhi* m.
law-book: *smṛti* f.; *dharmaçāstra* n.
law-suit: *vyavahāra* m.
lead, to: *nī.*
leader: *netṛ.*
learn, to: *gam* + *ava*; 1*vid*; *i* + *adhi.*
learned: *vidvāṅs*; *paṇḍita*; *kuçala.*
learning: *vidyā* f.
leather: *carman* n.
leavings: *ucchiṣṭa* n.
lesson: *adhyāya* m.
lick, to: *lih*; *lih* + *ava.*
life: *jīvita* n.; *āyus* n.; *carita* n.
light: *jyotis* n.
light (not heavy): *laghu.*
like: *iva.*

limb: *aṅga* n.
lion: *sin̄ha* m.
lip: *oṣṭha* m.
listen, to: *çru*.
live, to: *jīv*; *vṛt*; *an + pra*.
long: *dīrgha*; (adv.) *ciram*.
look at, to: *īkṣ + pra*.
lord: *īçvara* m.; *pati* m.
lotus: *padma* m. n.
love, to: *snih*.
love, god of l.: *kāma* m.
lunar mansion: *nakṣatra* n.

---

maiden: *kanyā* f.; *bālā* f.
maidservant: *dāsī* f.
make, to: 1*kṛ*.
man (*vir*): *nara* m.; *pumāṅs* m.; *puruṣa* m.; (*homo*): *jana* m.; *mānava* m.; *manuṣya* m.; *nara* m.
mankind: *jana* m. pl.
many: *bahu*; *prabhūta*.
march, to: *cal + pra*.
marriage: *vivāha* m.
marry, to: *nī + pari*.
master: *bhartṛ* m.; *pati* m.
mat: *kaṭa* m.
means: *sādhana* n.
medicine: *āuṣadha* n.
meet, to (intr.): *gam + sam* (mid.).
meeting: *samāgama* m.
melted butter: *ghṛta* n.
mention, to: *hṛ + ud-ā*.
merchant: *vaṇij* m.
merit: *puṇya* n.
mighty: *balin*; *balavant*; *vibhu*.
milk, to: *duh*.
milk: *kṣīra* n.; *payas* n.
mind: *manas* n.; *mati* f.
minister: *mantrin* m.
misfortune: *duḥkha* n.; *āpad* f.
modesty: *hrī* f.
moisten, to: *sic*.
monarch; *samrāj* m.
money: *dhana* n.; *vasu* n.
month: *māsa* m.
moon: *candramas* m.; *candra* m.; *indu* m.
mostly: *bhūyas*.
morning, in the: *prātar*.
mother: *mātṛ* f.; *ambā* f.
mother-in-law: *çvaçrū* f.
mountain: *giri* m.; *parvata* m.
mouth: *mukha* n.
much: *prabhūta*; *bahu*.
mouthful: *grāsa* m.
murder, to: *mṛ*, caus.; *han*; *han*, caus.
must: *arh*; cf. § 320 and Exercise 30.

---

name: *nāman* n.; by n.: *nāma*.
name, to: *vac*; *vad*; (reckon) *gaṇaya*.
neck: *kaṇṭha* m.
neglect, to: 1*hā*.
net: *jāla* n.
never: *na kadā + api*, *cid*, or *cana*.
news: *vṛttānta* m.
night: *rātri* f.
no one: *na ka + api*, *cid*, or *cana*.
north, northern: *udañc*; the N.: *udīcī* f., sc. *diç*.
not: *na*; *mā*.
nothing: *na kim + api*, *cid*, or *cana*.
now: *adhunā*; *sāmpratam*.

O: *he.*
obedient: *vidheya.*
oblation: *havis* n.
occur, to: *dṛç,* pass.; *2vid,* pass.
ocean: *udadhi* m.; *samudra* m.
offend, to: *han + prati; 1hā.*
offering (sacrificial): *havis* n.
old: *vṛddha;* older: *jyāyas.*
omnipresent: *vibhu.*
once: *sakṛt.*
one: *eka.*
only: *eva.*
opinion; *mati* f.; *mata* n.
or; *vā,* postpos.; *athavā.*
ordain, to: *kḷp,* caus.; *1dhā + vi;* ordained: *vihita.*
order, to: *jña + ā,* caus.
other; *anya; itara, apara.*
outskirts: *sīman* f.
overcome, to: *2pṛ.*
overwhelm, to: *vṛs.*
own, one's own: *sva.*
ox: *anaḍuh* m.
pair: *yugma* n.
palace: *prāsāda* m.
parents: *pitṛ,* m. du.
part: *bhāga* m.
path: *mārga* m.; *panthan* m.
peak: *çikhara* m.
pearl: *muktā* f.
peasant: *kṛṣīvala* m.
penance: *tapas* n.; *prāyaçcitta* n.
people: *jana,* pl.; *loka,* s. and pl.
perform, to: *sidh,* caus.; *car; car + sam ā;* (a sacrifice) *tan.*
perfume: *gandha* m.
perish, to: *naç + vi.*
pestle: *musala* m. n.
pierce, to: *vyadh.*
pilgrimage: *tīrthayātrā* f.
pious: *sādhu.*
place, to: *1dhā; dhā + sam-ā.*
place: *pada* n.; *deça* m.
plan: *abhiprāya* m.
plant, to: *ruh,* caus.
play, to: *dīv.*
please, to: *ruc.*
pleasure: *sukha* n.; with p., pleasantly: *sukhena;* (wish, choice) *icchā* f.; *kāma* m.; at p.: *svecchayā.*
plough: *lāñgala* n.; *hala* m. n.
plough, to: *kṛṣ.*
plunder, to: *luṇṭh; hṛ; lup.*
poem: *kāvya* n.
poet: *kavi* m.
point out, to; *diç.*
polluted, to be: *duṣ.*
poor: *daridra.*
possessions: *dhana* n.
post, sacrificial: *yūpa* m.
pot: *ghaṭa* m.
pound, to: *piṣ.*
pour, to: *hu.*
power: *bala* n.
powerful: *balin; balavant.*
praise, song of p.: *stuti* f.; *stotra* n.
praise, to: *çaṅs; stu.*
pray for, to: *arth.*
prescription: *ādeça* m.
presence: *samīpa* n.
previous; *pūrva.*
priest: *ṛtvij* m.
prince: *kumāra* m.
property: *vasu* n.; *dhana* n.
prosperity: *bhūti* f.
protect, to: *rakṣ; 2pā; pā,* caus.
protection; *çaraṇa* n.

protector: *rakṣitṛ* m.
punish, to: *daṇḍaya; çās.*
punishment: *daṇḍa* m.
put, to: *sthā*, caus.; 1*dhā; yuj* + *ni.*

---

quadruped: *catuṣpad.*
quarter: *pāda* m.; (of the sky) *diç* f.
queen: *devī* f.; *rājñī* f.; *mahiṣī* f.

---

rain: *vṛṣṭi* f.
rain, to (give rain): *vṛṣ.*
raise, to (the voice): *sṛj* + *ud.*
ray: *pāda* m.; *raçmi* m.
reach, to: *labh; āp* + *pra.*
read, to: *i* + *adhi;* (aloud) *paṭh; vac,* caus.
realm: *rājya* n.
receive, to: *labh; grah; grah* + *prati;* 1*dā* + *ā.*
recitation (private): *svādhyāya* m.
recite, to: *paṭh;* (tell) *kath.*
reckon, to: *gaṇaya.*
recompense, to: 1*kṛ* + *prati.*
reduced (in fortune): *kṣīṇa.*
region: *diç* f.; *deça* m.
rein: *raçmi* m.
rejoice, to: *tuṣ; mud.*
remember, to: *smṛ.*
restrain, to: *grah* + *ni.*
return, to: *vṛt* + *ni.*
rice: *taṇḍula* m.
reverence, to: *nam; pūj; ās* + *upa.*
reward: *phala* n.
rich: *dhanin; çrīmant; vasumant* (comp. and sup. sometimes *vasīyas, vasiṣṭha*).
riches: *dhana* n.; *vasu* n.; *çrī* f.; *rāi* m.
righteousness: *satya* n.
right (subst.): *dharma* m.
Rigveda: *ṛgveda* m.; *ṛcas* f. pl.
rise, to (of sun, etc.): *gam* + *ud; i* + *ud.*
river: *nadī* f.; *sarit* f.
road: *mārga* m.; *panthan* m.
rob, to: *muṣ, luṇṭh.*
root: *mūla* n.
rub, to: *mṛj; mṛj,* caus.
royal: *rāja-*, in cpd.
rule, to: *sthā* + *adhi; īç.*
run, to: *dhāv; dru.*
running: *dhāvana* n.

---

sacrament: *saṁskāra* m.
sacrifice, to: *yaj;* (for some one) *yaj,* caus.
sacrifice: *yajña* m.
sacrificial formula: *yajus* n.
sage: *ṛṣi* m.
sake of, for the: *artha* in cpd. (cf. 375, 3).
salt: *lavaṇa* n.
salvation: *mukti* f.; *bhūti* f.; *hita* n.
satiated: *tṛpta.*
satisfy, to: *tṛp,* caus.; (oneself) *tṛp.*
save, to: *hṛ* + *ud.*
Savitar: *savitṛ* m.
say, to: *vad; vac; brū.*
scatter, to: 2*kṛ.*
scholar: *çiṣya:* (learned man) *paṇḍita* m.
science: *çāstra* n.
sea: *udadhi* m.; *samudra* m.
seat oneself, to: *sad* + *ni.*

second: *dvitīya.*
see, to: *paç*; *dṛç*; *īkṣ*; *īkṣ + pra.*
seer: *ṛṣi* m.
send, to: *sthā + pra,* caus.
servant: *bhṛtya* m.; *bhṛtaka* m.
serve: *sev.*
set, to: (place) 1*dhā*; (intr., of sun, etc.) *i + astam*; *gam + astam.*
shade: *chāyā* f.
she, etc.: *sā*, f. of *ta.*
shine, to: *çubh*; *rāj*; *bhā + vi.*
ship: *nāu* f.
shoe: *upānah* f.
show, to: *dṛç*, caus.
shrewd: *paṭu.*
shut, to: 1*dhā + api*; 1*vṛ + sam.*
sick: *vyādhita*; *rugṇa.*
side: *pakṣa* m.
sin: *pāpa* n.; *enas* n.
sing, to: 2*gā.*
singing: *gīta* n.
sip, to: *cam + ā.*
sister: *svasṛ* f.
sit, to: *sad*; *sad + ni.*
situated, to be: *vṛt.*
six: *ṣaṣ.*
sixth: *ṣaṣṭha.*
skilled: *paṭu.*
sky: *div* f.; *diç* f. pl.; *ākāça* n.
slave: *dāsa* m.; *dāsī* f.
slay, to: *mṛ*, caus.; *han.*
sleep, to: *svap*; *çī.*
smell, to; *ghrā.*
smite, to: *hṛ + pra*; *han + abhi.*
so: *iti*; *evam*: *tathā.*
soldier: *sāinika* m.
some (pl.): *eka* pl.; some · · others: *ke cit* · · *ke cit.*
sometimes: *kva cit.*

son: *putra* m.; *sūta* m.
son-in-law: *jāmātṛ* m.
song: *gir* f.; *gīta* n.; (of praise) *stotra* n.; *stuti* f.
soul: *ātman* m.
sow, to: *vap.*
speak, to: *vad*; *vac*; *bhāṣ.*
spear: *kunta* m.
speech: *vāc* f.; *bhāṣā* f.
spoon: *juhū* f.
stand, to (intr.): *sthā.*
state, to: *brū.*
steal, to: *cur*; *muṣ*; *luṇṭh.*
steer: *go* m.
stick: *daṇḍa* m.
stone: *dṛṣad* f.; (precious) *maṇi* m.
stop, to (tr.): *rudh.*
strange (another's): *para.*
street: *rathyā* f.; *mārga* m.
strike, to: *taḍ.*
strive, to: *yat.*
strongest: *baliṣṭha.*
study, to: *i + adhi* (mid.); 2*as + abhi.*
subject: *prajā* f.
such: *īdṛç.*
suffering: *duḥkha* n.
suffused: *ruddha.*
suitable: *anurūpa.*
summit: *çikhara* m.
sun: *bhānu* m.; *āditya* m.
survive, to: *çiṣ + ud.*
sweet: *svādu.*
swift: *āçu.*
sword: *asi* m.

---

take, to: *dā + ā*; *grah*; *grah + prati.*
take place, to: *jan*; *bhū*

take refuge, to: *pad + pra*.
tasteful: *rasavant*.
tax: *kara* m.
teach, to: *i + adhi*, caus.; *diç + upa*.
teacher: *guru* m.; *ācārya* m.
tear: *açru* n.; *bāṣpa* m.
tell, to: *kathaya*; *vad*.
temple: *devakula* n.
ten: *daça*.
tend to, to: *kḷp*.
terrify, to: *bhī*, caus.; *vij + ud*, caus.
text-book: *çāstra* n.
that: *ta*; *ayam*; *asāu*.
then: *tadā*.
there: *tatra*.
thereupon: *tatas*.
thief: *stena* m.; *cāura* m.
think, to: *cint*; *man*; think on: *smṛ*; *dhyā*.
third: *tṛtīya*.
thirty: *triṅçat*.
thirty-three: *trayastriṅçat*.
this: *ta*; *ayam*.
thou: *tvam*.
three: *tri*.
threefold: *trivṛt*.
thrice: *tris*.
thus: *iti*; *evam*; *tathā*.
time: *kāla* m.
to-day: *adya*.
to-morrow: *çvas*.
tongue: *jihvā* f.
torment, to: *pīḍ*; *vyath*, caus.
touch, to: *spṛç*.
trade: *vyavahāra* m.; *vāṇijya*.
travel, to: *vas + pra*; *sthā + pra* n. (mid.).
treasury: *koṣa* m.
tree: *vṛkṣa* m.; *taru* m.
tremble, to: *kamp*.
true: *satya*; (faithful) *bhakta*.
truth: *satya* n.
twelfth: *dvādaça*.
twelve: *dvādaça*.
twenty-eight: *aṣṭāviṅçati*.
twenty-seven: *saptaviṅçati*.
twice: *dvis*.
twilight: *saṅdhyā* f.
twine: *bandh*.
two: *dva*.

---

umbrella: *chattra* n.
understand, to: *gam + ava*.
unite, to (intr.): *gam + sam* (mid.).
untruth: *anṛta* n.; *asatya* n.
upaniṣad: *upaniṣad* f.
useful, to be: *sev*.

---

vassal: *sāmanta* m.
Veda: *veda* m.
verse: *çloka* m.; (of Rigveda) *ṛc* f.
vessel: *pātra* n.
victorious, to be: *ji*.
victory: *jaya* m.
view (opinion): *mati* f.; *mata* n.
village: *grāma* m.
virtue: *dharma* m.; *puṇya* n.
visit, to: *gam + abhi*.
voice: *vāc* f.; *gir* f.

---

wagon: *ratha* m.
warrior: *kṣatriya* m.
wash, to: *kṣal*; *spṛç*.
water: *jala* n.; *vāri* n.; *ap* f. pl.
wave: *vīci* m.
we: *vayam*.

wear, to: *dhṛ*, caus.; *bhṛ*.
weary, to become: *çram*.
weave, to: *granth*; *bandh*.
wedding: *vivāha* m.
weep, to: *rud*.
west, western: *pratyañc*; the West: *pratīcī* f., sc. *diç*.
what (rel.): *ya*.
wheel: *cakra* n.
when (rel.): *yadā*.
when?: *kadā*.
whence?: *kutas*.
where (rel.): *yatra*.
where?: *kva*; *kutra*.
which (rel.): *ya*.
which (of two)?: *katara*.
white: *çveta*.
whither?: *kva*; *kutra*.
who (rel.): *ya*.
who?: *ka*.
whoever: *ya ka* + *api*, *cid* or *cana*; often by rel. alone.
whole: *kṛtsna*.
why?: *kutas*; *kasmāt*.
wicked: *pāpa*.
wife: *bhāryā* f.; *nārī* f.; *patnī* f.
win, to: *ji*.
wind: *vāyu* m.; *vāta* m.
winter: *hemanta* m.
wipe, to: *mṛj*; *mṛj* + *apa* or *pari*.
wish, to: *iṣ*.
with: *saha*, w. inst.; or by instr. alone.
withered: *mlāna*.
without: *vinā* (instr., acc.).
witness: *sākṣin* m.
wolf: *vṛka* m.
woman: *nārī* f.; *vadhū* f.; *strī* f.; *jāyā* f.
woman-servant: *dāsī* f.
wood: *kāṣṭha* n.; (forest) *vana* n.
word: *vāc* f.; *çabda* m.
work: *karman* n.; (literary) *grantha* m.
world: *loka* m.; *jagat* n.; *bhuvana* n.
world-spirit: *bráhman* n.
worship, to: *pūj*.
worthy: *sadṛça*.
wound, to: *kṣan*.
wreath: *mālā* f.; *sraj* f.

---

year: *saṁvatsara* m.; *varṣa* m. n.
yoke, to: *yuj*, caus.
yonder: *tatra*.
young: *yuvan*.

Appendix.

Hindu Names of Letters.

The Hindus call the different sounds, and the characters representing them, by the word *kāra* ('maker') added to the sound of the letter, if a vowel, or to the letter followed by *a*, if a consonant. Thus, *a* (both sound and character) is called *akāra; ū*, *ūkāra; k*, *kakāra;* and so on. But sometimes *kāra* is omitted, and *a*, *ū*, *ka*, etc., are used alone. The *r*, however, is never called *rakāra*, but only *ra* or *repha* ('snarl'). The *anusvāra* and *visarga* are called by these names alone.

Modern Hindu Accentuation of Sanskrit.

In the pronunciation of Sanskrit almost all Brāhmans employ, with insignificant variations, an ictus-accent, which is quite different from the older musical accent (*svara*) described in Indian and European grammars, and employed nowadays exclusively in the recitation of the Veda. The older system, moreover, as marked in the Vedic texts, has been subjected to very considerable modifications by the Hindus in the traditional recitations of the Vedic schools.

The modern ictus-accent is weaker than that of English. The more important rules governing its use are as follows:

1. *a*. In primitive verbs and derivatives from them the root-syllable is usually accented. *b*. But the accent never goes further back than the fourth place, and seldom back of the third. It may rest on the third syllable only if the penult be short; on the fourth, only if both antepenult and penult be short; thus, *káraṇam, káraṇāt*, but *karaṇéna; bódhati, kṣípasi, náçyatha*, but *bodhávaḥ, kṣipámaḥ, naçyánti; dúhitā, dúhitaram*, but *duhitṝṇām*.

2. Derivatives from nouns generally retain the accent of the

primitive, with the limitations given in 1. *b*.; thus, *ráñku*, *rā́ñkava*; *gárga*, *gā́rgyaḥ*, but *gārgyā́yaṇī*. A naturally short vowel in the penult, if followed by a group of consonants containing *y* or *v*, does not generally become long by position; thus, *prábala*, *prā́balyam*; *úkta*, *úktatvāt*.

3. In verbs and verbal derivatives joined with prepositions, in augmented and reduplicated forms, and sometimes in declensional forms, the accent is recessive, if the root or stem-syllable be short; thus, *ā́gamat*, *ā̆natam*, *anúṣṭhitam*, but *utkṛṣṭam*, *nirúktam*; *ágamat*, *ákṣipat*, but *bibhárti*, *tuṣṭā́ra*, *jagā́u*. Polysyllabic prepositions, when prefixed to other words, retain their own accent as secondary accent; thus, *úpagǎcchati*, *úpagǎmatām*.

4. In compounds, unless the first member be a monosyllabic word, each part generally retains its own accent, but that of the principal member is the strongest; thus, *rā́japǔruṣam*, *párvataçikharā̆kǎram*; *but únmukham*, *diggajam*, *praçiṣyam*.

The division of syllables is much more apparent in Sanskrit than in English. In reading Sanskrit prose the Hindus generally drop into a sort of sing-song *recitativo*. Verses are always chanted.